Getting Funded

Getting Funded

The Complete Guide to Writing Grant Proposals

FOURTH EDITION

Mary Hall, Ph.D., *and* Susan Howlett

PORTLAND STATE UNIVERSITY

EXTENDED STUDIES

CONTINUING EDUCATION PRESS

Portland, Oregon

Copyright © 1977, 1988, by Mary S. Hall, Ph.D.; 2003 by Mary S. Hall, Ph.D., and Susan Howlett
All rights reserved

First edition, *Developing Skills in Proposal Writing*, published 1971.
Second edition, 1977.
Third edition, *Getting Funded, A Complete Guide to Writing Proposals*, 1988.
Fourth edition, *Getting Funded, The Complete Guide to Writing Grant Proposals*, 2003.

ISBN 0-87678-070-1 (softcover)

Printed in the United States of America
10 09 08 07 06 05 04 03
11 10 9 8 7 6 5 4 3 2 1

Continuing Education Press, Portland State University

Library of Congress Cataloging-in-Publication Data

Hall, Mary S.
    Getting funded : the complete guide to writing grant proposals / Mary Hall and Susan Howlett — 4th ed.
        p.   cm.
    ISBN 0-87678-070-1 (softcover)
    Includes bibliographical references and index.
    1. Proposal writing for grants—United States. 2. Grants-in-aid—United States.
3. Proposal writing for grants. 4. Grants-in-aid.
    HG177.5.U6 H355   2003
    658.15/224 21

                                                                        2003682003
                                                                        CIP

Copies available from:
Portland State University
Extended Studies
Continuing Education Press
P.O. Box 1394
Portland, OR 97207-1394
P: 866-647-7377
F: 503-725-4840
www.cep.pdx.edu

Every effort has been made to provide current Web site information. All Web site URLs were current and correct at the time of publication. Due to the nature of the World Wide Web, URLs may change at any time and some pages may no longer be available.

Contents

About the Authors

Mary Stewart Hall, Ph.D. is a professor and founder of the Executive Master of the Not-For-Profit Leadership Program at Seattle University in Washington. She is also president of Stewart/Hall, a consulting firm serving U.S. and international private, corporate, and government grantmakers. From 1977 to 1995 she was president and trustee of the Weyerhaeuser Company Foundation and vice president of corporate affairs for Weyerhaeuser Company (a Fortune 500 firm). While there, Dr. Hall wrote the second and third editions of *Getting Funded*. Dr. Hall was previously associate superintendent of public instruction in Oregon and a staff member in the U.S. Congress. She authored the first edition of *Getting Funded* while serving as director of federal relations at the University of Oregon.

Dr. Hall has been chair of the Contributions Council of The Conference Board, an elected organization of the heads of the largest U.S. corporate grantmakers; a director of Independent Sector, a national collaboration of the largest philanthropic and nonprofit organizations; and president of Philanthropy Northwest, a regional association of private foundations and corporate grantmakers. She has served on the boards of several private foundations and numerous governmental grant advisory or peer review committees. She received her Bachelor of Science, Master of Science and Doctor of Philosophy degrees from the University of Oregon and is an alumna of the Executive Management Program at Stanford University's Graduate School of Business.

Susan Howlett has been helping nonprofits raise money joyfully since 1975, as a board member, development director, executive director, and freelancer. For the last 15 years, she has been a fundraising consultant to hundreds of nonprofits throughout the U.S. (especially non-institutional organizations, small nonprofits, and rural communities). From 1991 to 2001, Susan led the Seattle-based Puget Sound Grantwriters Association, bringing thousands of grantseekers and grantmakers together through presentations, conferences, workshops, and joint projects. The regional association of grantmakers often has Susan train new grantors.

She is adjunct faculty at the University of Washington, where she teaches the one-year Fundraising Management Certificate Program, as well as courses for faculty and staff. She developed the Non-Profit Management Certificate Program at Bellevue Community College, where she has taught grantwriting, fundraising, and board courses for more than 12 years.

Susan served on many boards and as a trustee with the Northwest Development Officers Association, which recently awarded her their prestigious Professional Achievement Award for a career of service to philanthropy and the development profession. Susan has served as a grant reviewer for local and federal government funders as well as private foundations. Often hired by funders, Susan speaks, trains, and consults nationally.

Acknowledgements

The authors would like to thank the following people whose wisdom, resources, and support were instrumental in the creation of this book: Goodwin Deacon, Ph.D., founder of the Puget Sound Grantwriters Association, prospect researcher, grantwriting consultant, and teacher; Jeannette Privat, creator of the Non-Profit and Philanthropy Resource Center of the King County Library System, and the regional Foundation Center Collection. In addition, Mary thanks her family, Sarah and John Hall, Pat, Kell, and Mark Brauer. Susan thanks her family, David, Katherine, and Ben Bauman.

Introduction

Proposal writing skills are now essential to many occupations and organizations. Since the third edition of this book was published in 1988, the world of grants and contracts has undergone many changes.

The content of proposals has evolved. The format for proposals has become much more standardized due to the adoption of common application forms. Requirements to state the purposes of a project as "outcomes" and include a logic model for "outcome-based evaluation" are now standard in many governmental and private funding sources. In addition, the preparation of budgets for proposals has become more complex as donors ask applicants to cost-share or to fund proposals from several sources. A growing number of grantmakers only want to support projects that show appropriate collaboration with various partners in both funding and implementation.

The relative availability of private versus governmental monies has also shifted. In inflation-adjusted terms, government support to nonprofits increased 195 percent between 1977 and 1997, boosting receipts from government from 31 percent of total grant revenue in the early 1980s to 37 percent by the end of the 1990s. By comparison, the overall Gross Domestic Product rose only 81 percent in real terms during this same period (1). State government has become a far more important site of decisions on funds flowing from the federal government, as well as those provided by local tax dollars.

In the private sector, private foundations now award more money than corporations. For 2001, private foundation grants were 12.2 percent of total charitable giving, compared to only 4.3 percent from corporations (2). Foundation budgets continue to grow at rates well in advance of inflation, while, in recent years, grants from corporations have stagnated. Yet, the wise proposal writer knows that, although the government clearly offers the largest amount of grant-in-aid monies, funding from the private sector is increasingly important in supporting innovation and experimentation.

A related trend has been the growing number of government and private funders that now wish to support only the "best" organizations to accomplish the grantmaker's particular goals. The sections of a proposal documenting the capability and reputation of the individuals and institutions to be involved in the project have never been as critical.

Not surprisingly, the competition for grants-in-aid continues to increase. The number of organizations in the United States qualifying for charitable, tax-exempt status rose 25 percent during the 1990s and more than 50 percent when compared to 1977 (3). This growth rate far outstripped increases in all types of public and private grant-in-aid sources during this same period. Many U.S. funding sources have begun accepting applications from not-for-profits registered in foreign countries or from social service-oriented, for-profit businesses here and abroad, slicing the pie ever thinner.

The Internet has significantly altered the circumstances of those seeking grant-in-aid funds. The words "proposal writing" used on any of the major Internet search engines results in more than one million listings which give advice on ways to research funding sources or write proposals. *Many government agencies, foundations, and corporations now require that proposals be submitted online.* Several, such as the National Science Foundation (4) and the National Institutes of Health, offer free tutorials (5).

For all these reasons, it is more important than ever to know how to prepare an effective proposal. This book shares ideas for how to do that by drawing on over sixty years of combined experience in making grants, writing proposals, serving as consultants to private foundations and on federal and state review committees, chairing professional grantmaking and grantseeking associations and teaching proposal writing. It also includes the results of recent interviews with more than 100 federal and foundation program officers.

The book is based on two fundamental assumptions:

1. **There is social value in writing proposals to seek funding from private and governmental sources.** The application process is still one of the most democratic means we know for matching those who have ideas for improvements in society with those who have the resources to support such progress. Individuals and organizations with the creativity, drive, perseverance, and capacity to submit successful requests not only deserve the additional resources and prestige that grants can bring, but they are a primary means of creating desirable social change.

2. **There is no special mystique about proposal writing.** Anyone with a good, well-planned idea who has done careful research on sources of support and is *able to communicate effectively in writing* can do a successful job of preparing a funding request.

There are, however, some ways of approaching this task that can be profitably adopted by the novice—or even someone with proposal-writing experience. This book shares a wealth of those ideas and provides many examples.

Despite all the changes that have occurred, **the basic steps of planning, preparing, and submitting a winning proposal remain essentially the same.** The preparation of a proposal follows a pattern which, in many respects, is analogous to the traditional planning process found in the literature on management. By viewing proposal development as a process, one can begin to recognize repetitive steps that must be completed for any application and can build a reservoir of experience to be applied to the development of any funded project.

To aid this recognition, the book is organized in a logical progression of steps and is divided into three major parts. Part I deals with the planning and information collecting that should be done in advance of the actual proposal writing. Part II focuses primarily on writing the proposal. It also touches on submission, negotiation, and project renewal. Appendix A includes a detailed checklist to ensure that all of the major steps have been completed.

Appendix B, new in this edition, contains advice for those who teach courses or workshops on proposal writing. It includes sample syllabi for a nine-session course and a one-day workshop. It also includes suggested assignments for each chapter in the book.

CHAPTER REFERENCES

1. Salamon, Lester M., *The State of Nonprofit America.* Washington, DC: The Brookings Institution Press, 2003.

2. AAFRC Trust for Philanthropy, *Giving USA 2002.* Sewickley, PA: Author, June 2002.

3. The Nonprofit World: Financial and Employment Trends, *Chronicle of Philanthropy,* March 21, 2002, p. 32

4. National Science Foundation, "Grant Proposal Guide." Retrieved from http://www.nsf.gov/home/menus/funding.htm

5. National Institutes of Health, "Grant Writing Tips Sheets." Retrieved from http://grants1.nih.gov/grants/oer.htm

Figure I-1. Diagram of Proposal Development Process

PROPOSAL DEVELOPMENT PROCESS

Phase 1: Essential Planning Steps

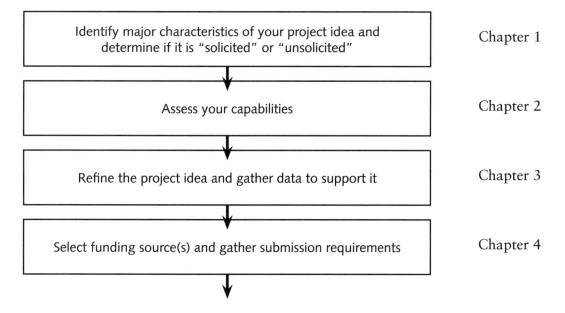

Identify major characteristics of your project idea and determine if it is "solicited" or "unsolicited"	Chapter 1
Assess your capabilities	Chapter 2
Refine the project idea and gather data to support it	Chapter 3
Select funding source(s) and gather submission requirements	Chapter 4

Phase 2: Writing and Submitting the Proposal

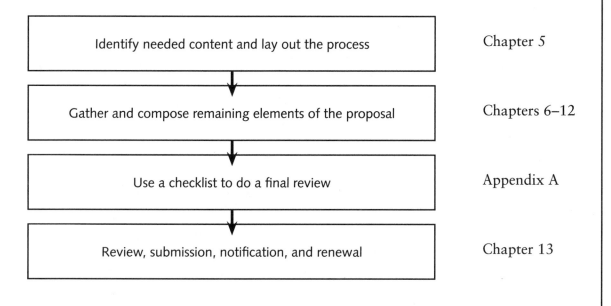

Identify needed content and lay out the process	Chapter 5
Gather and compose remaining elements of the proposal	Chapters 6–12
Use a checklist to do a final review	Appendix A
Review, submission, notification, and renewal	Chapter 13

PART ONE

Essential Planning Steps

Chapter 1

Getting Started

This chapter discusses how to begin planning a proposal by developing a profile to guide the assessment of capability, analysis of need, and search for possible funders. It discusses the impact that the source of the proposal's idea has on its timing and content, and defines basic terms used throughout the book.

BUILDING A PROFILE OF YOUR PROJECT

There are many different ways to begin planning a proposal. One of the most common is to identify the basic characteristics of the type of project you are seeking to fund. This will help guide the planning that is essential before actually writing an application. Knowing the profile of your proposed project will help you assess your capability, document the need for your project, identify similar efforts in the past, and search for likely sources of support.

Most sources of funding, whether public or private, have restrictions on what they will support by type of project, degree of innovation, field and subject matter, population to be served, and/or geography. To begin building a profile, answer the following questions:

- **What is the function of the project you are proposing?** Examples might include research, development, demonstration, training, service, technical assistance, facilities, equipment purchases, and so on.

- **Is your project unique?** It makes a big difference whether you are seeking a grant to try out a new idea or whether your need is for general organizational support. Many grant programs fund one or the other, but not both.

- **In what field is your project?** Some of the standard categories include education, health, social welfare, civic or community improvement, arts, culture, science and technology, religion, or environment/conservation.

- **Who will benefit from your project?** Types of clientele or project participants might include low-income persons, infants, youth, families, the elderly, the unemployed, the homeless, refugees, persons of a certain race, ethnicity, or sex, and so forth.

- **What are the geographical parameters of your project?** In what country will it be located? Is it local, statewide, nationwide, or international? It is oriented towards urban or rural areas?

Clearly identifying as many of the appropriate descriptive characteristics of your proposed project as possible will not only guide your search for funding sources, but help you identify others doing related work and sources of data to support the need for your project. These essential planning steps are described in Chapters 3 and 4.

Another starting place is to decide what type of grant (also called *award*) you are likely to be seeking. Some of the more common kinds are:

- **Project or program grant**—funds to achieve a specific outcome within a defined time frame. If this is a fairly limited initiative, it is usually called a *project*. Something of wider scope is referred to as a *program*.

- **Operating grant**—general financial support to the organization without expectations that the money will be used for a specific activity. This is also referred to as a *general purpose grant*.

- **Start-up award**—funds to help an individual or organization take the beginning steps for an initiative. This activity will help determine if it's feasible to proceed further and may help identify funding sources for the next phase of the project or program. Also referred to as a *seed grant*.

- **Challenge grant**—match of monies provided by the applicant or some other source.

- **Capital award**—funds to help build or remodel facilities or acquire equipment.

- **Endowment grant**—funds to be invested, with part of the annual income used for some specific purpose.

Most funding sources support only a few of these types of awards. These are spelled out in their written guidelines or on their Web site.

ORIGINS OF PROJECT IDEAS

It is crucial to know whether your proposal is for a project idea that originated primarily with you and/or your submitting agency or is for a purpose identified by the funding source. The former are usually called *unsolicited* and the latter *solicited*.

This distinction will have many implications that are discussed further in this chapter.

- An **unsolicited project idea** is one that is created by the person or organization seeking funds. From the viewpoint of the applicant, these are frequently the most interesting and important projects. However, they are often the most difficult to fund.

- A **solicited project idea** is one that has been suggested in at least general terms by the funding source itself, either as a specific initiative or as a general subject area in which it is interested. This is the most common type of project supported by both governmental and private sources. There are typically two ways in which solicited projects are initiated:

1. A **Request for Proposals (RFP)** describes the type of program to be mounted, the outcomes intended, and the criteria to be used in selecting recipients of the funds. The funder may also specify the time to be permitted for the project, a range of acceptable costs, the geographical area of clientele to be served, and, in some cases, the actual procedures or methods to be used. The document may also list the type of qualifications needed by those eligible to respond and detail the type of information to be submitted.

    Learning about RFPs issued by private foundations and corporations can be tricky. However, some foundations and corporations notify The Foundation Center when they issue an RFP and these can be found at http://www.fdncenter.org/pnd/rfp. You can also use your project's profile to identify foundations and corporations that have funded something similar in the past and periodically check their Web site to learn of any new RFPs.

    Monitoring the availability of RFPs from federal or state agencies is much simpler. All federal RFPs can be found at http://www.FedBizOpps.gov. Chapter 4 describes additional ways to learn about RFPs.

2. **Program announcements** are frequently used by governmental or private donors that want to support projects of a particular type or to address a particular need, but wish to leave considerable freedom to applicants in proposing how to design and carry out the program.

Program announcements come in many formats. Some federal agencies, for example, include all of their program announcements in an annual catalog or describe these on their Web site. Others (including most private foundations) issue separate booklets or pamphlets when they want to announce a particular program competition. They may also put the program announcement on their Web site. Chapter 4 provides more details on how to identify program announcements.

Whether issued by public or private sources, program announcements usually include a description of the nature of the problem the donor is trying to solve, the topics or categories in which proposals may be submitted, eligibility requirements for applicants, deadlines, what information must be submitted (and sometimes in what form), and the selection criteria and process. Occasionally, the announcement includes the amount of money available and whether priority will be given to applicants who have previously received funding from this source.

While the Internet has increased access to program announcements, it is also a good idea to contact those governmental or private sources that have previously funded projects with characteristics similar to yours and ask to be placed on their mailing list for all future program announcements.

IMPORTANCE OF SOLICITED VERSUS UNSOLICITED

Proposals take a great deal of time and effort to prepare. The closer your proposal matches the interests of potential grantors, the more likely you

are to receive funding. In the case of unsolicited ideas, you need to communicate with the funding sources well in advance of submitting a full proposal. It is unwise to send a completed application to a particular source for an unsolicited idea without first making a preliminary inquiry. Guidance on how to do this is provided in Chapter 4. **Do not waste your time or that of the funder with an inappropriate application.**

This distinction also matters in terms of the amount of time needed to plan and write the proposal. With applications for solicited ideas, a definite submission deadline and a date on which to expect notification of a decision are usually known. The sample timetable provided in Chapter 5 will help you decide how much time is needed to actually prepare the proposal.

In the case of unsolicited ideas, however, the applicant must first determine whether a proposal is even warranted. This requires additional time, ranging from only a few days if an inquiry can be made by telephone, to several months if the potential donor asks for a preliminary abstract before indicating whether a proposal would be welcome.

Finally, this distinction is important in determining the relative emphasis to place on various components of the proposal. In addition to the type of information required in a solicited application, three components are *critical* in an unsolicited proposal. It must convince the funding source of the merit of the idea, the need for the project, and the capability of the submitting agency.

MORE TERMS TO UNDERSTAND

There are three other terms, used frequently throughout the book, that you should understand: *contract, grant,* and *sponsored project*.

- **Contract** and **grant** are often used in conjunction with each other, yet legally they are two completely different devices for awarding funds. Typically, they also require different proposal formats.

  A **contract** is generally awarded for a project solicited through an RFP. The funder has already identified the need and the expected outcomes, selected an acceptable cost range and estimated the time required to complete the project. The object is to find eligible candidates and to choose the best possible candidate to carry out the project. The choice will be based on factors such as previous experience, geographical location, quality of personnel and/or lowest cost.

The funder also expects to exert fairly strict management control over the contract and may require frequent reports to or visits by the funder's contracting officer. This amount of control is one of the distinguishing characteristics of a contract. Several kinds of contracts commonly in use are *fixed-price, straight-cost reimbursement, cost plus fixed-fee,* and *shared-cost.* These are generally distinguished by how the budget for the contract is negotiated.

A **grant,** on the other hand, is typically awarded for a project where most or all of the above factors have not yet been determined. Some feel that grant proposals thus require more ingenuity and creativity than those for contracts. Grants are frequently awarded for research or experimental projects or for general support of organizations. They typically permit more latitude in shifting funds among budget categories, more flexibility in the timetable, and more freedom in procedures.

Whether a grant or a contract is most advantageous to the recipient has been debated for many years, and opinions still differ. In most cases, the funding source determines which type of award will be made. However, the applicant should know the characteristics of each type of award and the type most likely to be selected.

- A **sponsored project** is an activity or program financed by funds which have come from a source outside the applicant's own organization. The term *externally funded* is also used to describe this type of project.

Other terms unique to the field of proposal development will be defined as they appear throughout the book.

Chapter 2

Assessing Your Capability

This chapter provides a checklist to help you determine your general capability to engage in successful grantsmanship. It emphasizes why proposals should always help implement an organization's mission. It also discusses how to judge your ability to be competitive in responding to a specific Request for Proposals (RFP).

Let's face it—writing a proposal takes quite a bit work and expense. So, early in the process you need to ask, "Do I really want to do this?" and, "Can I be sufficiently competitive to make my investment of time, effort, and money worthwhile?" Equally important, you need to honestly answer the question, "If funded, will this proposal help implement my organization's mission?"

SHOULD YOU WRITE THIS PROPOSAL?

Proposal writing has positive and negative aspects. On the positive side, writing proposals is a great way for an organization to get its act together. Preparing an application requires you to think and plan, so writing proposals can always be beneficial to planning. Taking an objective look at the strengths and weaknesses of your institution or agency also helps you become more realistic about the types of sponsored funds you are likely to attract.

However, all applications have costs for the submitting institution or agency. Sometimes this is obvious, such as dollars required for matching funds or the allocation of staff time to write the proposal. Sometimes the costs are less apparent, such as the impact of assigning a key staff member to a sponsored project, or focusing on areas where external funds are available to the neglect of other more essential activities. Unfortunately, there are still too many examples of "the funding tail wagging the program dog."

Proposals for purposes that do not tie to mission are better left unwritten. Organizations can no longer support the submission of every project that interests one of their employees. Before you start, be clear that the proposal is for a really important purpose that is going to be considered a priority by your organization. And be realistic about whether you have the time and expertise necessary to do a winning job.

There is one type of proposal, however, that you should always think twice about before writing: A proposal soliciting funds to start a new organization. There has been a huge increase in the number of new nonprofit agencies created in recent years (50 percent since 1977). Some of these new agencies simply duplicated services or activities already being provided by others with just a different group of people "in charge." Since every new agency requires a separate administrative staff, facilities, board, and so on, funders now turn a wary eye on proposals to create a new organization. In fact, many now state that they will make grants only to "well-established" institutions (code for "an organization that has been around for several years"). So before you write a proposal to create a new entity, always find out who else is working in a similar field or serving a similar client and honestly explore whether you can affiliate with them. If you still decide to launch a new agency, be aware that you face an uphill battle convincing potential funders of the need.

Checklist 2-1 provides a list of questions to answer when deciding if your agency should submit a proposal.

All grants and contracts require that funds be expended within a specific period (even if an extension is sometimes an option). Usually, this is one calendar or fiscal year. Too many inexperienced proposal writers have stumbled because they didn't explore the availability of their organization's infrastructure before preparing the proposal or trying to implement the funded project. The level of such services will obviously vary from organization to organization. But individuals who do not have access to these basic systems, at least minimally, will find it more difficult to compete for external funds.

However, if you do not have such support systems, don't give up. On the contrary, a realistic assessment of your organization's capabilities may either prompt development of the necessary services or it may encourage you to plan submission of a project in cooperation with another agency that has the requisite competence. You may also want to consider contracting with another entity for the needed services. This is another benefit of developing appropriate collaboration. You could also consider asking another organization to serve as the project's *fiscal agent*. A fiscal agent is a public entity or 501(c)(3) nonprofit organization that agrees to serve as the financial home for a project and to assume all legal responsibility for the proper receipt, expenditure, and reporting on the grant or contract funds. Community foundations or organizations such as United Way are often good fiscal agents.

ASSESSING WHETHER TO RESPOND TO AN RFP

Requests for Proposals (RFPs) are increasingly being used by government agencies and some private foundations to announce opportunities for grants or contracts. The rise in the number of RFPs can be traced to the increased competition for funds and the wish by more and more donors to have more control over the types of projects they fund. Funding sources use RFPs to identify their highest priorities with more precision. They also believe RFPs may lead to more successful outcomes because they require applicants to do more detailed planning in advance. Finally, some agencies feel that the use of the RFP lessens the possibility of charges of unfair competition from unsuccessful applicants.

There is no uniform format for an RFP. Some Internet sources with examples are provided at the end of this chapter. Most RFPs contain the following information:

- Purpose of the project and desired outcomes.

- Amount of money to be awarded (may include a statement about the maximum for any single organization).

- Instructions for how and when to respond.

- Instructions for how the applicant is to demonstrate capability.

- Technical details on the content of the program, including expected tasks and products (usually called the *scope of work*).

- An explanation of legal issues or other requirements affecting the award.

- Instructions for preparing a budget (may require documentation of the projected person-hours).

Checklist 2-1. Assessing Your Institution or Agency

❑ **Do you have the proper legal status to receive funds from governments, private foundations, or corporations?** Very few funding sources will give grants or contracts directly to individuals. Only a small percentage will fund for-profit businesses (and those tend to be restricted to contracts for social services). Most insist that the application be submitted from a public agency or a private, nonprofit entity that has received 501(c)(3) status from the Internal Revenue Service. Check the eligibility requirements of the funders to whom you are likely to apply before going further with a proposal tailored to their requirements. If you do not qualify, see if there are other, legally qualified organizations that you can collaborate with to submit the proposal. Otherwise, take steps to get the necessary legal status before writing proposals. And a related point is to be sure that you have the licensing, accreditation, or permits required to do what you propose.

❑ **Is the purpose of the proposal consistent with the mission of your agency?** Some grantmakers feel that far too many organizations and institutions have simply chased external funds as a way of continuing the existence of their staff's employment. The days of submitting a proposal "just to get money," if they ever existed, are long gone. There needs to be an explicit tie between the purpose of the proposal and that of the agency submitting the proposal.

❑ **Does your organization have a strategic plan that positions you to achieve excellence?** Put succinctly, has your organization recently gone through the thoughtful discipline of reviewing its mission, including the needs or assumptions upon which the mission is based, and choosing its future goals, objectives, programs, and services? Can it document that you have analyzed the resources required to make your organization "one of the best" in its particular field and that you have realistic strategies for funding and implementation? Private foundations, corporations, and government agencies are increasingly looking for evidence that the applicants they fund are not only committed to performing at the highest level, but that they have the necessary plans and capability to make that happen.

❑ **Does your organization have a good governing structure or board?** Nonprofits are well aware that the quality of their board is a deciding factor in securing funds from individuals. It is also important in getting grants from foundations, corporations, and government agencies. Like individual donors, institutional donors want to see that you have experienced individuals at the helm. Grantors also expect that every board member will make an annual financial contribution to the organization.

❑ **Do you understand and can you explain the "competitive advantage" of your agency for this particular proposal?** All organizations have strengths and weaknesses. You want to write proposals for projects that build on your institution's strengths. Are there factors such as your mission, clientele, location, history, prior experience, and the qualifications of your staff or volunteers that you can emphasize to build the case for being the best recipient of an award? Part of this assessment of your strengths and weaknesses is to think through which aspects of your current operation are most likely to appeal to external donors, especially if funds are being sought for support of ongoing activities. As an example, one civic group repeatedly wrote unsuccessful proposals for grants to help defray the cost of their annual conference. They would likely have been more successful if they had sought grants to support their various service projects and then supported their conference through participant fees and sponsorships from for-profit vendors of services to their organization.

❑ **Do you know how the reputation of your organization will affect this proposal?** Have you examined records of previous grants or contracts received by your group, particularly from

Checklist 2-1. Assessing Your Institution or Agency (continued)

the funders you will likely approach, and do you know whether those sources were pleased with the results of prior awards? One program officer told of an organization approaching his corporation for an endowment gift without being aware that only 3 years earlier, their institution had misused grant funds from this same donor. Have you assessed other aspects of your organization's reputation that might enhance or impede your chances for grants and contracts?

❑ **Do you know who else in the community or field is doing similar work and can you articulate what makes your work distinct from theirs?** As we note in Chapter 3, you are unlikely to write a winning proposal if you have not done the basic homework on what others have done in the past or are currently doing that relates to your idea. And you need to be able to clearly explain how your project is going to supplement, replicate, build on, or improve these other efforts.

❑ **Do you have collaborative relationships with other entities doing similar work where those make sense?** Have you developed the appropriate partnerships? Both public and private grantmakers are now more interested in funding programs and projects that demonstrate effective collaboration because this means their money will not be used to duplicate existing activities. These collaborations also help with the need to address sustainability (your ability to continue the program in the future without continued support from the original donors).

❑ **Do you have or can you get (in time) the right staff for this project?** Since the assignments of experienced personnel are often fixed well in advance, you may not be able to shift them to this project if it is funded. If you must hire new staff, have you thought through the costs in both time and money? Does your agency have sufficient human resource staff to help you attract and hire qualified staff in time to mount the project? This is probably one of the biggest

errors made by inexperienced proposal writers who commit to project outcomes that do not allow the necessary time for startup.

❑ **Do you have the appropriate infrastructure to support the project and ensure that you can spend the funds within the required timeframe?**

❑ **Have you thought through the impact of your project on your infrastructure?**

(Answering the following questions requires careful assessment of all of the ways you will need to call on your organization to successfully implement the grant or contract.)

○ **Does your organization have experienced leadership who can make decisions quickly enough to allow you to compete in a timely manner?** This is now a real issue at some universities and large, centralized, nonprofit agencies, where it may take weeks and or even months to get a finished proposal through all the necessary review processes. You must have the ability to secure in advance the necessary buy-in from everyone at your agency who will be essential to the project's success.

○ **Can your organization quickly make decisions about the allocation of matching funds or the reallocation of other needed resources?**

○ **Does your organization have the necessary business systems to help define all types of resources needed for the project and provide the necessary fiscal reports?** This should be a real concern to small agencies and institutions that have limited accounting personnel. Donors typically require financial reports within a relatively short period after the end of a grant or contract. Those who haven't considered this requirement get themselves in trouble because of lengthy delays in their reporting.

Checklist 2-1. Assessing Your Institution or Agency (continued)

○ **Does your agency have the necessary space and equipment (or can they get it quickly enough) to meet your project deadlines?**

○ **Can the organization provide other types of assistance that may be essential to the**

proposal developer? Some of these are library or technical research support, secretarial services, editorial or media support, and printing or computer services.

- Required forms and a list of compliance statements.

In judging whether to respond to an RFP, the content of the document itself must be evaluated, as well as the capabilities of the potential applicant. In making this evaluation, it is helpful to apply the criteria of *relevance, eligibility, interest, feasibility, flexibility, capability,* and *competitiveness.* Checklist 2-2 speaks to these criteria.

Other information which it may be wise to collect prior to writing a response to an RFP is mentioned in Chapters 3 and 4.

A WORD TO BEGINNERS

About now, persons who have never written a proposal or responded to an RFP are tempted to throw up their hands. Is it really worth the effort to pursue the idea any further? The answer is "Yes," for the following reasons:

The preparation and submission of the proposal is of benefit to you even if the first attempt to get it funded fails. Experience only comes with trying. During each failure you gain valuable information and insight into how to improve future applications. Eventually this pays off. And the time and effort invested in preparing a proposal that is of real interest to you can pay off in other ways. You may find that a well-planned proposal that is strongly endorsed by your agency can be implemented, albeit more slowly, with the use of internal funds. And the effort invested in identifying prior research and related work may be translatable into a successful professional publication.

There are many things you can do to improve apparent areas of weakness.

- You can become more realistic in choosing likely sources of support. Going through the application process can help direct you to sources where the competition may be less keen, such as a discretionary fund within the organization itself, awards from state agencies, smaller or regional private foundations, local businesses and service clubs, or small grant programs within federal agencies.

- You can invite a more experienced colleague to serve as principal investigator or lead consultant in the application. This is a time-honored approach to help secure funds for ideas of interest to less experienced persons.

- You can collaborate with another agency that has the requisite support services, experience or reputation in the project area. By joining enthusiasm with experience, this team approach is often successful.

- You can ask a better-qualified organization to serve as "fiscal sponsor" for your project.

Every year, individuals and organizations that have never before sought external funds submit successful proposals. With proper homework and thought, you can, too.

Checklist 2-2. Evaluating Your Capability to Respond to an RFP

❑ **Is the RFP relevant to your agency's mission?** Answering this question at the outset is critical to a decision of whether to move ahead. The lack of a clear match between your mission and the purposes of the RFP will decrease your chance of success.

❑ **Are you eligible to respond to the RFP?** Most RFPs carry explicit eligibility requirements detailing the types of organizations that may submit a proposal. For example, the RFP may be limited to local government agencies or to nonprofits that have 501(c)(3) status from the Internal Revenue Service. Often, there are hints about implicit eligibility requirements, such as a statement that applicants have specific kinds of prior experience or will be able to mount a project within a particular geographic area. Organizations that cannot meet either the implicit or explicit eligibility criteria will not be considered.

❑ **Is the RFP compatible with your interests?** Your organization should focus on projects relevant to its current priorities. Because RFPs often require much more detail about proposed implementation plans and budget assumptions than other types of proposals, responding to them is particularly time consuming. Such proposals are also frequently more expensive to prepare. For example, funding sources issuing RFPs often invite potential applicants to attend a technical conference (sometimes also called a bidder's conference) that gives more information on the proposed program and provides an opportunity to ask detailed questions. However, potential applicants have to bear the costs of attending these meetings. It is much cheaper to access an on-line tutorial that some government sources of RFPs now provide. Therefore, you should probably ignore RFPs that do not match your top priorities.

❑ **Is the project in the RFP feasible?** Sometimes, RFPs are issued for projects that are very difficult for anyone to implement successfully. Think about the number and scope of products or activities that are expected, given the available time and funds; the availability of the necessary technology or knowledge; the environment in which the project must be implemented (funding sources sometimes overlook the impact of an unfavorable political climate or local opposition to a proposed project); the degree to which cooperation or participation by other agencies or individuals will be required and the extent to which you already have those collaborations in place; the decision-making process for the project and whether it appears to be stacked in favor of certain applicants; and the kinds and amount of monitoring, reporting, and evaluation data that must be furnished. Also, never overlook whether the proposed funding plan for the RFP is feasible. Does the funder offer sufficient funds to cover the entire cost of the project or will parts of it need to be subsidized by the applicant? If the RFP as originally written is not feasible, you should determine if the funding source is willing to entertain suggested modifications that will increase chances of the project's success. If it is not, don't apply for this one.

❑ **Is the RFP flexible?** At least two kinds of flexibility should be considered in assessing an RFP:

○ **How much flexibility is available to you in responding to the RFP?** Can alternative methodology or approaches be suggested for completing the work if you have a better idea for how to achieve the desired outcomes? This type of flexibility helps you determine whether your interest and capability matches the funding opportunity.

○ **How much flexibility appears to be available in managing the project?** Realistically, it is impossible to anticipate every event or factor that will impact a project. Does the funding source appear to be aware of this by specifying a process in the proposal (or at the technical conference) that can be used to negotiate needed changes once the project is underway? If not, you should carefully consider the consequences of responding to the RFP unless you are very

Checklist 2-2. Evaluating Your Capability to Respond to an RFP (continued)

experienced in planning and managing this type of project.

❑ **Are you capable of implementing the RFP?** Do you have on hand all the kinds of resources (including personnel) you will need to implement the project, or can you get them in time to meet the project's deadlines? Do you have the institutional infrastructure in place to make timely decisions? Most RFPs call for much tighter implementation deadlines and much more detailed performance requirements than other types of proposals. If you are working for an organization that does not have its act together with respect to making all kinds of program and resource decisions, you might want to pass on responding to RFPs.

❑ **Can you be competitive?** The evaluation criteria included in the RFP are important in considering the competitiveness of your staff and organization. These criteria usually indicate the extent to which factors such as previous experience, available support services, staff qualifications, and content of the proposal itself will be weighted in selecting recipients for the award. A major consideration is whether you can afford to submit a competitive budget.

❑ **Do you have the needed resources?** Some organizations have various resources or services that they can provide for the project without charge, while others must consider all externally funded projects to be essentially self-supporting. Some organizations have unionized staff, which impacts their per-person costs for such projects. Others are located in geographical areas where salaries are higher than elsewhere in the country. Still others will find that their distance from the funding source will result in much higher transportation costs than closer applicants. Cost is often a major criterion when a grantor evaluates competing responses to an RFP. Any applicant needs to think the costs through carefully before committing to a bottom line.

❑ **What is the political environment for the RFP?** You need to determine who else will be competing for the award and also understand the politics that will shape the selection of recipients. The names of the most likely competitors can usually be determined by attending the RFP's technical conference. Only the most serious applicants tend to attend such meetings. You should also identify whether there are certain individuals whose endorsements would be particularly useful in responding to the RFP, such as key elected officials, the heads of organizations that need to cooperate to make the project successful, or community leaders who are very familiar with key decision makers of the organization issuing the RFP. Try to determine if the RFP has been developed in response to criticism from a particular source or in response to legislative action sponsored by a particular group. What kinds of relationships do you have with these "influentials?" Can you work with them? Will they support you or someone else?

❑ **Does another organization already have the inside track?** In theory, if a government source intends to give a grant or contract to an already-selected recipient, it is supposed to declare the project a *sole-source offering*. For various reasons, this often doesn't happen. Identifying RFPs that are already "locked up" is sometimes difficult, even for organizations that have a good informational pipeline. But experienced proposal writers claim the content of the RFP itself may give the necessary clues. They look for

- The level of detail which the RFP mentions on projects already underway or work that has been completed by another organization prior to issuing the RFP.

- Evaluation criteria that can be met by only a very few applicants.

- A very detailed scope-of-work statement, indicating that the project has been tailored to the plans and ideas of a specific organization.

Source: *Getting Funded: The Complete Guide to Writing Grant Proposals* by Mary Hall and Susan Howlett. Available from Portland State University, Continuing Education Press, www.cep.pdx.edu.

SOURCES FOR SAMPLES OF RFPs

- A comprehensive listing of available RFPs from the federal government is available at http://www.FedBizOpps.gov

- The Foundation Center now provides an annotated description of foundations and corporations that have recently issued RFPs at http://www.fdncenter.org/pnd/rfp/index.html. You can then go to the Web site of the issuing grantmakers to view the full content of the RFP.

- Many state agencies now use Web sites to publish their RFPs. An example is New Hampshire's State Department of Education which has an easy-to-use site, http://www.ed.state.nh.us/RFPs

Chapter 3

Developing the Idea

This chapter indicates the steps to follow in developing the idea for a proposal and discusses the importance of gathering data and building the support and involvement of others during the planning phase.

The general progression of proposal development followed in this book is shown in Figure I-1, Diagram of Proposal Development Process, on page xi. Keep those steps in mind as you flesh out your proposal idea.

STEP 1: ASSESSING THE NEED

Before beginning to compose a proposal, the organization or individual developing the request must thoroughly assess the need for a proposal's idea. Consider organizational capacity, the local environment, the political climate, and societal problems as a whole. This is not an articulation of the need for the money, but the *need for the work to be done*. As there are not sufficient financial resources available to meet all of society's needs and desires, those dollars which *are* requested and approved should be used to the best possible purpose. Funders aren't interested in meeting internal organizational needs; a proposal bears weight if it articulates an *external need in the community*.

There are sound, pragmatic reasons why a thorough analysis of the proposed idea and its impacts, both good and bad, should be undertaken *before* the proposal document is started. Not the least of these is that if the project is funded, the applicant will be held responsible for delivering what may have unwittingly been promised. Important aspects you should consider in an assessment of need are given below.

External Considerations

- **The nature of the need.** All funders ask, "Is this project addressing the needs of the clients or the needs of the applicant?" If the needs of those to be served have not been assessed, it will be impossible to document a compelling rationale in your proposal. Such a proposal will not succeed.

- **Relevance of the project.** Among all the requests for support, will this one truly benefit society? Does it address a problem that really matters? Will it benefit enough people to justify the resources spent on it?

- **Duplication of efforts.** Many proposals submitted to funders seeking "innovative" ideas are for projects that have already been tried elsewhere. Grantors resent receiving proposals from several organizations at a time, each saying that it is the only one in the region doing what it does. This suggests that the applicants are not communicating, cooperating, or collaborating with one another, resulting in missed opportunities for cost savings due to economies of scale, shared information and activities, a more unified voice with decision makers, and more.

Internal Considerations

- **Prioritization.** Every organization or institution has a variety of problems that require attention. In meeting one need through the receipt of external funds, the organization may ignore or postpone working on another. Such a decision and its implications should be carefully considered. Funders want to know that the decision to focus on a particular issue or project reflects the organization's strategic plan and indicates that the proposed idea is a priority in relationship to other efforts of the organization.

- **Applicant resources.** In competing for sponsored project funds, an organization also commits some of its own resources. While this may involve only personnel and expenses for proposal development (in itself sometimes quite costly), it may also require matching dollars or services. Sometimes the agency is also expected to continue the project with its own revenue once the external funding ends. Or the funder may impose other conditions on receipt of funds, such as a particular type of audit or physical plant adaptations (such as handicap accessibility) or modified hiring policies, evaluation procedures, or reports. Applicants also need to ascertain if they can accommodate a newly funded project logistically. Consider the impact additional staff will have on use of space, phone systems, computers, copiers, administrative and bookkeeping staff, and so forth.

- **Impact on the applicant.** The receipt of a grant or contract always has some side effects, often unexpected, on the recipient. To the extent that these influences can be identified in advance, the agency can make decisions about how to ameliorate harmful effects or capitalize on beneficial results. For example, a new grant or contract may result in major changes in the structure of the organization. New types of expertise and professional interests may be brought into the agency, influencing values, interests, and expectations, even if the specific personnel involved are later terminated. It may mean that program priorities will be shifted, often for extended periods, as the community or population served comes to expect and demand continuation of a program started with outside funds. Facilities and equipment supported by the grant or contract will need to be maintained. The funder may require that the population to be served be involved in the project's planning and operation. This may dramatically affect future relationships between the organization and its community or clientele.

Factors to be considered in analyzing the need for a particular project's idea will vary. However, the following list may be useful in prompting other questions which should be asked during this process.

- **How do you know there is a need for the proposed idea?**

- **Who or what is affected by the need and in what way?**

- **How urgent is this need, in relation to others in the community?**

- **Is the need one of the top priorities in your institution's strategic plan?**

- **Who else agrees this is a problem worth addressing?**

- **Who else is working on the issue locally, regionally, or nationally?**

- **Have other ways of addressing the problem been tried?** This includes the applicant and others in the field. What worked, what didn't and why?

- **Why should these particular needs and this specific population receive attention at this time?** Is the political climate advantageous just now? Do newly released research results lead naturally to your premise? Has the topic been in the news lately, making it seem timely? Has the population to be served been particularly vocal or visible lately?

- **What is likely to happen if this particular project is not implemented now?**

- **Why are you best suited to do this work?** What makes you distinct?

- **Do you have the capacity to initiate this effort at this time?** Do you have a strong, connected board, competent staff, well-trained volunteers, organizational infrastructure, partnerships in the community?

- **Is the problem really solvable?** What evidence do you have that your efforts will make a lasting difference? Can the need really be met? Will the level (of service, research, exposure) you propose be enough to make an impact?

- **Is the need seen as especially important by those groups whose support and involvement are critical to your success?**

- **What constraints or difficulties should be anticipated in meeting the need?**

The end product of this process should include the items in Checklist 3-1 below.

Checklist 3-1. Results of Needs Assessment

❑ Proof that your project is unique, and reasons why you are best suited to do it.

❑ A compelling statement of the problem(s) the project will address.

❑ A clear description of the population(s) to be served.

❑ A list of factors which indicate why the idea should receive priority for funding, such as the current state of collaborations, economic or political environment, newsworthiness, timeliness.

❑ An understanding of the previous literature, research, or work that has addressed this same problem and knowledge of whether the specific project idea has already been tried in another context.

❑ Analysis of how the landscape may have changed in the recent past, due to events such as a natural disaster, an economic upsurge or downturn, or new research that upsets past assumptions, and how those things might affect the issue.

❑ A list of allies willing to support the proposal idea with political influence, funding, shared resources, support letters, and/or collaboration.

❑ Identification of additional data to be collected during the operation of the project.

Additional Considerations for a Research Project

While a needs assessment is most commonly associated with shaping demonstration, training, or service projects, it is also a critical step in the development of a proposal for a research project. In addition to answering relevant questions in the checklist presented earlier, the information collected is important later in shaping both the "problem statement" and the "related research" components of the proposal (see Chapter 8). The following list suggests some additional questions which might be considered in analyzing a research idea:

- **What is the problem?**

- **Why is the proposed research needed?** What gap in a body of knowledge or methodology does it propose to complete?

- **How significant is the proposed idea?**

- **How does it relate to the rest of the research and literature?**

- **Are there additional research breakthroughs that can be anticipated later because of this project's likely contributions?**

- **How important is the proposed activity to advancing knowledge and understanding within the field or across different fields?**

- **How well qualified is the proposer to conduct the project?**

- **To what extent does the proposed activity suggest and explore creative and original concepts?**

- **How well conceived and organized is the proposed activity?**

- **Is there sufficient access to resources to succeed?**

- **What aspects make the proposed project unique?** (the submitting institution, the individuals involved, the approach, the timing, the measurement methods)

- **What prior research has been done on either the proposed content or methodology and what have been its flaws?**

- **What is the theoretical base for the study?** What evidence exists that this base is sound or is at least worth further exploration?

- **What characteristics about the institution and/ or individuals engaged in this effort make this proposal more worthy of support than those of competitors?**

- **How might this endeavor further the top priority goals in the field?**

In order to complete the analysis of need, you may wish to consult one or more of the information sources listed at the end of this chapter. These sources are particularly useful in identifying previous research or securing regional or national data to be compared to local information about the problem.

STEP 2: DEFINING THE APPROACH

For any problem there may be multiple approaches to both the solution and its implementation. Once a need is clearly defined, the next step in refining the project idea is to consider many alternative methods for responding to it and to analyze the merits and disadvantages of each (see Checklist 3-2).

Example 1: A community faced with serious unemployment might either institute a large effort aimed at training people for existing occupations or emphasize the identification and development of new kinds of jobs. The former approach might more quickly decrease the level of unemployment, but it could also result in placing individuals in lower-paying positions, occupations that are seasonal or temporary, or jobs where there may shortly be an oversupply.

Subsequent decisions must be made about the best method of implementation. Some typical ones are:

- Should the job training be preceded by some type of educational activity?

- Should it be conducted in an institution or on the job?

- Should the employer be subsidized for hiring an individual trained in the project and, if so, for how long?

Example 2: In a community with a high rate of domestic violence, those addressing the issue must determine if the best approach is to:

- Protect the women and their children by sheltering them from harm.

- Counsel perpetrators so they won't re-offend.

- Work for more stringent laws that incarcerate offenders longer.

- Strengthen prevention education efforts in schools and workplaces.

- Work with young people to teach non-violent problem solving techniques.

If they decided that shelter was the answer, subsequent decisions might be whether to:

- Offer emergency shelter to the affected women and children.

- House the families in separate motel rooms or in a shared home setting.

- Provide longer-term housing to stabilize the situation.

Checklist 3-2. Selecting Among Options

In selecting possible options and weighing their merits, consider:

Feasibility & Effectiveness

❑ What has been the experience of other organizations or individuals in launching similar projects? Who else in the region or the field is doing this type of work and what has been learned from their experiences?

❑ What does the research or existing literature show about the success or failure of similar approaches in the past?

❑ How do the cooperating agencies view the different approaches? Would they cooperate more readily if you chose one over another?

❑ What do public policy makers see as potential barriers and benefits to each type of approach?

❑ What are the anticipated costs versus benefits for each approach?

Suitability

❑ Which approach is most suited to your organization's capabilities and interests?

❑ Does your approach fit the priorities and preferences of the potential funder? Is one approach clearly of more interest to them than another (e.g., prevention rather than crisis intervention, or preservation versus new construction)?

Uniqueness

❑ How is this approach innovative or distinct?

❑ How does it complement or further other work?

❑ Is there anything to be gained from a dramatic or unusual approach?

Anticipated Impact

❑ What will be the anticipated short-term and long-term impact of each approach in solving the particular problem?

❑ If a particular population or group of subjects is involved in the project, how will it be affected?

Utility & Sustainability

❑ Which approach will be easiest to sustain with contributed or earned income after a start-up grant ends?

❑ Which approach is easiest for other organizations to replicate? Many funding sources support only projects that will produce products or processes that can later be used by others.

- Include counseling, childcare, legal assistance or job training.

- Work with the children to prevent another generation of violence.

You can assume that, if personnel are doing a thorough job of refining the project idea, they will change their positions several times on the best solution for the need. New information causes the continuous reassessment of options. This will also be true once a project is underway. In fact, one experienced proposal writer pointed out, only partly in jest, that she always counted on her current project to prompt ideas for at least two future proposals. She said she was always thinking of better ideas or better approaches when it was too late to apply them to the current situation.

STEP 3: DOCUMENTING THE NEED

Many novices and even some experienced proposal writers overlook the importance of statistical data to the development and refinement of the project idea, or underestimate the role data should play in the application itself. Statistical data are needed, for example, to:

- Help prove the need for the project, particularly in your locale.

- Help refine an approach to the need.

- Document the degree to which your organization has previously been successful (with this or other clientele).

- Illustrate that you know what is going on locally and nationally.

While it is commonly understood that statistical data will be required by governmental funding sources, applicants often forget to provide them in requests to private foundations and corporations. These funders will not want to be bombarded with pages of charts and graphs, but they will want sufficient data included to answer questions which any sensible reviewer would ask.

Applications to national funding sources (whether governmental or private) should almost always contain some type of comparative data to place your needs in the appropriate context. For example, data showing that the juvenile delinquency rate in your town is twice as high as neighboring areas and five times as high as regional or national levels would help justify the need for a project more than any emotional appeals or political maneuvering. Comparative data are also useful in supporting a request to private funders for even a small portion of your agency's annual operating budget. All donors will want to know what impact your services are having and how this equates to others performing similar work.

Sources for such statistical data abound. Attachment 3-1 at the end of this chapter lists specific resources, but generically, grantseekers can turn to:

- Federal government agencies that oversee your field of work.

- Local government agencies that address similar problems.

- Elected officials whose staff may have done research or collected data.

- Colleges or universities where faculty or students may have done research in your field.

- United Way affiliates that may have conducted local research.

- Professional or trade associations related to your particular field.

- Librarians with access to on-line databases and reference materials.

It is inadvisable to take national statistics and apply them locally—though tempting in the absence of local documentation—because local factors may create vastly different circumstances. However, one can gather data sufficient for most grantors by polling or convening organizations, institutions, or agencies doing similar work in the community to gather their observations.

For example, an organization that served sexual assault survivors was planning to launch new child sexual assault services, but could find no documented proof of the problem in their county. So they gathered personnel from the state child protective services agency, the public health department, the county hospital, schools and day-care centers, the youth service bureau, police and fire departments, and religious institutions. They asked them if they had any knowledge of a problem. Not only were they able to gather sufficient anecdotal evidence to authenticate the need, but they also garnered the buy-in and support of the other agencies, which agreed that the proposed plan was sound and the host organization was uniquely suited to tackle the problem. Such corroboration of a need will appeal to funders, as it offers evidence that the applicant has a good relationship with colleagues and competitors and will probably not be duplicating services.

STEP 4: BUILDING SUPPORT AND INVOLVEMENT

Many stakeholders, both internal and external, should be included in developing the project idea. *Internal stakeholders* might include:

- **Those who will be carrying out the work.** They need to understand what the organization is promising and be willing and able to implement the idea as proposed.

- **Those responsible for managing the awarded contract or funds.** They may suggest that systems aren't in place for requested documentation or reporting, or that particular gifts must be spent within a specific budget cycle.

- **Legal counsel,** in case contracts or agreements need to be signed.

- **Risk management staff,** to assure the proposal doesn't expose the organization to liability.

- **Staff who will be evaluators at the project's completion,** to ensure that the applicant doesn't promise results they cannot measure.

- **Others in your organization who have received funds from the same source.** Not only will they have valuable information about the funder and the process, but they will feel included and informed, not competed with or slighted.

- **Top-level administrators or governing board members** who may be contacted by a grantor to verify that this project is indeed a priority of the institution.

Proposal writers sometimes find others reluctant to take the time to provide essential documents or help frame answers to important questions. Some find it best to garner the support and endorsement of the top person needed for the project to succeed, so that subordinates will be encouraged to cooperate. For example, an academic colleague noted that if his Dean supported an idea early in the process, other staff would as well; if not, they felt no compunction to cooperate or offer necessary information. Others believe that gaining the buy-in of each participant from the bottom up makes it easier to make their case to ultimate decision makers. Either way, you need to remind people that getting the grant will obligate the organization to conduct specific business, encumber funds in a particular way or time, and produce measurable results, so you don't want to promise something the organization isn't willing or able to deliver. (Enticing people with food and beverage during planning meetings also helps.)

External stakeholders might include:

- **Cooperating or affected agencies or groups within the community.** Private funders are particularly interested in the degree of local support for most projects and want assurance that the project will not duplicate others' services.

- **The population to be served or studied.** Their willingness to participate cannot be taken for granted and may, in fact, need to be documented in the application. They may also have suggestions for how to conduct the project so that it reflects the culture, values, or norms of those being served.

- **Relevant state agencies or organizations.** In many fields, a state agency or organization has been designated to oversee program development, resource allocation, or the provision of technical services to local groups planning projects. This may be a good source of information on the results of similar projects in the past, serve as a potential source of funds, or be willing to help with endorsements to regional or national sources.

- **The state agency that serves as a clearinghouse for some federal programs.** Some proposals for federal money must be screened by state personnel before your agency may submit them directly to the federal agency.

- **Local representatives of foundations or corporations you are likely to approach.** They can often spot issues that will strengthen your application and may be able to suggest other possible sources of support.

- **Program officers in a federal agency where you may be applying.**

ATTACHMENT 3-1.

SOURCES OF INFORMATION FOR IDEA REFINEMENT

Begin Locally

- **Federated funds** (such as United Way). See what research they have done locally, whom they have funded, and who else they know of in your field.

- **Phone directories.** Look in the government section and the Yellow Pages.

- **Elected officials.** Representatives and their staff people keep on top of who's doing what in their jurisdictions, and they may have done research or collected data themselves.

- **Local government agencies.** Department heads and their staff may have collaborated or communicated with groups doing similar work or done their own studies.

- **Nearby colleges or universities,** where faculty or students may have conducted research or worked with particular populations.

- **Professional or trade associations.** They will know who is addressing similar issues in your area.

Use the Library

Be sure to enlist the help of professional librarians, as they know of resources that may not be on the shelves or are stored in unexpected places. Libraries can have extensive print resources that are difficult for a novice to navigate, but may be precisely what you seek. Librarians have access to specialized tools that are oriented to their own locale. Many also subscribe to on-line databases, updated daily, that are not on the Internet. Use them to gain access to such things as:

- **Indexes of newspapers, magazines, and journals.**

- **Specialized encyclopedias.**

- **Sources of data** for domestic and international finances, economics, and trade.

- **Reference materials** on medicine, technology, mathematics, and health.

- **Data** on economics, geography, ethnic populations, and transportation.

Use the Internet

Some useful Web sites include:

Government Information Exchange
    http://www.info.gov

Local, state, and federal statistics
    http://www.firstgov.gov

Federal census information
    http://www.census.gov

Statistics from over 100 federal agencies
    http://www.fedstats.gov

National Center for Charitable Statistics
    http://www.nccs.urban.org

Chapter 4

Selecting the Funding Source

This section describes the types of funders, what distinguishes one type from another, how to identify and research funders appropriate for your proposal idea, and ways to initiate the relationship prior to submitting your proposal.

Many grantseekers want to jump directly into finding out who might fund their project. But this wastes time in the long run. Before you can identify which funders are appropriate to approach, make sure that you have first taken all the steps through Chapter 3:

- Identified an idea, analyzed its key characteristics, and decided whether it is a solicited (RFP) or unsolicited project.

- Reviewed your capability as an organization, secured the basic systems needed to support the proposal's development, and determined that the idea is compatible with the organization's mission and priorities.

- Substantiated the validity of the need for the project, developed a clear statement of the problem to be solved, and obtained appropriate statistical data and research.

- Brainstormed several options for meeting the need and implementing the project; tested against related research, local interest and capabilities, prior experience with similar idea,

possible impact, feasibility, and degree of innovation.

- Made a tentative decision about the best approach to the project and secured the buy-in of the cooperating agencies or departments necessary for implementation.

Now you are ready to begin your search for potential funders.

FINDING COMMON GROUND

Most project ideas could potentially be supported by several funding sources. So how do you select which one to approach? This is an important question to answer early because it takes significant time and effort to learn all you need to know about a funding source before actually writing the proposal.

Proposals that closely match a funder's goals—whether explicit or implicit—are much more likely to be funded. These goals could be prompted by legislation or politics, by the personal values and interests of a foundation's originator, or by a corporation's need to fund projects that will increase its visibility and stock value. But it's up to the grantseeker to do enough homework to be able to articulate why the proposed partnership makes sense.

Funders can tell when grantseekers have not narrowed their search enough to find good matches. Proposal reviewers (often called *readers*) may be reminded of someone in a bar using the same tired line to pick up anyone who might respond. Indeed, countless funders have received proposals with another grantmaker's name inadvertently left in the text. To convince a funder that your project is worth considering, you must explain why you believe there's a compelling connection between your goals and theirs, and why funding your proposal idea is an opportunity they won't want to miss.

Later in this chapter you will learn how to identify and research potential funders. As you narrow that search, here are some factors to look for:

Shared Mission

The grantor's goals clearly relate to the goals of the proposal idea. Two examples: The foundation of a real estate agency funds a homeless shelter or a Habitat for Humanity project; the local arts commission offers seed money to pay the artist in an arts education program in a low-income neighborhood school.

Shared Constituency

The people connected to the funder (employees or customers of a corporate entity or the members of an association) share the same characteristics or experiences as those to be served by the project. Two examples: A union whose membership is predominantly immigrants supports a program championing immigrants' legal rights; a toy manufacturer funds a group dealing with family support.

Shared Culture

The decision makers share the core values of the applicant organization, such as how it's governed or the ethnic makeup of the population served. Two examples: A company run by Chinese immigrants funds construction of a nursing home for Chinese elders; an alternative medicine clinic supports a group exploring nonpharmaceutical approaches to depression.

Shared Image

The funder and applicant share the same name or perceived status, or the corporate tag line could be applied to the program. Two examples: A cellular phone company whose tag line is "Imagine No Limits" supports a ski program for people with disabilities; a timber company whose tag line is "The Tree Growing Company" supports a neighborhood tree-planting project.

Shared Market

Who's making money from your constituents? Regardless of the economic status of the people you serve or those who support you, someone is making money from them. Are they partial to a particular clothing line, model of car, or vacation destination? Is there a type of beverage they usually drink, an information management system they prefer, a leisure product they enjoy? Are there pharmaceuticals they take due to their age or medical condition? Picture a sugar substitute company sponsoring an event for a group fighting diabetes.

Who would *like to be* making money from your constituents? Corporations can position themselves powerfully in front of the people you associate with by giving a gift that affords them signage at an event or logo placement on your materials. Look for products or companies seeking visibility, possibly because they're new to your community, and be prepared to define the demographic profile of your constituency so they can see the value of a partnership.

Damage Control

Sometimes a funder's image may have suffered for political, economic, or environmental reasons. An invitation to support your work gives them an opportunity to reposition themselves among your constituents. Examples: a transportation provider that recently had an accident; a food purveyor responsible for a food poisoning incident or a manufacturer accused of polluting.

Figure 4-1. Public and Private Funding Sources and Differences Between Them

FUNDING SOURCES

Public	Private	
• Federal government. • State government. • Local government (county, borough, municipality).	• Foundations. • Corporations. • Service clubs. • Professional associations.	• Trade associations. • Unions. • Special interest groups. • Faith communities.

WAYS THEY DIFFER

• Where the money comes from. • Why they're giving money away. • Who's involved in the decision-making process. • What the decisions are based on.	• Method to initiate contact. • Size of awards. • Reporting procedures. • Acknowledgement procedures.

Advantages

Public	Private
• Purpose set by legislation. • Focus on functions usually affecting significant groups in society. • Have the most money. • More likely to make big grants/contracts. • More likely to pay all project costs. • More likely to cover indirect costs. • Easier to identify and research. • Have known application processes and firm deadlines. • Use prescribed formats for proposals. • Have policies about renewal. • Lots of staff, with resources for technical assistance. • Funds available to wider array of organizations (e.g., profit, nonprofit, other public entities). • Accountable to elected officials if funders obviously don't follow the rules.	• More likely to focus on emerging issues, new needs, populations not yet evolved into special interest groups. • Will often allow their funds to be pooled with other sources. • Some can make very large grants. • Better source of funds for start-up or experimental projects. • Proposals need not be complex or lengthy. • Can be much more flexible in responding to unique needs, circumstances, time frames. • Seldom have bureaucratic requirements to follow in administering grants. • Can help leverage large public grants. • Can often provide forms of help other than just cash. • Usually have fewer applicants. • Can generally be much more informal. • Often better sources for more local needs and smaller agencies.

Source: *Getting Funded: The Complete Guide to Writing Grant Proposals* by Mary Hall and Susan Howlett. Available from Portland State University, Continuing Education Press, www.cep.pdx.edu. Copyright © 2003. All rights reserved.

Figure 4-1. Public and Private Funding Sources and Differences Between Them (continued)	
Disadvantages	
Public	**Private**
• Much more bureaucratic. • Proposals must be longer and require compliance with a variety of stipulations. • Often require institutional cost-sharing and matching. • Many more requirements to follow once funds are received. • Reviewers tend to favor established applicants. • Sometimes difficult to sell really new ideas or high-risk approaches. • Cost to applicant of securing such funds and carrying out projects usually much higher. • Changing political trends affect security of some programs and continued availability of funds.	• Average grant size usually smaller. • Priorities can change rapidly, making continued support harder to predict. • Applicants have limited influence on the decision-making process. • Information on policies and procedures harder to track; requires more lead time for research. • Some unwilling to pay all project costs and most do not cover indirect costs. • Limited staff size lessens opportunities for preliminary discussion/site visits. • May not explain a rejection, making it harder to compete more effectively next time.

UNDERSTANDING THE TYPES OF FUNDERS

All funders fall into one of two categories: public (government) and private. This section describes the various types of funders and what distinguishes them from one another. Figure 4-1 shows the types of funding and the differences between the two. More detailed distinctions follow:

Public Funders

Government funders make grants to carry out purposes established by their respective legislative bodies (federal, state, county or borough, municipality, etc.) and generally support projects that help a large number of individuals.

Federal Government

There are hundreds of separate grant programs supported through the federal government, and managed by a large bureaucracy of departments, bureaus, and offices. Although the growth rate of such funds is declining, the federal government

still represents the largest source of support for those seeking external funding.

Organizations new to grantseeking should be cautious about approaching federal funders, as the process is elaborate, complicated, and time-consuming, and one of the first questions federal funders will ask is, "Do you have evidence of local support for your proposal?" Gathering the necessary items (see Checklist 4-1) will help you determine which federal funders may be most appropriate for your proposal idea.

State and Local Governments

State and local government agencies have at least four reasons for serving as sources of grant or contract funds:

- They are designated as recipients for federal monies (usually block grants) which must then be redistributed to local applicants.

- They receive a grant or contract themselves and want to identify others to perform part of the project's requirements.

- They are designated as the administrator of a grant program established by the state legislature, county, borough, or city council and must then choose recipients for these funds.

- They wish to purchase a particular product or service to help implement some nongrant aspect of their responsibilities.

State and local governments have two distinct advantages over federal agencies, even though the availability and size of awards may not match those of federal funders: Their personnel are usually more accessible and the competition for funds is likely to be less intense.

Don't assume that state or local agencies are not interested in supporting research. They routinely fund studies on issues appropriate to their jurisdictions. While they may not offer grants-in-aid for research, they frequently arrange for consulting contracts, personal services agreements, or internships, sometimes tied to doctoral dissertations.

Characteristics of Government Funders

Government funders must be accessible to the public. Don't hesitate to contact them to ascertain the suitability of your project idea, perhaps asking about the most propitious time to apply, a reasonable amount to request, or what aspect of your work might appeal most to reviewers. Because so many grantseekers request this information too late in the process, some government agencies are now stipulating dates (a month or two prior to the deadline) after which they will not accept such contacts.

Government grants reflect the priorities of governmental leaders or bodies. These could shift, depending on who is in leadership, what is the most pressing community problem, or the political climate, but the goals usually address a need for research or delivery of services that improve the current situation in the nation or community (e.g., research on disease, or low-income housing).

Who makes the decisions varies. Some government funders have permanent, full-time program officers whose job it is to issue RFPs, review them, determine who gets funding, and maintain those relationships throughout the course of the grant. Others hire reviewers, usually professionals from the field, who receive a stipend for their effort. Others seat a panel of volunteer peer reviewers with expertise in various aspects of the topic.

The review criteria are clearly articulated, with explicit scoring procedures. The review process is transparent, and grantseekers can request specific information justifying the ranking they received and how they could strengthen the proposal another time.

Federal grants and contracts constitute the largest amounts of money being awarded in the nation, but state and local awards can range from the low thousands of dollars to hundreds of thousands.

Reporting requirements are most stringent among public funders, who expect detailed accounts of how the money was spent and how the project is progressing. Acknowledgement is expected on printed documents and resulting reports.

Most government funding resources can now be found through the Internet. Specific sites are listed at the end of this chapter. Also consider these other ways of searching for grant opportunities:

- Call the offices of elected officials (members of Congress, state legislators, county or city council members) who can suggest departments and agencies.

- Look under the government listings in your phone book to see the options.

- Ask librarians.

- Check the Web sites of your state or community.

Sometimes government funding comes from unlikely sources, so don't write off a department because it doesn't sound like it would fit. Recent grants were made by the Defense Department for breast cancer research and by a city's utilities division for tree planting projects.

Private Funders

Foundations

Foundations carry out purposes established by their founders or their trustees and, generally, support efforts in a specific field, issue area, or community. Each year they must award an amount

Checklist 4-1. Information to Gather on Potential Federal Funders

- ❑ Correct name of the grant program or program category.
- ❑ Correct name and contact information of administering agency.
- ❑ Major purpose of legislation that authorized the program.
- ❑ Eligibility requirements for applicants.
- ❑ Details on any restrictions placed on use of the program's funds.
- ❑ Particular geographic regions that may be higher priority for this funder.
- ❑ Requirements for matching funds or cost sharing.
- ❑ Latest regulations governing program (and any indication they may change).
- ❑ Current priorities of the program and whether they may change.
- ❑ Appropriations in current fiscal year (FY) and amount projected for following year.
- ❑ How much of available money is earmarked for continuation of prior awards.
- ❑ Pertinent compliance requirements of funding agency or Office of Management and Budget (OMB) policies.
- ❑ Whether a preliminary step is required to gain permission to submit full proposal.
- ❑ Name, title, and contact information of key administrator.
- ❑ Application deadline(s); there may be more than one per year.

- ❑ Dates of anticipated review and notification.
- ❑ Required proposal format and accompanying forms.
- ❑ Application and review process, including selection criteria and rating form.
- ❑ A list of grants or contracts awarded recently, including amounts.
- ❑ Names and affiliations of recent proposal reviewers, so you can see what types of people they use, with what affiliations, backgrounds, and interests.
- ❑ Whether a state or local government plays any role in the selection process or program administration and, if so, the relevant names and contact information.
- ❑ The tendency of the agency to cut budget requests: find funded proposals, which are public record, and compare the requested amount to that awarded.
- ❑ Whether they fund indirect costs and, if so, what percentage.
- ❑ Whether they fund overhead costs in a project budget.
- ❑ What percentage of the total project cost they are likely to cover.
- ❑ Policies about renewals.
- ❑ What obligations (reports, administrative requirements) follow the grant or contract.

Table 4-1. Types of Foundations and Their General Characteristics					
	Private Foundations		**Public Foundations**		
Characteristic	Independent or family	Company-sponsored corporate	Operating	Community	Other public
Description	Independent grantmaking organizations established to aid social, educational, religious, or other activities chosen by founder.	Legally independent grantmaking organizations with close ties to the corporation providing the funds.	Organizations which fund the programs, research, or services of an institution (such as a university or hospital).	Organizations which make grants to address the needs of a specific community or region.	Organizations formed to serve specific population groups (e.g., women or gays) or specific fields or issues (e.g., human services, social justice).
Source of funds	Endowments from a single source such as an individual, a family, or a group of individuals.	Endowment and/or annual contributions from a profit-making corporation.	Endowment provided by the sponsoring institution, but eligible for maximum tax-deductible contributions from the public.	Contributions from many donors; eligible for maximum tax deduction. Established ones have endowments.	Contributions raised from a large number of individuals who share their goals.
Decision-making body	Donor(s), donor's family, an independent board, or a bank or trust officer acting on donor's behalf.	Board composed of corporate officials or local company; some may have no corporate affiliation.	Usually an independent board of directors.	Board of directors representing the community.	Peer review panels representing donors and constituents; sometimes includes grantees.

Table 4-1. Types of Foundations and Their General Characteristics (continued)					
Grant-making activity	Broad discretion allowed, but may have specific guidelines and give in only a few specific fields. 80% limit to local area.	Give in fields related to corporate activities and/or in communities where the corporation operates. Usually give more grants for smaller amounts than independent foundations.	Give grants directly to the foundation's program, but occasionally fund outside organizations with mutual goals.	Grants generally limited to charitable organizations in the local community.	Grants often made in conjunction with training or technical assistance, sometimes for multiple years.
Reporting requirements	IRS 990-PF available to public annually. Some issue separate annual report.	IRS 990-PF available to public. May publish guidelines and annual report.	IRS 990-PF available to public.	IRS 990 available to public. Many publish full guidelines or annual report.	IRS 990 available to public.

equal to a specific percentage of the interest earned from their principal, and they must file reports on their activities annually with the Internal Revenue Service. There are several types of foundations: Their general characteristics are listed in Table 4-1.

Emerging Developments in Foundations

The world of foundations has changed dramatically in the last two decades. Enormous amounts of wealth changed hands as "baby boomers" began to inherit their parents' fortunes and created foundations with their newfound resources. Many corporations and their employees and stockholders benefited from unprecedented gains in the stock market and invested their assets in new foundations. Three-fifths of the larger foundations in the U.S. were formed in the last 20 years. Table 4-2 details this growth.

These huge shifts have altered how foundations behave, reflecting the attitudes and interests

of a new wave of funders. Where foundations seldom used to offer grants for operating support or multiyear funding, we're now seeing an increase in both. And many of the newer foundation donors are getting more engaged in the work of the grantees, viewing themselves as "venture philanthropists" as they infuse nonprofits with their own financial and intellectual capital, resources, and contacts.

Giving circles, new "social investment clubs," have emerged throughout the country. Groups of individuals pool their financial resources to make a joint contribution that will have greater impact than a single gift. Some are taking the steps to become bona fide foundations.

Types of Foundation Awards

Awards offered by foundations range from $100 to several million dollars. The gifts fall into the following categories:

Table 4-2. Changes in Foundation Giving, 1980 to 2001

	1980	2001	% Change
Number of foundations	22,099	61,810	180%
Total assets ($billion)	48.2	476.8	890%
Total giving ($billion)	3.4	30.5	788%

Source: The Foundation Center, Foundation Yearbook, © 2003. Total giving includes grants, scholarships, and employee matching gifts; excludes set-asides, loans, program-related investments (PRIs), and program expenses

- **General support or operating funds,** to assist with applicant's normal ongoing work.

- **Seed money or startup funds,** to help launch a new organization or enterprise.

- **Program or project grants,** designated for a specific type of activity, service or effort, including research.

- **Pilot or demonstration grants,** to help show the effectiveness of a model or approach that could be replicated by the grantee or others using continuation funds from elsewhere.

- **Capital building or equipment costs,** for construction or purchase of tangible items.

- **Program-related investments,** direct gifts of assets for investment in program-specific areas, such as economic development, low-income housing, or minority enterprises with the expectation that the sum will be paid back with or without interest.

- **Fellowships/scholarships/internships,** given to applicants who offer them to students.

- **Challenge or matching grants,** contingent on the applicant generating additional monies from other contributors.

- **Training, technical assistance, or capacity-building expenses** enhance the ability of the applicant to function better or become more self-sufficient.

- **Endowments** help the applicant garner substantial capital reserves so that the earnings can pay for program or operating costs.

- **Loan guarantees,** use the good name of the grantmaker to secure a loan. While money may not ever change hands, the grantmaker must record a guarantee as if it might have to cover the loan if the nonprofit defaults.

Table 4-3 shows a typical breakdown of the types of awards foundations offer.

Foundation Award Recipients

Most foundations must limit their awards to private, nonprofit, tax-exempt organizations that have been certified by the Internal Revenue Service as qualifying under Section 501(c)(3) of the Code. Some foundations will make awards to public entities as defined under Section 170(c) of the Code. A small number of foundations will also make grants directly to individuals. If a foundation wishes to support an organization that has not yet earned the appropriate designation, it may offer a grant pending qualification or ask the organization to find a *fiscal sponsor* (an entity to which the grant can be awarded on behalf of the applicant).

While the actual amounts vary from year to year, the pattern of what types of organizations various foundations have funded has been relatively consistent. Figure 4-2 presents a broad overview of that pattern.

Figure 4-3 shows the recent distribution of grants by subject area among foundations

Checklist 4-2 offers a list of kinds of information to gather on potential foundation funders.

Specific resources for identifying foundations

Table 4-3. Types of Support Awarded by Foundations, ca 2000

Type of Support	Dollar Value of Grants 2000		No. of Grants 2000		Average Dollar Value of Grants
	Amount	%	No.	%	
General Support	**$2,100,341**	**14.0**	**23,293**	**19.4**	**$90,170**
General Operating	1,722,125	11.5	19,673	16.4	87,537
Annual Campaigns	41,764	0.3	452	0.4	92,398
Income Development	131,024	0.9	1,295	1.1	101,177
Management Development	205,428	1.4	1,873	1.6	109,679
Capital Support	**3,396,964**	**22.6**	**14,216**	**11.9**	**238,954**
Capital Campaigns	532,116	3.5	1,843	1.5	288,723
Building/Renovation	1,585,664	10.6	7,175	6.0	220,998
Equipment	183,588	1.2	2,364	2.0	77,660
Computer Systems/ Technology	186,320	1.2	1,260	1.1	147,873
Land Acquisition	133,517	0.9	253	0.2	527,735
Endowments	729,514	4.9	1,106	0.9	659,597
Debt Reduction	10,247	0.1	70	0.1	146,386
Collections Acquisition	35,999	0.2	145	0.1	248,269
Program Support	**6,870,895**	**45.8**	**44,941**	**37.5**	**152,887**
Program Development	5,119,532	34.1	33,965	28.4	150,730
Conferences/Seminars	174,610	1.2	2,101	1.8	83,108
Faculty/Staff Development	349,085	2.3	2,113	1.8	165,208
Professorships	101,965	0.7	298	0.2	342,164
Film/Video/Radio	103,330	0.7	693	0.6	149,105
Publication	159,822	1.1	1,189	1.0	134,417
Seed Money	235,280	1.6	867	0.7	271,373
Curriculum Development	222,786	1.5	1,250	1.0	178,229
Performance/Productions	57,073	0.4	721	0.6	79,158
Exhibitions	88,290	0.6	623	0.5	141,717
Collections Management/ Preservation	58,455	0.4	215	0.2	271,884
Commissioning New Works	16,757	0.1	144	0.1	116,368
Electronic Media/Online Services	183,910	1.2	762	0.6	241,352
Research	**1,588,386**	**10.6**	**6,498**	**5.4**	**244,442**
Student Aid Funds	**1,065,565**	**7.1**	**4,965**	**4.1**	**214,615**
Student Aid	33,019	0.2	297	0.2	111,175
Fellowships	296,719	2.0	1,415	1.2	209,695
Internships	23,001	0.2	320	0.3	71,878
Scholarships	602,206	4.0	2,361	2.0	255,064
Awards/Prizes/Competitions	110,621	0.7	572	0.5	193,393

Table 4-3 continued on next page

Table 4-3. Types of Support Awarded by Foundations, ca 2000 (continued)

Other	**336,146**	**2.2**	**1,521**	**1.3**	**221,003**
Technical Assistance	216,291	1.4	987	0.8	219,140
Emergency Funds	1,321	0.0	28	0.0	47,179
Program Evaluation	118,534	0.8	506	0.4	234,257
Not Specified	**2,503,148**	**16.7**	**36,023**	**30.1**	**69,487**
Qualifying Support Type[1]					
Continuing	3,552,517	23.7	29,765	24.9	119,352
Matching or Challenge	501,665	3.3	1,366	1.1	367,251

Source: Foundation Giving Trends (2002), The Foundation Center. All dollar figures expressed in thousands; due to rounding, figures may not add up.

*Based on grants of $10,000 or more awarded by a national sample of 1,015 larger U.S. foundations (including 800 of the 1,000 largest ranked by total giving). For community foundations, only discretionary grants are included. Grants to individuals are not included in the file.

[1]Qualifying types of support are tracked in addition to basic types of support, i.e., a challenge grant for construction, and are thereby represented separately.

Types of Support Award by Foundations, circa 2000: http://fdncenter.org/fc_stats/pdf/07_fund_tos/2000/15_00.pdf

are listed at the end of this chapter, but here are some rules of thumb about searching for foundations. Since the federal government requires private foundations to make their financial information (including grant details) available to the public, grantseekers can locate and research private foundations more easily than any other type of private funder. Seasoned grantseekers rely heavily on both hard-copy and on-line directories compiled by national resources such as The Foundation Center, and by regional resources such as Regional Associations of Grantmakers. While corporate *foundations* will appear in listings of private foundations, corporate *giving programs* are not required to report their activity and may be harder to identify. Community foundations can be identified through The Grantsmanship Center, the Council on Foundations and other resources listed in the next chapter.

Characteristics of Foundation Funders

The monies awarded by private foundations are usually the interest income generated by massed capital, and the priorities for awards are stipulated by the donors of that capital. Look at where that money came from, as the original source will often have an enormous impact on the grantor's goals and procedures. For example, the foundation of a company that makes its money in resource extraction may not be interested in proposals from environmental organizations.

Independent foundations must carry out the specified intent of the original founder, while family foundations are established to create a shared family activity, to garner tax benefits, or to facilitate giving to groups with whom they are already involved. Public foundations emerge to address the unmet needs of their particular constituency, such

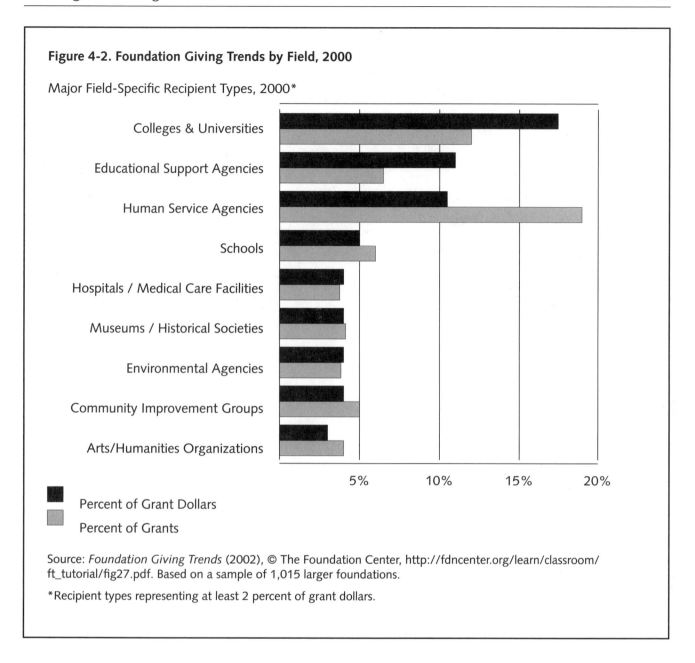

Figure 4-2. Foundation Giving Trends by Field, 2000

Major Field-Specific Recipient Types, 2000*

- Percent of Grant Dollars
- Percent of Grants

Source: *Foundation Giving Trends* (2002), © The Foundation Center, http://fdncenter.org/learn/classroom/ ft_tutorial/fig27.pdf. Based on a sample of 1,015 larger foundations.

*Recipient types representing at least 2 percent of grant dollars.

as gays and lesbians, African Americans, or people living with AIDS.

Depending on their size, private foundations may have professional *program officers* who are instrumental in the selection process, but leave the final decision to the trustees. Again, depending on size, some family foundations have staff who are pivotally involved in the decision-making process, but most use unpaid family members to make determinations. Since operating foundations exist primarily to fund an institution, individuals from the board and staff of the institution make these decisions. Community and public foundations want their reviewers to reflect the community or population they serve. Many family foundations and giving circles choose to operate without paid staff and limit their accessibility to protect their privacy.

Foundations base their decisions on more subjective criteria than government funders. They may put more emphasis on who's on the board of a nonprofit, how the alliance might reflect on them in terms of politics or marketing, and whether leaders or volunteers in the applicant organization

Figure 4-3. Distribution of Grants by Subject Category, 2000

Grants by Major Subject Categories, 2000

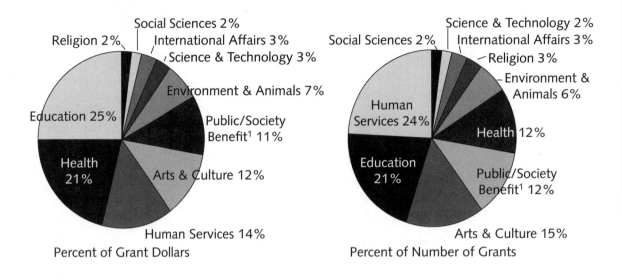

Percent of Grant Dollars   Percent of Number of Grants

Source: *Foundation Giving Trends* (2002), © The Foundation Center, http://fdncenter.org/learn/classroom/ft_tutorial/fig02_2000.pdf. Based on a sample of 1,015 larger foundations.

[1]Includes civil rights and social action, community inprovement, philanthropy and voluntarism, and public affairs.

are part of their own organization. Reputation, clarity of purpose and presentation, and a sense of capability all affect opinions. Ultimately, all decisions hinge on whether the proposal furthers the funder's goals, whether clearly stated or not.

Community, public, operating, and larger private foundations usually accept calls from potential applicants. While corporate and family foundations may *wish* to be accessible to the public, they are often overwhelmed with inquiry calls.

The size of foundation awards varies greatly, from low hundreds to hundreds of thousands or millions of dollars. The *average* foundation gift in the last decade was $5000. Foundations have lower expectations about reporting and acknowledgement, but do expect to hear how their grant monies were spent and to be acknowledged in print materials. The larger the gift, the more rigorous they will be about accountability, asking for receipts, audits, professional evaluations, frequent communication, and reports.

Private Funders

Corporations

Corporations, owned by and accountable to their stockholders, support nonprofit organizations and institutions to further the interests of the company. They can provide that support through many channels:

- **A corporate foundation,** as described above.

- **A corporate giving program,** similar to a corporate foundation but not required to publicly disclose its grantmaking activities nor to grant a certain percentage of its assets each year. Giving programs work closely with marketing, community relations, and government relations departments of the company.

- **Employee gift matching.** The company matches (often dollar for dollar up to a maximum amount) contributions employees make to

Checklist 4-2. Kinds of Information to Gather on Potential Foundation Funders

❑ Correct name and contact information for the foundation.

❑ Eligibility requirements for applicants.

❑ Restrictions that might eliminate you (geography, affiliations, prior funding).

❑ What kinds of organizations are eligible to apply?

❑ Primary stated purposes of the foundation.

❑ Subject areas in which they make awards (education, health, arts).

❑ Program categories and current priorities (prevention, direct service, research).

❑ Types of organizations they have funded (grassroots, institutional, emerging).

❑ Types of awards they seem to prefer (challenge, seed, capital, capacity building).

❑ Types of grants or purposes they will NOT fund (religion, publicly funded organizations).

❑ Low, average, and high amounts of grants awarded in previous cycles.

❑ Minimum or maximum amounts awarded.

❑ What percentage of a project budget they will consider.

❑ Whether they pay indirect costs and, if so, what percentage.

❑ Name and contact information for primary contact person.

❑ Name and address to which application should be submitted.

❑ Names and backgrounds of donors, trustees and officers.

❑ Names, titles and contact information, and background of staff, if any.

❑ Local or regional representative you could contact and that person's role.

❑ Amount of their assets.

❑ Amount they granted last year.

❑ How much of last year's granting went to continuation awards.

❑ Their application process.

❑ How you initiate contact.

❑ Their fiscal year.

❑ Their deadlines.

❑ Do they request a letter of inquiry prior to submission of a full proposal?

❑ Do they have an application form?

❑ Do they want attachments? Which?

❑ Do they have selection criteria and, if so, what are they?

❑ Who are the reviewers (staff, family members, community members)?

❑ What can you find out about them and their priorities?

❑ What is their policy on renewal? How many years might they support a project?

❑ Will they support a project that also receives federal or other public monies?

❑ Who do you know who has received funding from them who could offer advice?

❑ Do you have contacts who could help influence their opinion of your proposal?

❑ What cultivation strategies might be appropriate with this funder?

Source: *Getting Funded: The Complete Guide to Writing Grant Proposals* by Mary Hall and Susan Howlett. Available from Portland State University, Continuing Education Press, www.cep.pdx.edu. Copyright © 2003. All rights reserved.

nonprofits of their own choice (sometimes restricted to particular fields).

- **Contributions in-kind** of goods or services. In-kind support includes access to loaned executives and other employees, such as graphic designers, computer experts, printers, or program staff who contribute their services at no cost. Companies also make gifts-in-kind of equipment or supplies, especially whatever they make or sell. Many grantseekers overlook the fact that their budget requests could be significantly reduced if they simply asked manufacturers and purveyors of products and services for in-kind gifts. This would also provide evidence of other support, which most grantmakers want to see. As you identify your budget line items, look for opportunities to garner in-kind rather than cash support.

- **Encouragement of employee giving groups.** Employees collect contributions from their peers and determine among themselves whom to fund.

One thing to keep in mind when considering corporate funders is that they are ultimately accountable to their stockholders, and their primary goal is to make money. Many grantseekers approach corporate funders with a sense of entitlement: "You make money in our community. Therefore you owe it to the community to support its charitable organizations and institutions." This attitude will not strengthen your chances of receiving an award.

Many factors influence corporate decisions about partnerships with nonprofits. Some characteristics of a strong corporate/nonprofit alliance are listed in Figure 4-4.

Another consideration is that historically, corporate support has constituted a very small percentage of charitable giving, consistently under 10% of all nongovernmental money received by nonprofits. When strategizing which prospective funders to approach with your proposal, don't plan for a disproportionately high amount to come from corporations.

Characteristics of Corporate Funders

Corporate giving is generally aligned with the company's goals:

- **Marketing and public relations goals,** such as corporate sponsorship of an event where the audience mirrors the company's new target market.

- **Financial goals,** such as an insurance company supporting efforts that reduce accidents and thefts.

- **Human resource goals,** such as engaging employees in charitable causes to build loyalty and camaraderie.

Decisions may be made by upper-level managers, professional foundation administrators, or a group of employees who serve for a year or two at a time. Some businesses will also consult their risk management staff, their government relations staff, their union leaders, and other stakeholders as they determine whom to fund.

It is wise to find out who will review your proposal, since you might present your case differently, depending on the level of professionalism, knowledge of the field, or perspectives of the reviewers. For example, a representative from an employee giving group in a manufacturing firm told a group of grantwriters, "Your proposal may impress a foundation officer, but our factory workers aren't going to contribute their hard-earned pay to a nonprofit where the top staff earn more than they do and enjoy offices with views."

Corporate contributions staff are generally also responsible for many other functions, such as public relations, government relations, employee giving campaigns, in-kind contributions and corporate volunteers, in addition to the work of the company, so they can be hard to approach in person. However, grantseekers should always try to make contact with the staff of corporate funders before submitting any kind of proposal.

Corporate awards can range from low thousands to hundreds of thousands of dollars, but the *average* corporate gift in the last decade was $2500. Corporations generally want maximum visibility for their support, especially logo place-

---

Figure 4-4. Characteristics of a Corporate/Nonprofit Partnership

- It promotes internal pride.

- It involves participation by employees, therefore promoting a feeling of ownership.

- It has organic growth potential—a built-in ability to develop in unanticipated and unplanned directions—and is flexible and adaptable.

- It relates to the commercial interests of the corporation.

- It can become part of the corporate culture.

- It can be positioned as a logical extension of the corporation's accepted belief system.

- It reinforces values/beliefs the members of the public want to have, think they have, or want others to think they have.

- Benefits to the nonprofit organization extend beyond money to include enhanced image, expanded management capacity, strengthened skills, etc.

- It can involve the nonprofit constituency (members and service recipients) in promoting the program.

- It allows for benchmarks during the decision-making process so the company can see how plans are unfolding and influence their direction.

- It can last over time.

---

ment (on printed materials, clothing, or Web sites, with a link to theirs), signage (banners or more permanent signs) and acknowledgement at gatherings, including product sampling, public recognition by the MC or the opportunity to greet the audience.

Checklist 4-3 is a list of the types of information you should gather on potential corporate funders.

Other Private Funders

Service organizations. Regardless of their location or particular interests, these organizations share a common goal: to serve their communities by developing leadership, offering volunteer time, skills, contacts and expertise, and raising and contributing funds. A partial list of such organizations includes: Rotary, Kiwanis, Lions, Junior League, Soroptimists, Optimists, Altrusa, Civitan, Zonta, PEO, Links, Sertoma, and Exchange Club.

Some service clubs have chosen a particular area of interest to fund, focusing nationally on issues such as child abuse and neglect or the loss of sight. But others welcome unsolicited propos-als. Depending on the size and sophistication of the group, awards can range from a few hundred dollars to hundreds of thousands of dollars, from one-time gifts to long-term partnerships.

Professional and trade associations and labor unions generate the money they give away by collecting dues or donations from their members or creating earned income through products or services such as conferences or publications.

- Professional associations number in the thousands and range from large, well-known organizations (e.g., a bar association for lawyers) to lesser-known groups connected with specific academic disciplines. Many of these offer grants, scholarships, and fellowships, or have significant annual award competitions. Professional associations often invest in programs that will enhance their own fields (e.g., women engineers have supported a program that engages girls in science) or that serve their own constituency (e.g., associations of landscape, interior, and fashion designers have supported groups serving AIDS patients because they have lost so many colleagues to the disease).

Checklist 4-3. Information to Gather on Potential Corporate Funders

❏ Full name of the firm and contact information.

❏ Name, title, and contact information for the person in charge of corporate giving.

❏ Name, title, and contact information for marketing, public or community relations.

❏ The firm's philanthropic interests and priorities.

❏ Their annual contributions budget.

❏ Their gift range and average gift amount.

❏ Their fiscal year: When do they have the most discretion to award funds?

❏ Do they prefer organizations or grants of a particular type?

❏ Do they have guidelines? An annual report?

❏ Restrictions that might make you ineligible (geography, type of organization).

❏ The best way to approach them (phone call, email, letter of inquiry).

❏ Is there a formal application process? A required form? When are deadlines?

❏ What role does local management play in the process for a company headquartered elsewhere?

❏ Should the initial approach be made to local management or headquarters?

❏ Who makes the decisions (management, foundation staff, employee committee)?

❏ What criteria are decisions based on?

❏ What kinds of resources have they given others (product, in-kind goods or services, employee volunteers)?

❏ Do they offer corporate sponsorships? Whom have they sponsored in the past?

❏ What kinds of acknowledgement have others offered? What could you offer?

❏ Will they give awards to organizations receiving annual support from federated campaigns the company supports (like United Way)?

❏ Who are their major competitors in the community and how do they distinguish themselves from the competition?

❏ What is the demographic profile of their customer base? Their employee base?

❏ Does the company have a presence in the community (a facility, employees, customers)?

❏ Is the nature of their business related in any way to the proposed project?

❏ Does your organization produce research with any tie to their business?

❏ Does your organization deal with issues that are of unique importance to them or their industry?

❏ Does your institution educate or train significant numbers of people employed by the firm?

❏ Does the firm sell substantial products or services to your primary constituency?

❏ Would they gain any unique benefit by association with your project?

❏ Would your project truly help further their corporate giving goals?

- Trade associations, composed of businesses in the same industry or product lines, sometimes form their own foundations or make cash or in-kind gifts to organizations doing related work. For example, a contractors' association might support new playscapes for childcare centers, home repairs for elderly shut-ins, or low-income housing.

- Labor unions are an often forgotten but growing source of project support, particularly for services or issues of direct relevance to their membership. Examples might be those who want to support independent policy studies on the impact of imports on their employment or those who are interested in medical research on some health-related issue of particular concern to their workers.

Special interest groups, which may be nonprofit organizations themselves, fund projects that their members deem worthwhile.

- Fraternal organizations, such as Elks Clubs or Shriners have contributed millions of dollars to children's health care and community projects.

- Greek-lettered professional societies support their specific fields (social work, journalism).

- Heritage organizations, such as Colonial Dames or Daughters of the American Revolution, have supported historic preservation efforts.

- Military organizations such as American Legion or Veterans of Foreign Wars, military wives groups or retired officers clubs have funded aircraft and naval museums.

- Hobby groups have offered gifts to groups who could benefit from their partnership. For example, quilters offer assistance to abused children, birders invest in habitat restoration.

Student-based groups offer support too.

- High school or college service clubs.

- Groups studying a particular profession or industry (e.g., Future Farmers).

- Special groups such as foreign students.

- Sororities and fraternities. Members of Panhellenic sororities and fraternities often make significant grants to nonprofits nationally. Some have alumni associations that also contribute.

Faith communities, including temples, mosques, churches, and other spiritual groups, support food banks, family services, homeless shelters, and other social services that enhance the quality of life in their community and abroad. Some have large formal foundations and others have less sophisticated giving practices.

Specific resources for locating and researching all the types of private funders listed above can be found at the end of this chapter. However, the best way to identify and approach these funders is through individuals in your own constituency—people who know someone at the foundation, work at the corporation, or belong to the service club, association, or group. *People give to people,* so use your own contacts whenever possible.

Characteristics of Other Private Funders

The money offered by these types of funders has usually been generated by contributions from the members, or funds they have generated through conferences, fees, or fundraising events. Those who decide on awards could be volunteers from the community without much experience with philanthropy or the nonprofit sector, and their decisions may reflect that.

Clubs, organizations, and faith communities usually prefer to accept inquiries from their own members, so explore who among your own leaders, colleagues, or constituents might belong to such a group before appealing to it. Ask them to champion your proposal among their peers.

Gifts from these groups may range from low hundreds to hundreds of thousands of dollars. It is wise to begin by applying to more local sources for smaller grant amounts, in order to gain experience and credibility with both program and grant management, before requesting more significant grants from larger or national sources. Many grantseekers automatically aim for large sums, but big grants can cripple grantees who are not equipped to manage them.

IDENTIFYING AND LOCATING FUNDERS

Now that we have explored what types of funders exist, what distinguishes them from one another, and what kinds of information you should be learning about them, we can turn to the process of identifying and locating suitable prospects.

Use all the resources available to you. You can search for appropriate funders through several mechanisms. Don't rely on just one or two, because a grantor perfectly suited to your idea may not have a Web site and may not show up in a directory which includes only funders who award $10 million or more a year.

On-line Resources

Nearly all government grantors will have a Web site and they can also be found through other government entities. Foundations may not have Web sites of their own, but will probably show up on other sites because they must report their activity to the IRS annually, making it public information. While corporations may have a Web site, their corporate foundation or giving program may not be covered on it or on other sites that compile corporate data. And since grantmaking isn't the primary function of some of the other private funders mentioned earlier, there might not be any reference to their giving on the Web. But countless resources do exist on the Internet, and an attachment at the end of this chapter lists many of them. While some electronic databases charge a fee, they may be available through a local library.

Print Directories

Hard copy directories of grantmakers vary greatly. Entries are nearly always cross-referenced by geographic area and by field (e.g., education, social services, environment), or by type of grant (e.g., capital, project, loan). Be careful to check for limitations that would disqualify you immediately (e.g., community or population served, area of interest, type of funding sought, such as debt re-

duction, capital, or operating). The most widely respected directories are listed in the attachment at the end of this chapter, but good local directories may be available from your regional association of grantmakers or other local sources.

Your Local Library

Libraries hold treasure troves of information about grant sources. Some will have printed directories for use on-site as well as on-line databases. Look for industry-specific newsletters and specialty publications and databases. Check with your local public library, the libraries at nearby colleges or universities and even librarians in private corporations. Library Web sites may offer helpful resources. In addition to actual listings of potential funders, libraries will have background information on the government agencies, companies, foundations, or organizations you're considering, including their history, their leaders, financial and stock information, business relationships, and more.

Your Own Constituents

Grantseekers often neglect to consult their own stakeholders when searching for funding options. Board members, co-workers, volunteers, those served by the organization, members, donors, and vendors belong to service clubs and professional associations, work for businesses and government agencies, and socialize or worship with corporate funders. Don't forget to ask your own people to help identify sources.

Elected Officials

Contact the staff of elected officials who represent your community on the local, regional, or national level to see if they know about funding opportunities. It's in their interest to help attract money that will serve their constituents. Ask if they periodically notify organizations of RFPs or if they know of other potential sources, especially governmental agencies, that might be suitable for you.

Similar Organizations

Research other organizations and institutions that do similar work to see who has funded them in the recent past. Your search could be as simple as calling known organizations to request an annual report, which should list their grantors. Or you could consult some of the on-line resources listed at the end of this chapter to see who else is doing similar work and who has supported them in the past.

Prior Funders

If grantmakers have already invested in your organization or your proposal idea, they want it to succeed and carry on. Approach those who have supported you in the past and ask for suggestions, introductions, or referrals to other funders.

Vendors

Firms you do business with want you to succeed so you can continue doing business with them. They may have their own corporate giving program. Or they could introduce you to others in their industry or firms *they* do business with.

RESEARCHING IDENTIFIED FUNDERS

You will want to learn as much as possible about potential funders before deciding who is most appropriate for your proposal idea. In addition to the resources listed at the end of the chapter, be sure to look into the items specified below.

Their Guidelines

Grantmakers craft guidelines to inform applicants of their goals and procedures, but few applicants read them closely. Savvy grantseekers pay careful attention to the guidelines or the RFP, watching for the funder's overarching rationale for awarding grants or contracts. Do not try to squeeze your round program into a grantor's square hole. If they state that they fund only education reform efforts in local school districts, don't ask them to fund an after-school arts program. Make sure that your proposal truly helps them accomplish their own goals.

For example, some groups applying to a city's Department of Neighborhoods complained that the funder created hardships for them by requiring collaborations among the local chamber of commerce, schools, and community councils. But one of the stated goals of that department was to strengthen neighborhoods by increasing communication and cooperation among existing neighborhood groups while they worked toward a common goal. Look for the funder's goals. *Nobody will give you money just because you need it.*

You can save valuable time and money by ensuring your eligibility before approaching a prospective grantor. Since one of the most prevalent complaints among grantors is receiving proposals from applicants who don't fit the guidelines, set yourself apart from other applicants by pointing out how you *do* meet them.

Study their procedures. Some funders will eliminate applications that don't follow instructions. If they state that they don't accept phone calls or unsolicited proposals, don't try to bend the rules. If they require a *letter of inquiry* (also called a *query letter* or a *pre-application*) before accepting a full proposal, don't try to leap ahead to a full proposal. All the details in the guidelines are there for a reason. Pay attention to them.

Their Annual Reports

Public companies must report certain financial information to the Securities and Exchange Commission and their shareholders. You can review annual reports, quarterly reports or ownership filings on-line or by requesting them directly from the company. Annual reports can contain useful information for potential grantseekers which will provide clues about the appropriateness of your proposal idea to them. These items include:

- What types of people comprise the leadership of the organization.

- What they showcase as their accomplishments.

- What their total assets are and how their stock is doing.

- How those numbers relate to previous years.

- How much they gave away last year, to whom, and for what.

- The range of grant amounts.

- Whether they make their case using stories and photos, or statistics and citations.

- Whether they emphasize products and outcomes, or process and anecdotes; partnerships with others, or distinctions from others.

Their IRS Form 990-PF

Private foundations must submit a Form 990-PF (Return of Private Foundation) annually to the Internal Revenue Service. This document includes a list of all their grantees, details on finances, giving interests, restrictions, application procedures, and deadlines. It is viewable at Foundation Center libraries. Checking which organizations a foundation has funded in the past, for what projects and for what amounts will clarify whether your idea is suitable for this funder.

Their Web Sites

While fewer than 5 percent of foundations have Web sites, most government and corporate grantmakers offer extensive information on the Internet. Here are some things to look for as you investigate your potential funder.

- Their stated goals (in general and concerning their funding).

- How they present themselves to the world (folksy or formal).

- Whether they make themselves accessible (by phone or e-mail) or make it difficult to reach them.

- Whether they prefer more traditional means of communication (phone, mail) or electronic communication (asking you to download and submit applications on-line or contact them by e-mail).

- How they position themselves among similar organizations.

- Indications of their history, core values, and future goals.

Their Industry Publications

If you're approaching a company, association, religious group, or special interest group, you may be able to find articles about them and about trends in their field in industry or association newsletters, journals and magazines, or on Web sites.

Individuals Who Know Them

You can glean more subjective information by contacting program officers at government agencies, recipients of previous grants and previous reviewers for answers to the following questions:

- Do they agree that your project addresses an important need?

- Does it seem that you have thought of a good way to solve this problem?

- What could be changed to strengthen your chances?

- How closely does the project match the program priorities and selection criteria of this particular funding source?

- Are there political factors you should know about before applying?

- How many of the grants awarded recently went to first-time applicants?

- What components of the proposal seemed most important to the last reviewers?

- What were the most common mistakes made by applicants?

- What information do applicants typically leave out that the funder wants to see?

- Are there any discretionary funds, unsolicited proposal funds, or as yet unannounced programs you might qualify for?

- Do they know of other programs that might be more appropriate to apply for?

MAKING CONTACT WITH A FUNDER

Grantmakers don't want to hear from you for the first time on deadline day. How you initiate and cultivate the relationship with them greatly affects their opinion of the ultimate proposal. Here are some steps to take to optimize the relationship:

- **Do your homework.** Find out as much as you can about the funder before contacting them. The more you know about them, the more receptive they will be to your advances. Your familiarity with their guidelines demonstrates your respect for their time, and your acknowledgement of recent developments in their world shows that you're paying attention to *them*, not just thinking about your needs.

- **Approach them as they wish to be approached.** If a directory listing says, "No phone calls," don't call. If their guidelines say, "Send a two-page letter of inquiry first," don't call. If there is no phone number for a family foundation, don't try to find the president at home.

- **Make a good first impression.** If your first contact is a phone call or e-mail, plan it ahead of time, making sure that you introduce yourself clearly and compellingly, without rambling. Tell them the reason for the contact right away: "I've read your guidelines and I have some clarifying questions."

- **Send a letter of inquiry,** if appropriate. These letters help funders screen out applicants who don't fit the guidelines or have a proposal idea that won't be competitive. They are usually one to two pages long. You'll find two sample letters in the following pages.

- **Cultivate a relationship** with the grantor before asking for support. Nobody wants to think you only want their money. Send copies of articles you see about them in the news with a note congratulating them on the coverage. Invite them to an event that showcases your mission or offer a tour of your facility. If you find an article in a trade publication that illustrates the need for your proposed idea, send them a copy to educate them ahead of time. Just make sure that whatever you do to invest in the relationship is indeed adding value for them, offering something they couldn't get anywhere else.

- **Follow the rules** when you apply. If they say applications are due by 5:00 pm on Friday, don't ask for an extension at the last minute. If they ask for multiple copies without binding, respect their instructions. These things ultimately affect how they perceive your organization.

- **Don't bother them soon after the deadline.** Once your proposal has been turned in, let them take the time they need to process it. You will most likely hear from them as soon as they have an answer. However, if you haven't heard after several months, it is appropriate to contact them to check the status.

- **Send a thank you note** as soon as you hear from them, regardless of the outcome. Express your appreciation that they took the time to review your proposal.

- **Follow through** with promises of acknowledgement and reporting. Invite them for a site visit to see their money in action. Let them meet or hear from participants. Send photos for them to use in their own publications or share with their donors. Turn reports in on time, even if the news isn't what you'd hoped to share. Thank them again.

- **Keep in touch** after the grant or contract is over. How you steward the relationship affects your reputation as they talk with other potential funders in the community.

HOW TO WRITE A LETTER OF INQUIRY

Many grantmakers require a letter of inquiry before giving permission to submit a full proposal. This type of letter can make a strong initial impression on funders, who often will determine within seconds whether they like an idea or not. Occasionally, a grantor will decide to fund an organization based on the query letter alone. A favorable impression can hinge on how the letter looks on the page (white space is good), how readable it is (long words, long sentences, and long paragraphs are bad), and how clear and compelling the request is. If you have only seconds to capture the attention of busy reviewers, make it easy for them to feel engaged by your plans. Checklist 4-4 shows the elements that constitute a strong letter of inquiry.

Checklist 4-4. Elements in a Strong Letter of Inquiry

❏ Acknowledgement of the funder, funder's behavior, guidelines, or goals.

❏ Name, mission, and founding date of applicant organization.

❏ Brief statement of the problem, need, or issue.

❏ Brief statement of the proposed solution.

❏ Who else agrees this is a problem and/or is working with you to address it.

❏ Cost of total project and who else is being approached for funding.

❏ Amount requested and what it will cover.

❏ Name and contact information for person best able to answer questions.

❏ Signature of most senior individual connected to the request.

Tips for making your letter more engaging:

- **Keep it brief,** one or two pages total.

- **Avoid big blocks of text.** Have paragraphs of varying lengths, use indented, bulleted lists, and signal important items with boldface, italics, or underlining.

- Avoid the words "we need." Talk about needs in the community, but not your needs as an applicant. Funders are concerned about the needs of your clients or their own needs. Your job is to *meet* those needs.

- **Use action verbs,** avoiding weak "to be" constructions (is, are, was, were).

- **Use active voice,** not passive constructions ("we will initiate," not "the program will be initiated by"—remember "Mistakes were made"?).

- Use simple, easily understood words and avoid jargon.

- Let the reader feel your enthusiasm and passion without overdoing it.

- Connect the goals of the funder with the goals of the project or organization.

- Make sure the requested amount can be located immediately on the page.

- Have the problem flow into the solution, which leads naturally to the request.

ATTACHMENT 4-1.

SAMPLE LETTER OF INQUIRY TO A FOUNDATION

Dear [Name of Funder],

Thank you for all you have done for women and children in our region. We applaud your recent work with the Children's Advocacy Center and the award you received for your role in it. With this query letter, we invite your support of our related work.

The People's Law Center, founded in 1978, ensures equal access to the justice system for citizens who could otherwise not afford legal counsel. We serve about 1,250 families from our county each year, through:
- information and referral services with our 800 number;
- free legal clinics at county-wide community-based venues;
- sidewalk advocacy tables at a busy street corner on Saturday mornings; and
- pro bono attorney services for those needing representation in court.

As with 24 of the 26 similar programs throughout our five-state region, the majority of our clients needing direct representation are women with children in domestic abuse situations, often complicated by other factors like poverty, unemployment and housing issues. Since our county is predominantly rural, the number of attorneys available to take pro bono cases is small to begin with. And because these cases are time-consuming, emotionally draining and complex, the pool of volunteer attorneys knowledgeable in family law and willing to take them shrinks each year.

Last year, a strategic planning process conducted by our board determined that our top priority for the coming year would be to launch an in-house program, with a full-time staff attorney, dedicated to family law cases. The program was designed by members of our board and staff, volunteer attorneys, judicial staff, colleagues from the local crisis center and battered women's shelter and law enforcement personnel.

We anticipate that setting up and running this program for the first year will cost $85,000. In addition to the $5,000 we agree to absorb in our operating budget, we have garnered $30,000 from the local bar association, two churches, a service club, and three long-term individual donors.

Your guidelines state that your top priority is improving the lives of women and children in our region. Our program will provide direct representation to 50 domestic violence victims and their children in the next year. We seek approval to submit a full proposal for a grant of $10,000.

We intend to raise the remaining $40,000 from a start-up grant from United Way, two law firms and the Apex Corporation. Funds to sustain the program will be generated by grants the first two years, then individual donors, through mailed appeals, events and personal solicitation.

If you have questions about our organization, our new program or this request, please contact our Executive Director, Shelley Smith, at 555-123-4567. Thank you again for supporting families in our community. And thank you for your consideration.

Joshua Jordan
Chair, Board of Directors

ATTACHMENT 4-2.

SAMPLE LETTER OF INQUIRY TO A CORPORATION

Dear [Name of Corporation],

Congratulations on your recent merger with Axis. We at The Community College thank the leaders of both companies for your past support of education in our region. We will soon gather 1,000 education supporters for a benefit performance and we invite you to join us by becoming a corporate sponsor at the $5,000 level.

Our college has been providing affordable, accessible education to the students of our tri-county area for 45 years. Eighty-eight percent of our graduates find employment in the area immediately upon completion of their 2-year curriculum. Many of the employees and countless customers of your company are Community College alumni.

When the primary employer in the region closed the plant last year, scores of families who had dreamed that their children would be the first generation to attend college gave up hope. But The Community College isn't giving up hope. We're raising enough money in the next year to offer 100 scholarships to graduating seniors at the local high schools.

One element of our fundraising strategy is to host a concert, featuring the well-known jazz singer Stella Raye, who graduated from the college in 1967. The concert will be May 6, in our campus auditorium. We expect the event to attract an audience that would be enthusiastic about your new product line.

To acknowledge your corporate sponsorship, we would be pleased to offer the following benefits to your company:
- your name and logo on promotional posters in a three-county area;
- your name and logo on newspaper ads purchased four weeks prior;
- your name and logo on the front cover of the program at the concert;
- signage and table space in the lobby to display company literature;
- front-row-center tickets for you to distribute to eight guests;
- an invitation for those eight guests to attend a backstage reception;
- the opportunity for a company representative to introduce Ms. Raye;
- acknowledgement in our college newsletter and our annual report.

Your gift will ultimately affect the livelihood of hundreds of families among your employee and customer bases, hopefully anchoring some of our bright young people in the community. We hope that your abiding interest in the economic vitality of our region will encourage your participation in this effort to help educate the next generation of students. If you have questions about the college, the concert or this request, please contact our Advancement Director, Sam Smith, at 555-1212. Thank you for your consideration.

Jean Worden,
College President

Source: *Getting Funded: The Complete Guide to Writing Grant Proposals* by Mary Hall and Susan Howlett. Available from Portland State University, Continuing Education Press, www.cep.pdx.edu. Copyright © 2003. All rights reserved.

ATTACHMENT 4-3.

ELECTRONIC AND PRINT RESOURCES FOR RESEARCHING FUNDING SOURCES

ELECTRONIC RESOURCES

The electronic resources are organized as follows:

1. Gateway Web sites that cover many types of sources.

2. Government (federal, then state and local).

3. Foundations.

4. Corporations.

5. Organizations.

6. General Resources.

7. Listservs.

Most of the sites listed below are free of charge. **Those that charge a fee are marked with "$$".** You may be able to access some of them through your public or university library, which may offer them free to their patrons through the library Web site. You can access these with your library card. This method is especially useful for business and biographical research. (Print resources and some CD-ROMs may also be available at the library.)

The Internet is a tremendously useful research tool, but it can also lead to a bewildering mass of data. If you want the Web to be a useful tool, you must organize your collection of resources, just as you would a set of books on a shelf. This means bookmarking your favorite Web sites and organizing them into folders.

1. Gateway Web Sites

Because the world of Internet research is always changing, it's often best to begin your search for information with a "gateway Web site," which leads to many other Web sites. Gateways organize the resources for you and stay up to date when URLs change.

David Lamb's Prospect Research Page

The bible of prospect researchers; also useful for grantseekers. Web sites for foundations, corporations, executives, and more.
http://www.lambresearch.com

King County Library System, Nonprofit and Philanthropy Resource Center

A well-designed Web site with links to national resources as well as local.
http://www.kcls.org/sc/nprc.cfm

University of Washington

Designed for faculty use, with links to many sources for research grants. A few sections are restricted to UW faculty, but most are open to the public. Many other research universities have similar Web sites.
http://www.lib.washington.edu/gfis/resources/webstuff.html

Society of Research Administrators Grants Web

Many great links to sources of funding for research grants.
http://www.srainternational.org/newweb/grantsweb/index.cfm

CSC Non-Profit Resource Center

Thousands of links to foundations, corporations, and other nonprofit resources. Includes a glossary of fundraising terms.
http://home.attbi.com/~cscunningham/links.htm

Internet Public Library

Useful resources for nonprofit organizations.
http://www.ipl.org/div/subject/browse/bus60.00.00

Fundsnet

Links to funders sorted by field, such as arts, children, education, etc.

> http://www.fundsnetservices.com

$$ GrantStation

Membership provides access to funder search engine, weekly bulletin of grant opportunities, government deadline alert, and more.

> http://www.grantstation.com

$$ GrantSelect

Research grants database, run by Oryx Press. More expensive than GrantStation, but better suited to academic users.

> http://www.grantselect.com

2. Government Resources

Federal agencies now expect grantseekers to search for sources on the Internet. While there may be some useful resources at local libraries, you will find the most information on Web sites such as these.

Federal Register

The *Federal Register* is the official daily publication for rules, proposed rules, and notices of federal agencies and organizations, as well as executive orders and other presidential documents. To look for grants, click on Browse, then HTML, and you will see the table of contents of the *Federal Register*. Look under each category for "Grants." Then move to the right and click either text or pdf for the full contents of the RFP.

> http://www.access.gpo.gov/su_docs/aces/
> aces140.html

Catalog of Federal Domestic Assistance

A searchable database of information about all types of federal assistance programs.

> http://www.cfda.gov

Fundsnet Services

Government funding resources.

> http://www.fundsnetservices.com/gov01.htm

Notices of Funding Availability

These appear in the *Federal Register*, printed each business day by the U.S. government, and are available for on-line searching by broad subject categories or by agency.

> http://ocd1.usda.gov/nofa.htm

FirstGov

Provides easy one-stop access to all on-line U.S. Federal Government resources, including government grants information.

> http://www.firstgov.gov

Federal Gateway

Not a government site, but a nonprofit that clearly knows its way around the government. Links to every federal department, as well as many local governments.

> http://fedgate.org

University of Washington Grants and Contracts Services

Federal Internet resources.

> http://depts.washington.edu/gcs (Scroll down
> to "Federal Internet Resources")

Community of Science (COS)

Funded research database allows you to search grants given by the National Institutes of Health (NIH), National Science Foundation (NSF), United States Department of Agriculture (USDA), Small Business Innovation Research (SBIR), and the Medical Research Council (MRC) in a variety of ways.

> http://www.cos.com

Other Federal Resources

In addition to searching the Internet for Web sites of federal agencies you think might be appropriate, contact your member(s) of Congress or their staff to ask for suggestions of other sources to investigate. Conversations by phone or e-mail with *program managers* (staff who manage the granting process) in federal agencies may lead you to unlikely-sounding departments with surprisingly suitable funding opportunities.

State and Local Funders

These can be found by looking up the home page of your state, county, borough, or municipality and clicking on Services or Resources for the appropriate field. Check with elected officials or contact agencies you think might be suitable and ask the staff for guidance. Local librarians will know where to direct you as well.

Look in your phone directory for state and local government agencies to see what exists before researching them on the Internet. Check the Web sites of the Council on State Governments and your state's secretary of state. Contact the offices of elected officials (state legislators or city council representatives) to let them know your plans and see if they can suggest departments that might be relevant.

State Home Pages

Find your state home page, then search for grants. Every state is different, but the home page may allow you to search for terms such as "grants" or "community resources."

http://www.tgci.com/STATES/states2.htm

3. Foundations

The federal government requires foundations to make their financial information (including grant details) available to the public via the IRS 990-PF form. Since these forms became available on-line in 1999, they have been a treasure trove of information for grant researchers. Foundation information is also organized into a wide variety of directories in print, on CD-ROM, and on-line.

You will have no trouble finding foundation Web sites and information about foundations through free resources. But if you want to do a targeted search—for instance, to find potential sources of grants for a library at a community college in Oregon—you will probably have to use a fee-based research tool such as FC Search or the Foundation Center Directory On-line.

The only drawback to the wealth of foundation information is that it includes many small foundations that do not accept unsolicited grant proposals. These foundations are usually family giving vehicles; they support organizations already known by the donor families. You may attempt to cultivate individuals who give through family foundations as you would any other potential major donor. But don't send them a grant proposal unless they've invited you to do so.

To eliminate records of "Do Not Solicit" Foundations in FCSearch (see below), insert "applications not accepted" (with quotation marks) into the text search and then select "NOT" from the drop-down menu in front of it.

The Foundation Center

The Foundation Center is the definitive national resource for information on foundation funding. They have exhaustive libraries in New York, Washington, D.C., Atlanta, Cleveland, and San Francisco, as well as cooperating collections in 220 libraries in all 50 states, the District of Columbia, and Puerto Rico. These library locations are listed on their Web site.

The Foundation Center Web site includes links to foundation and corporate grantmakers, information on how to write a grant, further on-line and Web resources for grantseekers, and much more. The Web site is free.

http://fdncenter.org

$$ The Foundation Center Printed Directories

These offer profiles of grantmakers with recent grants, and their subject guides list funders by field (art, health), while their grant guides list grants of $10,000 or more awarded by the largest foundations. FCSearch, their CD-ROM resource, and Foundation Directory On-line subscription service offer unparalleled information. These resources are available for free in many Foundation Center libraries.

http://fdncenter.org/learn/faqs/index.html# research

GuideStar (990s and 990-PFs)

GuideStar has a very useful advanced search feature, which allows you to search by keyword, category, and city and state. It doesn't replace FC Search or similar fee-based databases, but it may help you find foundations of interest. Unlike GrantSmart (see below), GuideStar includes 990 forms from grantseeking organizations as well as the 990-PFs that private foundations are required to file.

> http://www.guidestar.org

GrantSmart (990-PFs)

GrantSmart includes 990-PF forms. It also has an advanced search feature with keywords.

> http://www.grantsmart.org

Note: GuideStar and GrantSmart overlap a great deal in their 990-PF databases, but occasionally you will find a listing on one that you will not find on the other, so it's a good idea to check both. Some people find GuideStar's interface easier to use. You can also find 990-PFs through The Foundation Center's Web site, which uses GrantSmart as its provider.

State and Local Foundation Directories: A Bibliography

This is a very useful list of hardcopy and on-line directories of local grants. If your area is included, the local directory will be an essential resource.

> http://fdncenter.org/learn/topical/sl_dir.html

Community Foundations by State

A user-friendly guide to community foundations all over the country.

> http://www.tgci.com/resources/foundations/ searchGeoLoc.asp

Foundations On-line

Another listing of foundation and corporate Web site links.

> http://www.foundations.org

CSC Non-Profit Resource Center Foundations List

> http://home.attbi.com/~cscunningham/ Foundation.htm

Association of Small Foundations

Links to small foundations
> http://www.smallfoundations.org

Charitable Trust Listings

In many states, a state agency, often a "charities" division of the secretary of state or attorney general, registers charitable trusts (entities holding assets that are invested to produce income that is then allocated to a charitable purpose). Directories of registered trusts are sometimes available to the public. Search for "charitable trusts" and "your state."

Council on Foundations

This association of grantmakers provides a directory of community foundations. Search for "community foundation locator."

> http://www.cof.org

Regional Associations of Grantmakers

Foundations throughout the U.S. belong to regional associations of grantmakers (RAGs), nonprofit membership associations that strengthen philanthropy in their respective geographic areas. In addition to having helpful Web sites, many RAGs also publish directories of their members.

> http://www.rag.org

4. Corporations

Unlike foundations, corporations are not required to publicize their charitable giving. Corporate foundations must obey the same disclosure rules as private foundations, but not all companies give through a corporate foundation. Many companies, of course, are eager to let the public know about their good works and the community causes they support. These corporations often include information about their charitable activities in their annual reports or in a special report about their "community relations," as their grant-making departments are often called. These reports may or may not include the dollar amounts of their grants.

Corporate giving information may be available on the company's Web site, but it can sometimes be hard to find. Go through the Foundation Center's list of corporate giving Web sites or check the other gateway resources listed below.

If the corporation you are interested in does not publish a list of its grants, you may still be able to find information about its giving history by checking the local newspapers and business journals. If these are available on-line, search for "company name" and "grants," "contributions," or similar terms. (Remember to check your library's databases for news sources.)

Researching Companies On-line

This Internet tutorial on how to research companies is a good place to begin.

http://home.sprintmail.com/~debflanagan

Corporate Grantmakers

http://fdncenter.org/funders

CSC Non-Profit Resource Center

A list of corporations.

http://home.attbi.com/~cscunningham/Corporate.htm

Fundsnet: Corporate Philanthropy and Foundations

http://www.fundsnetservices.com/corp02.htm

$$ Hoover's Online

The most comprehensive resource for research on corporations. Not aimed at grantseekers, but many prospect researchers use it extensively.

http://www-2.hoovers.com

Business.com

Search for company information by type of business such as automotive, law, pharmaceuticals, etc.

http://www.business.com

Corporate Information

Links to public and private companies by state or country.

http://www.corporateinformation.com

EDGAR Database

This site includes corporate Securities and Exchange Commission (SEC) filings.

http://www.sec.gov/edgar/searchedgar/webusers.htm

$$ 10KWizard

A more convenient way to search SEC documents.

http://www.tenkwizard.com

5. Organizations

American Society of Association Executives Directory

A free database of thousands of associations. Search in your area of interest to see if some give grants.

http://info.asaenet.org/gateway/OnlineAssocSlist.html

Internet Public Library: Associations on the Net

http://www.ipl.org/div/aon

$$ Directory of Associations

http://www.marketingsource.com/associations

Directory of Unions

http://www.labornet.org/links/directory.html

Directory of Service Clubs

http://directory.google.com/Top/Society/Organizations/Public_Service

6. General Resources

The Grantsmanship Center

The granddaddy of grants training organizations. The Web site sells many useful publications very cheaply (everyone should own the $4 *Program Planning and Proposal Writing*). They also have helpful archives of *Federal Register* notices.

http://www.tgci.com

$$ Chronicle of Philanthropy

A highly respected weekly periodical about national philanthropy and grantmaking. You can subscribe to the print or electronic versions. The Web site also contains useful free information, including current headlines and articles. The *Chronicle* publishes a Guide to Grants, an electronic database of all grants listed in the *Chronicle* since 1995.

> http://philanthropy.com

Specialized Newsletters

Particular areas of interest may have periodicals that list grants available in that field, such as the *Chronicle of Higher Education.*

7. Listservs

Listservs are professional Internet discussion groups with a stated subject, such as grants. You can join them on-line for free. Once you have subscribed, every message sent to the list by any subscriber will appear on your e-mail. (If you don't want your e-mail box flooded, you can request the "Digest" version, which bundles all the day's messages together and delivers them to your box in a single e-mail once a day.)

Many of the frequent contributors to listservs are experienced professionals who are very generous with their time and expertise. You can learn a great deal from a listserv. You can also waste a huge amount of time. As with anything on the Internet, it's up to you to glean the useful information and prevent yourself from getting sucked into the vortex.

Charity Channel: Grants Forum

Charity Channel has over 70 forums related to nonprofits and fund-raising. You may be interested in more than one.

> http://charitychannel.com/forums/GRANTS.
> htm

PRSPCT-L

Prospect research issues. Much of the research is focused on individuals, but there is also much discussion of foundations and corporations. The folks on this listserv really know how to do research on the Internet.

> http://groups.yahoo.com/group/PRSPCT-L

CFRNet

A listserv focused on building partnerships between educational institutions and corporations and foundations. May also be useful for development officers at large institutions such as museums and hospitals.

> http://cfrnet.wustl.edu

PRINT RESOURCES

1. General

Directory of Biomedical and Health Care Grants, 2002. 16th edition. Phoenix, AZ: Oryx Press, 2002.

The Grants Register. 21st edition, 2003. Chicago: St. James Press, 2002.

Annual Register of Grant Support: a Directory of Funding Sources, 2002. 35th edition. Chicago: Marquis Academic Media, Marquis Who's Who, 2001.

Directory of Grants In The Humanities, 2001/ 2002. 15th edition. Phoenix, AZ: Oryx Press, 2001.

Directory of Research Grants, 2001. Phoenix, AZ: Oryx Press, 2001.

Operating Grants for Nonprofit Organizations. Phoenix, AZ: Oryx Press, 2001.

The Foundation Center's Guide to Grantseeking on the Web. New York: The Center, 2001.

Brewer, Ernest. *Finding Funding: Grantwriting from Start to Finish, Including Project Management and Internet Use.* 4th edition. Thousand Oaks, CA: Corwin Press, 2001.

Seltzer, Michael. *Securing Your Organization's Future: A Complete Guide to Fundraising Strategies.* New York: Foundation Center, 2001.

Bauer, David G. *The "How to" Grants Manual: Successful Grantseeking Techniques for Obtaining Public and Private Grants.* Washington, DC: American Council on Education; Phoenix, AZ: Oryx Press, 1999.

The Grantseekers Handbook of Essential Internet Sites. 4th edition. Orem, UT: Aspen Publications, 1999.

National Directory Of Grantmaking Public Charities. New York: The Foundation Center, 1998.

2. Government

Government Assistance Almanac, 2002–2003. 16th edition. Washington, DC: Foggy Bottom Publications, 2002.

Sears, Jean L. *Using Government Information Sources: Electronic and Print.* Phoenix, AZ: Oryx Press, 2001.

Loans and Grants from Uncle Sam: Am I Eligible and for How Much? 8th edition, 2001–2002. Alexandria, VA: Octameron Associates, 2000.

Ramsey, Leslie A. *Winning Federal Grants: A Guide to the Government's Grant-Making Process.* Gaithersburg, MD: Aspen Publishers, Inc., 1999.

3. Foundations

The Foundation Directory, 2002. 24th edition. New York, Foundation Center; distributed

Guide to U.S. Foundations, Their Trustees, Officers, and Donors. 2002 edition. New York: Foundation Center, 2002.

The International Foundation Directory, 2002. 11th edition. Detroit, MI: Gale Research Co.; London: Europa Publications, 2002.

Directory of Operating Grants. 6th edition. Loxahatchee, FL: Research Grant Guides, 2001.

Glass, Sandra A., Ed. *Approaching Foundations: Suggestions and Insights for Fundraisers.* San Francisco: Jossey-Bass, 2000.

Foundation Fundamentals. 6th edition. New York: Foundation Center, 1999.

4. Corporations

Corporate Foundation Profiles. 12th edition. New York: Foundation Center, 2002.

Corporate Giving Directory 2002. 23rd edition. Farmington Hills, MI: The Taft Group, 2001.

National Directory of Corporate Giving. 8th edition. New York: Foundation Center, 2002.

National Directory of Corporate Public Affairs. Washington, DC: Columbia Books, Inc., 2002.

Directory of Corporate Affiliations 2001. Washington, DC: National Register Publishing, 2001.

Austin, James E. *The Collaboration Challenge: How Nonprofits and Businesses Succeed Through Strategic Alliances.* San Francisco: Jossey-Bass Publishers, 2000.

The Directory of Corporate and Foundation Givers, 2000. Detroit: Taft Group, 2000.

National Committee for Responsive Philanthropy. *Grants: Corporate Grantmaking for Racial and Ethnic Communities.* Wakefield, RI: Moyer Bell, 2000.

Buzzard, Shirley. *Partnerships with Business: A Practical Guide for Nonprofit Organizations.* Sterling, VA. (45449 Severn Way, Suite 161, Sterling 20166): Corporate Community Investment Service (CorCom), 1999.

How to Find Information about Companies, Part 1. Arlington, VA: Washington Researchers, Ltd., 1999.

Weeden, Curt. *Corporate Social Investing: The Breakthrough Strategy for Giving and Getting Corporate Contributions.* San Francisco: Berrett-Koehler Publishers, 1998.

The Complete Guide to Corporate Fund Raising. Detroit, MI: Fund Raising Institute, 1991.

5. Associations

Encyclopedia of Associations: National Organizations of the U.S. Detroit: Gale Group, 2002.

National Directory of Grantmaking Public Charities. New York: Foundation Center, 1998.

National Trade and Professional Associations of the United States. Washington, DC: Columbia Books, Inc., 2002.

PART TWO

Writing and Submitting the Proposal

Chapter 5

Writing the Proposal

This chapter indicates some of the reasons why planning is so essential, suggests a process and timetable for proposal development and discusses the major components of various types of proposals. It ends with a discussion of preparing a proposal to fund research.

REASONS FOR A GOOD PROPOSAL

A well-planned and well-written proposal is essential if you are to receive funding. Your proposal needs to demonstrate that you have:

- Identified a need or problem that is really important.

- Done your homework to show how your work differs from others.

- Understood and can demonstrate its relevance to the funder(s).

- Planned an effective and feasible approach that will result in useful outcomes.

- Justified the requested resources.

- Shown, in compelling terms, that your organization and staff have the skills and experience to succeed.

Proposal writing is both an art and a science. There *are* specific techniques and processes of preparing an application that can be acquired and im-proved with practice. And, obviously, the proposal needs to be well written, clear, concise, readable, and free of jargon. ***But, most importantly, the proposal must (1) prove you are knowledgeable in your field, and (2) engage the funder in your excitement about the project.***

A well-planned and well-written proposal can also:

- **Allow you to develop a useful schedule for implementing the project.** Many startup problems can thus be avoided.

- **Provide a framework for management of the project** by establishing the rules of the game within your organization. For example, if staff from another part of the agency are essential to the success of the project, this can be negotiated at the time the proposal is written and evidence of this referenced in the application.

- **Force you to make certain that adequate resources have been anticipated.** These include time, money, personnel, facilities, and so forth.

- **Serve as a vehicle for informing others** about the goals and intended operation of the project.

- **Test the degree of real internal commitment to the project,** especially among your organization's top leadership. By the time all of the internal reviews and signatures have been obtained, you should know whether your organization is enthusiastic about your project and will honor commitments made in the proposal. You should not submit a proposal if you think your agency might not deliver on its promises. Your professional reputation is at stake.

PREPARING TO WRITE THE PROPOSAL

There are many helpful sites on the Internet that give useful suggestions for preparing proposals to private foundations, corporations, or government sources. Some are listed at the end of this chapter.

The following checklist was developed from answers to a survey of over 100 private foundation and government program officers.

Checklist 5-1. Steps for Preparing a Proposal

- ❏ Read all of the forms and instructions provided by the funding source and pay close attention to those regarding format, length of each section, required style manual, overall number of pages, required content, and so forth.

- ❏ Think through all of the information you must have to complete the proposal. Develop an outline and the major points you want to make. Contact anyone else who must furnish information well in advance and give him or her an early deadline so that you're not held up at the last minute by critical missing details.

- ❏ Verify that your organization can and will sign any compliance statements required by the funder on such things as anti-discrimination policies, subject protection, animal research, drug-free status, and so forth. Identify who in your organization must provide these assurances and contact them early in the process.

- ❏ Find out if electronic forms or templates are available for certain parts of the proposal, such as the compli-

ance statements or budget. This will simplify your task.

- ❏ Determine if certain parts of the proposal, such as the evaluation section, need to be prepared by consultants and arrange to get that input.

- ❏ Ensure that the proposal flows logically from one section to another. You are telling a *story* about what needs to be done, why, and how. (Table 5-1 shows how these elements should fit together.)

- ❏ Maintain a balance between conciseness and sufficient detail to effectively explain the project. Admittedly, this is hard to do if the potential funder severely limits the length of your proposal. All proposals must deliver critical ideas quickly.

- ❏ Ensure that your citations are relevant.

- ❏ Be compelling, but do not oversell your idea. Promise only those outcomes and activities that you can definitely accomplish given the requested resources.

- ❏ Guide the reviewers to the most important parts of the proposal. Use subheadings if necessary. Include a table of contents for lengthy proposals. Number all the pages.

- ❏ Avoid lengthy introductory phrases that bury your most important points.

- ❏ Use language appropriate to the funding agency. Explain technical phrases and terms for the lay reader, if possible. Avoid abbreviations and acronyms (unless very common in your field).

- ❏ Keep the type size readable and use sufficient margins and spacing to make the proposal attractive. Unless your proposal is easy to read, it will not be.

- ❏ Use drawings, charts, or statistical tables in the proposal as appropriate to the funder. Check with the funding agency in advance if you want to include multimedia products or CDs as part of your application. Find out what platform and equipment are available to the reviewers.

- ❏ Have someone else do a final edit of the proposal, especially if that person has written successful grant proposals to your proposed funder. Get the spelling and grammar right. Do not rely on spell-check; do a visual review.

- ❏ Check the final proposal against the funder's requirements and forms before sending it. Be sure to include everything that is required.

Ensuring Internal Logic in the Proposal

Novices often struggle with having each section of their proposal relate to the previous section. You can avoid this problem by thoroughly understanding the main purpose of each component in the proposal. Experienced grantwriters suggest creating a detailed worksheet to guide the writing by identifying the key points to be made in each part of the proposal. This makes writing the proposal much easier and ensures that the content of the components relate well to one another. Table 5-1 is an example of this type of worksheet.

MAJOR COMPONENTS OF A PROPOSAL

There is no such thing as a proposal or proposal format suitable to every funding source. However, there is growing consensus on the major elements that should be included. More and more government agencies are encouraging applications online, and this has led to more standardization in proposal formatting. Many private foundations and corporate donors now accept common grant applications developed by national or regional associations of grantmakers. **Always remember that private foundations and corporations typically want less information and shorter proposals than do government agencies. They often have small staffs and are not required to request much of the information that government funders must collect to comply with regulations.**

Proposals to Government Agencies

In some ways, proposals to state or federal agencies are easier to prepare than those to private sources. Not only do public agencies usually provide detailed forms and instructions, but they seldom expect proposals to be as short as do private foundations or corporations.

However, public agencies are more demanding that their forms be completed precisely as directed. If required documentation is omitted or major questions are not answered, they may defer consideration of the proposal until the next application deadline or (much more likely), reject it completely.

Table 5-2 describes the elements commonly found in applications to government agencies and lists the information normally contained in each section.

Proposals to Foundations and Corporations

The Internet has made possible greater use of forms and proposal guidelines by foundations and corporate giving programs. Always verify that you have the latest version of the funder's requirements. Stay within the number of pages specified and use attachments for other information you think is essential. If the funding organization does not tell you what questions it wants answered and in what format, either follow the suggestions in Table 5-3 or use the "Common Grant Application" from the National Network of Grantmakers that can be found at http://www.nng.org/html/resources/cga_table.htm. Better yet, call and ASK!

TIMELINE FOR PROPOSAL DEVELOPMENT

As with everything else in this field, there is no perfect or uniform model for the proposal development process. You just have to do the best job you can with the time that is available. **A critical step early in the process is to develop a detailed work plan that specifies the major information needed for the proposal, who will prepare it, when and in what sequence, and when the necessary internal reviews must be completed in order to meet the application deadline.**

Private foundations and corporations are increasingly establishing deadlines for their grant programs, as has been the case in government agencies for many years.

Typically, it takes funders at least six months to a year from when the proposal is submitted to make their decision. For some, delays may be even longer. Appropriation levels must be known before the funder can decide how much money it will

Table 5-1. Example of a Proposal Content Worksheet

Component	Question	Rationale
Purpose	What do we want to do?	To reduce the high school dropout rate in x community by x percent by x date.
	To what end?	So that more young people can be self-sufficient, be prepared for college and/or higher paying employment, become better citizens and parents, and be physically and mentally healthier.
Need	Why do this?	An increasing number of youth are dropping out of high school in x community at rates well above the state's average. Research shows that high school dropouts have low self-esteem and a limited sense of future opportunity; are often unemployed or in low-wage jobs; are most likely to engage in crime, become poor parents, and perpetuate a cycle of poverty; and have more physical and mental health problems.
Procedures	How will we do it?	Combine existing community services for tutoring, recreation, counseling, health education, and parent training into a new center and add mentors assigned to troubled youth. This approach has been tried successfully elsewhere.
Evaluation	How will we know if it worked?	School attendance records, test scores, and the degree of change on self-esteem inventories will be used to measure progress towards the project's outcomes. Records will also be kept on the number of mentors matched with teens, and the number of parents who complete training. Over several years, we expect to see an increased graduation rate among those served by the center.
Qualifications	Why choose us?	Our agency has prior experience in managing after-school programs and in working with teens. It has previously collaborated with all of the other agencies whose services would be combined in the new center and has a large number of volunteers.
Budget	How much will it cost?	As most of the services are already budgeted by other agencies, the project will cost $100,000 annually for operating the new center and $10,000 for evaluation. The new mentoring program will be managed by an existing staff person. The involvement of other agencies will add to the center's sustainability.

Table 5-2. Major Components of a Proposal to State and Federal Agencies

Element / Information Usually Provided	Approx. Pages
Title Page	1 page

Title Page   1 page
Title of project, name and contact information of the project director, name and address of submitting organization, name of the program and agency to which the proposal is being sent, inclusive dates of the project, total budget and amount requested in this proposal, signatures of persons authorizing submission.

Signed Assurances   varies
All government sources will describe what assurance or compliance statements are required for their programs. Be sure you meet every one completely.

Abstract   ½ page
A self-contained, ready-for-publication description of the project, covering purpose/outcomes/ objectives, need and significance, procedures, evaluation, dissemination. This should stress the end products and benefits of the project if funded. Normally this is 200–250 words long. It will be used verbatim by the program manager to describe your effort.

Statement of Purpose   1½ pages
Specific description of the expected outcomes, goals, and objectives to be achieved through this project. This section is usually quite detailed.

Statement of Need   1 page
Well-documented description of the problem to be addressed need and why it is important. Should establish significance, timeliness, generalizability, and contribution to other work. Credible sources should be used for all statistics supporting and explaining the needs.

Procedures   3 pages
A plan of action for how the purposes will be achieved and why this approach is the most effective. Discuss how it is different from or complementary to similar efforts by others. Stress collaborations, if possible. Tell how the results will be disseminated to others.

Sustainability   ½ page
Government funders want to know how these activities will be supported after this grant ends. Some agencies ask that this be discussed as part of the procedures or in the budget. Others want it to be a separate component. Be specific about your plans for future funding, including other grantors, individual donors, and earned income.

Evaluation   2 pages
Details the means by which the applicant and funding source will know what the project has accomplished. Should describe the questions to be asked, the methods to be used in gathering and analyzing the data, and how the information will be used and reported. Many government sources are now requiring that this section be formatted as a logic model for outcome-based evaluation (see chapters 7 and 10 for a discussion of logic models).

Qualifications/Personnel   2½ pages
Provides an overview of the mission, history, programs, and relevant experience of the sponsoring organization and documents why it is ideally suited to undertake this work. Describes specific personnel who will work on the project, their qualifications, their duties, and, if not covered in the budget, the

Table 5-2. Major Components of a Proposal to State and Federal Agencies (continued)

percentage of time they will spend on the project. Most government sources want résumés of major project staff and often require a specific format or template. This section should list any consultants to be used, what they will do, and how they are qualified to participate. It should also discuss any cooperating organizations and give evidence of their willingness to participate.

Budget   2 pages

The cost of the project for each year of its operation should be displayed by major line items (government sources usually have detailed budget forms). Itemize what is being provided by the sponsoring organization, what is being requested from the government, and what will be contributed by other sources. There is increased interest among government sources in supporting projects that are also funded by private foundations and/or corporations. A plan of action for any additional fundraising should be provided. You may also want to use footnotes or a budget narrative to explain how various costs were computed.

Attachments   varies

Nonprofits should attach their 501(c)(3) letter unless told in the guidelines that this is not necessary. All organizations should include the names and affiliations of their boards. The program guidelines will describe what other attachments are desired, such as an audited financial report of the organization. Letters of support or agreements to participate should be provided from any organizations or groups whose involvement is essential to the project's success. In some cases, it is useful to get a letter of support from your Congressional delegation or, if applying to the state, from key legislators. Ask the program officer if this would be appropriate. Be very careful to follow the funder's guidelines about what can go into attachments.

---

have for new awards versus for paying continuation awards.

Ideally, work on a proposal should begin at least a year in advance of when the project or program is expected to begin. This provides ample time to explore related work, develop a compelling needs statement, clearly think out a project's outcomes and approach, negotiate any cooperative arrangements, develop plans for evaluation, create a detailed budget, identify and prepare requests to others that may co-fund the project, gather the necessary compliance or assurance statements, and complete internal proposal review and approval processes. One federal program officer observed that lack of sufficient time to prepare a good proposal is the single biggest reason for proposal failure.

Table 5-4 (page 67) displays the major activities involved in a proposal's development and shows how they are typically sequenced.

WRITING WITH A COMMITTEE OR TEAM

Sometimes, writing a proposal with a committee is the only way to develop a competitive application in a very short period. The following suggestions were provided by a foundation program officer who was previously a university faculty member and who routinely prepared proposals using committees.

- Have an initial meeting with a few colleagues to brainstorm the project idea and do a preliminary assessment of capability. If the proposal is to be submitted in response to a Request for Proposals, critique this document using the criteria provided in Chapter 2. Make a checklist of all of the information you will need to complete the application.

Table 5-3. Major Components of a Proposal to Foundations and Corporations

Element / Information Usually Provided	Approx. Pages

Title Page   1 page
Name of project or program; legal name of applicant organization; name of project director with title, address, phone, FAX, and e-mail; beginning and ending dates of project; total project budget and amount requested from this source; amount already secured for this project from other sources (if any) and, if space permits, the names of others who are being approached to co-fund this project; the name and signature of the person authorized to approve submission of the proposal on behalf of the organization (such as the president of the university, executive director, or board chair of a nonprofit agency).

Executive Summary   ½ page
This section determines whether the reviewer will read the rest of the proposal, so write it carefully. Summarize the project outcomes, the problems, the approach, and why these are relevant to the funder. The executive summary must make a compelling case for why this is a significant project that should be funded by this entity. Include a short description of your organization and why it is the "best" choice for this project.

Purpose/Needs Statement   1½ pages
Describe the problems, needs, or issues that are to be addressed; goals and objectives or outcomes that will result from the project and why these matter; target population; and geographic scope. This section must show how the project's purpose and the needs are relevant to the funder's guidelines. It must also answer the "so what" question (i.e., why this project, why now, how will it benefit society, what will be the impact of the project?). Either as an introduction to this section or at its end, summarize your organization's mission, history, major programs and services, and how these relate to the project.

Approach   1½ pages
Describe the strategies and methods to be used and justify why these are the most effective. Show how your work differs from or complements similar efforts by others. Emphasize collaboration whenever possible. Discuss dissemination and replication. Include a timeline with major milestones. Mention how the donor will be recognized.

Evaluation   1 page
Provide a brief description of your plan for judging the success of the project or your organization's work. What questions will the evaluation address and how will you measure them? Will an outside consultant conduct the evaluation? How will you use the results? What reports will the donor receive and when?

Qualifications/Personnel   1 page
Describe why you and/or your organization are the best suited to do this project. Describe the organizational structure for the project. Provide a sentence or two on the duties of each project staffer. Give the names and summarize the backgrounds of those who will fill key staff and consultant positions. List any partners or cooperating agencies (a letter indicating their support for the project and willingness to participate should be included as an attachment). Briefly describe your board and be sure to mention if they all make an annual gift to your agency. Direct the reader to an attachment showing the names and affiliations of your board. More detailed job descriptions for key project staff may also be included as attachments, particularly for larger projects.

Table 5-3. Major Components of a Proposal to Foundations and Corporations (continued)

Budget   1–2 pages
Develop a detailed budget for the project that shows what is being requested from the funder, what will be contributed by your organization, the names of other donors and amounts of funds received from them, pending requests to others, and what parts of the project their grants will cover. Make sure the funder understands that he/she is not the only supporter. If you haven't described this earlier, include a footnote explaining how you intend to raise any additional income needed to implement the project. If relevant, describe how the project will be continued after the grant ends. The budget display should show planned expenditures and income for each 12 month period if the project is to last more than one year.

Sustainability   ½ page
Describe how your project will be supported once the funds you are requesting end. Be specific. Do not say, "We'll raise additional monies to support this." The most convincing strategy is to show that your agency's budget will begin absorbing an increasing percentage of the project from its beginning.

Attachments   1–2 pages
501(c)(3) letter for your organization; names of your board of directors and their affiliations; your organization's latest audited financial statement; your agency's current budget and major sources of revenue; your latest annual report; letters of support/commitment (up to three); recent newspaper clippings or press releases.

- Verify that the project addresses your agency's mission and priorities. Have preliminary discussions with top administrators to get buy-in.

- Assign one person to check professional literature and informational sources on related work, and to create a preliminary statement of how your project is different from or complementary to others.

- Select who will be "lead" for the proposal development. This person should lay out the work plan for completing the proposal, make assignments and oversee completion, secure compliance documents, determine what internal reviews are necessary, and serve as the project's spokesperson. Ideally, this individual will also be the project director.

- Schedule as many brainstorming and progress report meetings as needed and as time permits. Otherwise, use memos and/or e-mail to check on and report progress. Much of the grantwriter's time will be spent encouraging other members of the team to complete their assignments on time. You should either meet or communicate with your team every week or the momentum evaporates.

- Arrange a final "mock-up" meeting that lays out the proposal in outline form. Use the elements in Figure I-1 to be sure that there is internal logic to the flow of ideas. Different individuals can then quickly write various parts of the proposal knowing that their work will be consistent with others. At this point, have someone who is experienced in preparing budgets create the financial plan for the project. This should be laid out for each twelve months of the project. It should specify what will be sought from the funding source, what is already in hand or will be sought from other donors, and what will be contributed by your organization. The "lead" person should begin discussing any financial commitments needed from the organization with key administrators as soon as possible. Make certain they are

Table 5-4: Timeline for Proposal Development

Month	Activity
1st	Identify need. Hold preliminary discussions with colleagues to determine interest and significance and to assess your capability to successfully pursue this idea. Decide whether to proceed further.
2nd	Identify project director and others to be involved in planning and/or writing the proposal. Approach other agencies whose involvement is critical to the project's success and determine their role in the proposal's preparation. Prepare a detailed work plan. Make preliminary assignments. Conduct needs assessment. Identify prior work or related activities of other organizations. Develop a case for how your work differs from or complements others. Begin to identify potential funders. Discuss optional approaches to the problem. Hold meetings with top administrators to get buy-in. Establish legal eligibility of your organization. Make contact with other organizations that could serve as the fiscal agent.
3rd	Complete work on potential funding sources and send letters of inquiry to the best prospects, even if you intend to call or meet in person. Few funding sources will indicate interest before receiving something in writing. Many will not schedule a personal meeting until they've received a written inquiry.
4th	Reach agreement on final version of project idea, need, and approach. Develop first draft of proposal and seek feedback from colleagues who have previously received funds from this source, agency administrators, partners, and collaborators. Follow-up on any letters of inquiry that haven't received a response. Contact legal personnel to discuss any legal issues that might arise if a grant document or contract is negotiated. Internal legal staff need to buy off early in the process.
5th	Modify the proposal using input received during previous months. Complete final version and translate into formats required by funder(s). Project director submits the proposal for internal reviews. Seek review and clearance as necessary from other agencies. Submit the proposal to funding source(s).
6th–9th*	Verify receipt of the proposal by the funder and find out when a decision is likely to be made. Funders conduct initial review of proposal and request additional information or clarification. Site visits sometimes scheduled.
10th–12th*	Approval or rejection is received. In either case, obtain comments of reviewers. Funder may ask to negotiate parts of the project or its budget.
13th*	Check or authorization to expend funds is received. Project starts. If funding is for only one year, begin planning for refunding efforts.

*The activities conducted by the funding source during the latter half of this process are not under the control of the grantwriter. It is a good idea, however, to include these steps in your timeline so you know that you've started early enough on the proposal's development, given the date on which you'd like to start your project.

comfortable with the indirect costs (overhead) allowed by the funder. If that rate is less than normal, discuss with them the types of expenditures and amounts to include in the budget as a direct expense.

- Simultaneously, identify one person to do research on potential funders. This person should find out if letters of inquiry are needed, secure all necessary forms, verify deadlines, and arrange preliminary contact with potential sources.

- Ask a colleague to do a thorough and objective critique of the final draft. Assess persuasiveness and the proposal's internal logic. Have someone with good editing skills look for grammar, consistent style, flow, and readability.

- The "lead" proposal developer should gather all of the components and translate them into the various formats required by the different funding sources. Given the ease of editing on the computer, this can usually be done fairly quickly. If time is really tight and proposals to several different sources are needed simultaneously, the task of filling out the different forms and preparing the various narratives can be shared among the committee using ironclad internal deadlines.

- Secure early approval from your institution's internal legal staff if the proposal is for a project that will require a written contract with the funder or has any unusual legal issues. Do not wait until you hear from the funder before discussing your plans with your internal lawyers. Otherwise, you may not be able to start your project when planned.

- Make certain that someone who is very careful about details gives each proposal a final check before it is submitted to your top administrator for signature. This check should verify that all of the required information is included and that the proposal package is complete. Determine how many copies of the proposal need original signatures. After you've secured the signatures and the copies of the proposal are returned to you, do one final review to ensure they are all complete. Pieces of a proposal sometimes get lost or mislaid during the internal review/ signature processes. It is up to you to ensure that the full package is sent to the funding source.

RESEARCH PROPOSALS

Components of a Research Proposal

While there are similarities between applications to fund research and other types of proposals, there are also some significant differences. Table 5-5 shows the typical parts of a research proposal.

Tips on Writing Research Proposals

Internet Resources

The Internet provides a wealth of resources with guidance on writing research proposals. Some of the most useful include:

An interactive tutorial on writing proposals designed specifically for those in elementary and secondary education.

http://www.schoolgrants.org/WriteGrant.htm

A gateway site on writing proposals maintained by the University of Wisconsin at Madison.

http://www.library.wisc.edu/libraries/ Memorial/grants/proposal.htm

An online collection of articles suggested by Michigan State University.

http://www.lib.msu.edu/harris23/grants/ 4acfrais.htm

Duke University's inventory of sources on how to write research proposals.

http://www.ors.duke.edu/fundopps/fndopps. htm

The National Council of University Research Administrator's site.

http://www.NCURA.edu/resources/prep.htm

National Institute of Allergy and Infectious Diseases, "Faculty and Research: Writing a Grant Proposal."

http://cpmcnet.columbia.edu/research/writing. html

Table 5-5. Elements of a Research Proposal

Element / Information Usually Provided	Approx. Pages

Title or Cover Page — 1 page
A title for the project that signals the purpose and significance of the research; the names and contact information of the principal investigator and this individual's department chair or program director; the name and contact information for the submitting organization; name of program and agency to which the proposal is being submitted; proposed starting date and budget period; and total funds requested. Some agencies want the title page to specify whether the proposal is for a new or continuing project. Others ask that the title page list other sources also being approached for support. Generally, the principal investigator, a departmental representative, and an official representing the submitting organization sign the title page.

Abstract — ½ page
A clear, short, logical summary of your proposal including the expected outcomes or aims of the project, the most important research questions to be asked, the project's background and significance, and key elements of the research design and methods.

Table of Contents — 1 page
A table of contents should always be included in lengthy research proposals.

Statement of Need — 1 page
Outlines the problem(s) and why this problem needs to be addressed at this time, and builds a case for the importance of the research.

Purposes — 1 page
Lays out what you hope to accomplish by clearly identifying the goals, objectives (or aims), and hypotheses or research questions.

Background and Literature — 2 pages
Establishes the context for your project and demonstrates your understanding of the field with a critical analysis of pertinent past work and scholarly literature. Make certain that the significance of your project in filling a "gap in knowledge" is established. Don't forget to include your own previous work on the topic and that of any likely reviewers.

Research Plan — 2½ pages
The study design, methods, sample selection, data size, data measurement, data collection, and analysis. This section should include a timeline. It also needs to make clear why the approach you are proposing is the best way to tackle this research.

Dissemination of Results/Practical Significance — ½ page
Disciplines differ on what kinds of claims should be made to justify the value of research, but many funding sources want this information.

Qualifications — ½ page
Makes the case for why you and/or your organization are the best suited to do this research. Discuss factors such as superior facilities, access to specialized equipment, the availability of a pool of highly talented people, existing relationships with organizations whose cooperation is essential to the research, access to scarce types of study populations, and so forth. The unique capabilities of the principal investigator may also be presented here. If not requested as a separate attachment, this section should also provide a list of references of people who can evaluate the researchers' capabilities.

Source: *Getting Funded: The Complete Guide to Writing Grant Proposals* by Mary Hall and Susan Howlett. Available from Portland State University, Continuing Education Press, www.cep.pdx.edu.

Table 5-5. Elements of a Research Proposal (continued)

Personnel   1 page
A description of the project's positions and duties, who will fill them (or how those individuals will be recruited and selected), and the background and related experience of the key personnel. Show what percentage of each person's time will be allocated to the project. Provide a rationale for any consultants to be involved, their roles and backgrounds.

Budget   1 page
Itemized costs of the project, both annual and overall. Most funding sources that support research specify the various categories that must be used in displaying the budget. Show how the costs were calculated.

Attachments   varies
Copies of compliance documents required by the funding source, such as:

- the certification on ethical treatment of human and/or animal subjects.

- a nonprofit's 501(c)(3) letter (unless told not to include this).

- letters of recommendation (it is helpful if you draft these so each covers the points you want made).

- letters of agreement from collaborators and consultants.

- newspaper clippings or articles in professional publications reporting on related work of the principal investigator and/or institution. Always check with a program officer whether attachments and appendices are counted in the overall allowable length.

The Environmental Protection Agency's interactive proposal writing tutorial.
> http://www.epa.gov/seahome/grants/src/grant.htm

The National Science Foundation's "A Guide For Proposal Writing."
> http://www.nsf.gov/pubs/1998/nsf9891/nsf9891.htm

Social Science Research Council.
> http://www.ssrc.org/programs/publications_editors/publications/art_of_writing_proposals.page

Other Tips for Research Proposals

Other tips offered by experienced research proposal authors are:

- **Develop a thorough outline of your proposal before writing the first draft.** Then write the entire first draft before you start to edit.

- **Include as much information as possible in your first draft to ensure that you don't leave things out:** Shrinking is easy; remembering is not.

- **Use language that hooks the reader's interest early in the proposal.** Starting proposals with a question is a great way to do this. But make certain the question is one you will answer through your proposed project.

- **Use language familiar to the funder.** This is especially important when responding to a Request for Proposals. Whenever possible, repeat back the language in the RFP. Also, explain any technical terms. While reviewers will be experienced researchers, they may not be experts in your particular field. Straightforward and active verb prose is always best.

- **Make it obvious early in the proposal that your project matches the interests of the funding agency.** Staffs of both government and private

---

funding sources say that the lack of a clear fit with their priorities is the single most common reason for rejecting applications. You can emphasize this fit in the research project title, in the abstract, and in how you write the introduction. Most funding agencies support either a particular type of research (such as basic versus clinical), research in a particular field or discipline, research carried out by certain individuals (young faculty members, students), or studies conducted in a certain way (like international collaborations or university faculty-practitioner partnerships). Make your proposal's compatibility obvious.

- **Make certain your proposal gives obvious answers to essential questions.** Reviewers essentially want your proposal to quickly tell them three things: What are we are going to learn as a result of the project that we do not know now? Why it is worth knowing? How will we know that the conclusions are valid?

- **Be logical and "linear" in your presentation.** Organize your goals, aims, hypotheses or research questions, and research design. Make certain that the research plan clearly links to the specific objectives.

- **Have a statistical experimental design that provides for an adequate number of samples to be evaluated.** This is essential in developing a reasonable timeline and budget. Unfortunately, it is typically one of the weakest sections of many proposals.

- **If the research involves human subjects, be certain that your proposal adequately addresses the inclusion of minorities and women in the project.** It is no longer acceptable to simply state that "no individual will be discouraged from participating based on race or sex." You must estimate the distribution of potential males and females within the study population as well as the number or percentage of individuals in different racial groups.

- **Consider protection.** Discuss how you will protect yourself, your personnel, and the public, if the research involves hazardous materials or procedures.

- **Observe the page limitations.** Do not try to push the limit by using small type or by putting information that should be in the body of a proposal into appendices. Reviewers may legitimately decide that if it isn't in the proposal, it doesn't exist.

- **Pay close attention to instructions.** Note what to submit, the number of copies, and the binding. With the proliferation of proposals, funders cannot afford to make copies for all reviewers, and will probably eliminate your application from the running if you neglected to send the appropriate number or you failed to follow instructions not to staple or bind your proposal.

CHAPTER 6

Title Page, Abstract, and Accompanying Documents

This chapter outlines considerations in selecting a title and discusses the contents of a title page and abstract. It also provides examples of forms which frequently must accompany a proposal.

CHOOSING THE TITLE

An experienced proposal writer once remarked, only partly facetiously, that the most important choice in developing a successful project was a good title. A title that aptly describes the primary goal of the project in words that will be easily remembered and often repeated is a definite asset. Here are several Do's and Don'ts:

Do's

- **Do make the title fit the funder.** A technical sounding title might be appropriate for submission to the National Science Foundation or one of the National Institutes of Health, but would be much less appropriate for a social service project submitted to a private foundation or a curriculum development project sent to a state education agency.

- **Do describe the purpose of the project,** giving the reviewers a clear idea of what the project is about.

- **Do keep the title short.** Remember that the project will normally be indexed or entered into some type of informational system. Brevity helps and, at least in the private sector, is mandatory. Reviewers in the throes of a decision-making meeting usually refer to proposals by shortened nicknames—make it easy for them to remember yours.

- **Do use imagination and flair.** Select words that draw a picture in the mind of the reader, words people use in everyday conversation.

Don'ts

- **Don't use the name of the funder in the project title.** Naming a project after a sole donor is usually mutually agreed upon after a decision has been made to fund a project, rather than at the initial application stage.

- **Don't select a title which begins "A Project to . . ."** This shows lack of imagination and adds unnecessary length.

- **Don't select a title that is likely to have been used by others.** One funder recalled receiving 17 applications called "New Beginnings." Sixteen were not funded.

- **Don't choose a title that can be considered comical.** Funding sources are sensitive to the fact that politicians have skimmed project titles listed in annual reports or government documents and based criticism on jargon-filled or flippant titles.

COVER AND TITLE PAGE

Cover and Binding

Increasingly, both private and public funding sources discourage covers on proposals, and federal agencies now prohibit bound or stapled applications. **Pay close attention to binding instructions.** Funders will probably eliminate your application from the running if you failed to follow instructions not to staple or bind the proposals. With private foundations or corporations, the presence or absence of a cover or binding is usually dictated by the funding source. The size or complexity of the application, and possibly the amount of monies requested, can also have a bearing. For example, a university presenting an elaborate case study to justify an endowed chair will usually enclose its material in some type of cover. A folder with pockets for accompanying documents is another alternative.

Whatever the decision, never use a binding that makes it difficult to disassemble the proposal (something frequently done during the review process). And never select a cover that appears inappropriately elaborate or expensive.

Cover Sheet

The cover sheet provided by many federal programs doubles as a title page, as a summary, and occasionally, as a guarantee of compliance with various federal regulations. Attachments 6-1 and 6-2 at the end of this chapter give two examples—one for a nonresearch proposal and one for a research proposal.

Title Page

There is no standard format for a title page. Usually, directions on whether or not to include one are provided by the funder. If not, a title page normally includes:

- Title of the project.

- Name of the agency submitting the application.

- Name of the funding source to which the proposal is submitted.

- Beginning and ending dates of the project.

- Total project budget and amount requested from this source.

- Names, contact information, and signatures of the project director or principal investigator.

- Name and signature of the applying organization's official authorizing that the proposal has been approved.

ABSTRACT OR EXECUTIVE SUMMARY

Although this is one of the first items in a proposal, the *abstract*—also called an *executive summary*—is usually among the last to be written, because all aspects of the proposal must be clearly defined before they can be summarized succinctly. A good way to write a proposal is to draft a dummy summary, then use it to guide preparing the body of the proposal, and then redo it for the final draft.

While most abstracts are between 250 and 500 words, some funders expect an executive summary of only one or two paragraphs. Neither should be more than one page in length.

The abstract, a cogent summary of the proposed project, should be prepared with care. It must tell the entire story simply and clearly. Many novices make the mistake of using the abstract as an *introduction* rather than as a *synopsis* of the proposal.

The abstract plays several important roles:

- Funders frequently use it to make the basic determination of whether the project is eligible for, or even worthy of, further consideration. One experienced foundation executive says that, in nine out of ten cases, she never reads beyond the summary page before deciding whether to reject a project or retain it for further analysis.

- It is often taken out and circulated separately to key funding officials (public or private) who have asked to see a digest of all incoming projects.

- Funding sources use it for the various national information systems that provide citations to sponsored projects.

- Grantors may use it to secure input from others in their organization who serve in an advisory role. For example, corporate foundations will consult their local manager in the community from which an application is submitted. The manager is often provided only with the summary unless the project is very extensive or complex.

- Proposal writers can circulate it to others within the organization who should know about the project, but who do not need the entire proposal.

Most federal programs, many state sources and an increasing number of private funders now provide pre-printed summary or abstract pages that must preface the proposal. These forms, usually available on-line, call for details such as where the project is to be carried out, the number of project participants, budget information on other sources of funds, and assurances that the applicant agency has complied with various regulations. Examples of such forms from both public and private sources are provided in the attachments at the end of this chapter.

If no format is specified, the summary should:

- Describe briefly the problem the proposal intends to address.

- Give a quick overview of the proposed solution, the timeframe, and who will be affected.

- Present a concise description of the project's significance or replicability.

- Indicate why the applicant organization and staff are especially qualified to conduct the project.

- Highlight required funding and any other funders who are involved.

- Show how the project is consistent with the funder's goals.

FORMS AND ATTACHMENTS

Use Only Appropriate Attachments

Be sure to attach only what the funder requests. Some reviewers eliminate applications based on inclusion or omission of attachments. Foundations almost always want board lists, IRS determination letters, and audited financials, while government funders do not. Read the guidelines.

Proof of Compliance with Government Regulations

Federal and state applications require a plethora of forms which assure that the applicant agency is in compliance with an array of government regulations on such issues as nondiscrimination, and protection of human or animal research subjects, the public, and your institution. In some cases, compliance must be established **before** the full proposal is submitted. Prior approval is normally documented through a checklist (see Attachment 6-2) or through entering the number assigned to the organization for a specific compliance on the proposal's title page.

Proposal writers **must** familiarize themselves with such requirements well in advance of the application deadline. The applicant organization, not the project director or proposal writer, is responsible for establishing compliance procedures or internal review processes, and the process often takes weeks or months to finalize. If you need these approvals, allow your organization plenty of time to prepare for and meet such institution-wide requirements.

Some public agencies will accept proposals from organizations whose compliance processes are still under review. The agencies signal this by indicating that you may enter the word "pending" in the space for the organization's documentation number. Some funders require that the process be finished prior to receipt of the grant and others by the end of the project's grant cycle. Renewal funds are seldom granted without compliance.

Proof of Nonprofit Tax Status

The most common attachment to proposals to private grantors is a copy of the organization's letter of determination from the IRS indicating that the organization is a *private, nonprofit agency* qualifying under section 501(c)(3) of the tax code and not a *private foundation* defined under section 509(a), since the latter cannot receive funds from another private foundation. A copy of the determination letter should be included by all applicants unless they are public agencies, such as a federal or state agency, or a public school or university, which often have different IRS determinations but are still eligible for grants.

Check your IRS determination letter to make sure that:

- The determination has not lapsed. The IRS sometimes offers new organizations a preliminary ruling of nonprofit eligibility. The official determination letter may have an expiration date by which the organization must get a permanent designation.

- The organization name is current. Organizations sometimes change their names and neglect to get a new determination letter. They must renew their status through refiling certain information by a specified date. Currently, re-establishing 501(c)(3) status is handled by the IRS's regional offices and can take several months to complete. Foundations may pledge a grant to an organization whose filing has

lapsed, but they cannot disburse the funds until this status is reinstated.

- There is no confusion about who has been granted tax-exempt status. Applicant organizations sometimes fall under the umbrella of a larger non-profit, whose name appears on the determination letter. If you are applying under the aegis of another group, explain your relationship to them clearly.

You may also be asked to include proof of status as a nonprofit corporation issued by the state in which your organization was incorporated. However, IRS tax-exempt status usually suffices.

Board of Directors List

Many funders will ask who serves on a nonprofit's board of directors. Apart from wanting to see if they know anyone on the board, funders want to know why you've chosen each individual to help govern your organization. You may want to indicate:

- Where they work, if there are certain employers in your community who lend credibility to a board.

- Where they live, if you're proving that your statewide organization is led by statewide leaders, not just people in the largest or capital city.

- Their area of expertise, assuming they will share their wisdom shaping your finances, communication, legislative relations, or program development.

- Their relationship to the mission, as a parent, client, student, patient, or colleague in the field.

- What constituency they represent, providing access to—or proving partnership with—cooperating entities.

What you list as your board's affiliations will depend on what your organization values and what might appeal to that grantor. Look for clues in their guidelines, the RFP, and their printed and online materials.

For example, one nonprofit organization, wishing to demonstrate that its board reflects the community it serves, identifies the ethnic or cultural heritage of each board member, while an ecumenical religious group lists the denominations of their board members.

Financial Statements and IRS Form 990

Some funders require that you include a copy of your most recent financial statements audited by an outside reviewer. Some grantors require a full audit for you to be eligible for funding. Others simply want to see that an external expert has reviewed your finances recently, so you can submit either a less stringent *review* or a *compilation*. (Check with your CPA to determine which is best.) Information in your audit may help answer questions raised by your organizational budget. Be prepared to include your organization's most recent annual IRS Form 990, Return of Organization Exempt from Income Tax. It lists key financial information about an organization, including revenue and expenses, and salaries of key staff. Many grantors will request your current organizational budget and balance sheet. They want to see what your organization has projected for expenses and revenue for the year and how it is doing against projections.

Organizational Chart

You may be asked to submit a chart illustrating the hierarchy or chain of command in your organization or institution. This shows funders who is accountable to whom and where, in the scheme of things, your project fits. It also shows them how many individuals will be supporting the proposed project and in the context of what other activities.

Letters of Support or Endorsement

If your project can succeed only with the cooperation of other entities, funders may ask for letters of endorsement from key personnel in those entities. For instance, if your program is based in the court system, they may want to know that the presiding judge thinks you're competent and cooperative. If your program depends on a reciprocal arrangement with a state agency, funders will want to see proof that the relationship is collegial and respectful. Verify that you have built strong, healthy relationships with others. If the funder does not require letters of support (some grantors don't want support documents they haven't requested), simply include a list of agencies or institutions from which you have letters and offer to share them.

Securing a letter of support from another entity can take weeks or months, so **plan ahead.** Let the endorser know how to address the letter, what types of things you want included (it helps to offer some sample wording), and when you need it. To be safe, you may want to specify a deadline well before your own. Ask endorsers to send their letters to you, not directly to the funder. If an endorser has a particularly close relationship with the funder, suggest sending a separate message (by phone, mail, or email) in addition to the formal letter of support.

Estimates from Vendors

If you are requesting money for capital expenditures, you may be required to submit estimates from three potential vendors so the funder can see that you've shopped around and the numbers proposed in your budget reflect reality. If you include only one estimate, reviewers may wonder how that bid relates to prices from other suppliers in your area.

FORMS AND ATTACHMENTS FOR A RESEARCH PROPOSAL

Research proposers may be asked to supply additional information, including:

- Findings from a pilot study, if applicable.

- Samples of letters to project participants explaining the research project.

- Résumés or curricula vitae of the investigators/researchers and staff.

- A diagram of the research design.

Research proposals will need to include assurances that the applicant institution complies with all relevant laws and guidelines. These forms, including explanatory notes, can usually be downloaded from the funder's Web site. The most common concern human subjects, vertebrate animals, inventions and patents, debarment and suspension, drug-free workplace, lobbying, delinquent federal debt, misconduct in science, civil rights, handicapped individuals, and sex and age discrimination.

ATTACHMENT 6-1.

SAMPLE COVER SHEET FOR A STANDARD PROPOSAL

Common Application Form

Provide the following grant information in this order. For your convenience, you may choose either to copy and fill out this cover summary, or create your own using the headings listed below.

Funder applying to: _____ Date submitted: _____

Total proposed project/program budget: _____ Amount requested: _____

Program name: _____

Duration of project/program: from _____ to _____ When are funds needed? _____

Nature of request: ❑ capital ❑ project ❑ operating ❑ program ❑ endowment other

Organization information:

Name and address: _____

_____

Phone number: _____ TTY: _____ Fax number: _____

E-mail: _____ FEI number: _____ Date of incorporation: _____

Chief staff officer/title: _____ Phone number: _____

Contact person/title: _____ Phone number: _____

Board chairperson/title: _____ Dates of organization's fiscal year: _____

Organization's total operating budget for past year: _____ and current year: _____

Has the governing board approved a policy which states that the organization does not discriminate as to age, race, religion, sex or national origin? ❑ Yes ❑ No If yes, when? _____

Does the organization have federal tax exempt status? ❑ Yes ❑ No If no, please explain.

Has the organization's chief executive officer authorized this request? ❑ Yes ❑ No

An officer of the organization's governing body must sign this application:

The undersigned, an authorized officer of the organization, does hereby certify that the information set forth in this grant application is true and correct, that the federal tax exemption determination letter attached hereto has not been revoked and the present operation of the organization and its current sources of support are not inconsistent with the organization's continuing tax exempt classification as set forth in such determination letter.

_____   _____   _____
Signature   Print name/title   Date

Enclose all required support materials with the application (see page 1 General Instructions).

Source: *Getting Funded: The Complete Guide to Writing Grant Proposals* by Mary Hall and Susan Howlett. Available from Portland State University, Continuing Education Press, www.cep.pdx.edu. Copyright © 2003. All rights reserved.

ATTACHMENT 6-2.

SAMPLE COVER SHEET FOR A RESEARCH PROPOSAL

Research Grant / Consultancy Application Cover Sheet

A copy of this form must be submitted to the Grants Office with **ALL** applications for research or consultancy funds. Please provide the number of copies of the application required by the funding agency, plus an additional copy for our records (to which this cover sheet should be attached).

Please note that you **MUST** apply the university overheads of 15% to your budget (unless the funding agency is exempt or it is a Nationally Competitive Scheme).

PROJECT CLASSIFICATION

Project status:
❑ Renewal
❑ New project
Broad research type:
❑ Pure basic research
❑ Strategic basic research
❑ Applied research
❑ Experimental development

Project classification:
❑ Research grant
❑ Scholarship
❑ Fellowship
❑ Consultancy
❑ Research consultancy
❑ Progress report*
❑ Prelim proposal*
    *cover sheet not needed

RFCD code: %   **SEO code:**   %
_____ _____   _____ _____
_____ _____   _____ _____
_____ _____   _____ _____

Projects AOU (e.g., AVE, BIN, All, etc):
_____

Project's area of research strength:
_____

PROJECT DETAILS

Project title: _____

Applicant name(s):	Staff number:	Early career researcher?	Project time (total # days):
_____	_____	❑ Yes ❑ No	_____
_____	_____	❑ Yes ❑ No	_____
_____	_____	❑ Yes ❑ No	_____

Funding agency / Contracting party / Client: _____

Total amount requested ($):	Application date:	Commencement date:	Termination date:
_____	_____	_____	_____

ETHICS APPROVAL

Does the project involve			Has approval been obtained?	What is the permit number if received?
The use of animals?	❑ Yes	❑ No	❑ Yes ❑ No	_____
The use of human participants?	❑ Yes	❑ No	❑ Yes ❑ No	_____
The *in vitro* production of recombinant DNA molecules?	❑ Yes	❑ No	❑ Yes ❑ No	_____
Potentially hazardous procedures and situations?	❑ Yes	❑ No	❑ Yes ❑ No	_____
The use and disposal of potent teratogens or carcinogens?	❑ Yes	❑ No	❑ Yes ❑ No	_____
The use of ionizing radiation?	❑ Yes	❑ No	❑ Yes ❑ No	_____
Intellectual property rights or confidential material?	❑ Yes	❑ No	*Will be referred to Contracts Officer*	
Other matter of a hazardous nature— please specify:	❑ Yes	❑ No	❑ Yes ❑ No	_____

Attachment 6-2. Sample Cover Sheet for a Research Proposal (continued)

It is the chief investigator's responsibility to obtain approvals from the appropriate university committees or state or federal authorities before commencement of the research, or as otherwise specified by the funding agency. The most common matters requiring approval are listed below, together with the appropriate body that would consider the issue.

Ethics situations as listed above	Relevant committee
The use of animals or human subjects	Animal or Human Research Ethics Committees
Potentially hazardous procedures and recombinant DNA	Institutional Biosafety Committee
The use and disposal of potent teratogens or carcinogens	Hazardous Chemicals Sub-Committee
The use of ionizing radiation	Radiation Sub-Committee
Intellectual property rights or confidential material	Pro Vice-Chancellor (Research)
Other matter of a hazardous nature	Occupational Health and Safety Policy Committee

CHAPTER 7

Writing the Purpose Statement

This chapter discusses how to present what you want to accomplish with the funds you are seeking, explains different types of purpose statements and provides tips on writing and presenting them in applications. It also discusses how purpose statements should be written in a research proposal.

The *purpose statement* section of a proposal needs to originate in a knowledge base, so it must be written by someone who truly knows the field. It tells the funding source what you want to do and what will change as a result of their award.

While all components in a proposal are important, this section is among the most critical. It is the fundamental building block for every proposal. If your purpose statement is not clear and compelling, matched to the grantmaker's interests, and appropriate to the scale of the project, it is unlikely that your proposal will be funded. Having a clear idea about what you want to achieve is critical to the writing of all other parts of an application and lack of clarity here can doom the proposal. To paraphrase Alice (in Wonderland), "If you don't know where you are going, then it doesn't matter which way you go." Grantmakers tend to support proposals that demonstrate a sense of direction.

The scale of your purpose is particularly important. One of the most common problems in many proposals is the practice of taking on too much. Even experienced proposal writers often fail

to strike a proper balance between promising to achieve important impacts and stating outcomes that can really be achieved given the time, staff, and budget included in the application. Admittedly, this balance is difficult, but it is critical to preparing an effective and feasible proposal. Being honest (in every sense) about the purpose of a project is essential to you and your organization's professional reputation.

DIFFERENT TYPES OF PURPOSE STATEMENTS

One must choose carefully how best to describe the purpose of a project. You can usually tell which approach a particular funding source prefers by paying close attention to the language used in its application guidelines and forms.

Increasingly, purpose statements in well-crafted proposals include *goals, objectives,* and *outcomes.* This approach quickly signals the overall intent of the project, the tangible results to be achieved, and the benefit to the client and community. In the following example, a nonprofit community development agency is applying to a private foundation for funds to help guarantee loans for its low-income clients who want to become first-time homebuyers. Its proposal purpose section might look like Figure 7-1:

Figure 7-1: Example of Purpose Statements

Goal	Increase the number of low-income homeowners in XXX city.
Objective	Expand the pool of guarantees for low-interest home loans to poor first-time homebuyers in XXX neighborhood by 30 percent within 12 months.
Outcome	Thirty percent of low-income individuals in XXX community will become first-time homeowners by XXXX date.

Now let's look at how these terms differ.

Goal

A *goal statement* is a broad description of the intended consequences of the project. It helps the reviewer gain an overall orientation to the longer-term purposes of the project, but does not address the specifics of what will be accomplished or what the applicant will be held accountable to produce. Typically, proposals have only one, or at most two, goal statements.

Example: This project will help parents be more engaged in their children's education.

Objective

An *objective statement* describes a specific and measurable result of the project. There are at least four types of objectives:

- **Behavioral.** A human action will result. The statement should specify who is going to perform the behavior, what behavior will occur, under what circumstances will the behavior be observed and how the behavior is to be measured.

  Example: Thirty of 50 parent participants will learn how to use checklists to monitor their children's reading progress.

- **Performance.** Adds a specific time frame and expected level of proficiency.

  Example: Within three months of participating in two types of training programs, all of the parents will pass a skills test on the use of checklists to monitor their children's reading progress.

- **Process.** The manner in which something occurs is an important result, such as an effort to determine the best procedures. This kind of objective should say who will perform the process, what is intended to result from the process, and how the process will be evaluated.

  Example: The project staff will document two different methods of training parents to use checklists and, through follow-up interviews, determine which method the parents prefer.

- **Product.** A significant tangible item will result. This kind of objective should say who will produce the product, what the product is, the intended audience, when the product will be available, and how the quality of the product will be measured.

  Example: The staff will prepare four different types of performance checklists by the third month of the project and determine, through follow-up interviews, which checklist parents prefer.

Most proposals include behavioral and performance objectives. Process and product objectives are normally presented only when they are requested by the funding source, are essential to explaining the significance of the project, require a considerable amount of the project's resources, or are an important element in the proposal's evaluation design.

Outcome

An *outcome statement* describes what will change in the lives of individuals, families, organizations, or the community as a result of the project. It should also be stated in measurable terms.

Example: The reading skills of all children in the program will increase at least a grade level and their parents will be using new skills in coaching, monitoring, and encouraging their children's education.

Outcome statements help grantmakers answer the "so what" question, namely, will anyone (other than just the applicant) be better off as a result of this project?

Beginning in the mid-1990s, many funding sources began to require outcome statements because they wanted to change the emphasis in proposals from the needs and interests of the applicant agency to the intended benefits to clients, the community, or society as a whole. This was a real paradigm shift in the thinking of both private and governmental grantmakers and must be addressed by any successful grantwriter.

Funders essentially got tired of people saying, "You give us the money and we will do this cool program," when it became obvious that just repeating a program wasn't necessarily making a change. We can all think of examples of much-heralded and very expensive programs that were later proven to have made absolutely no difference. Grantors are now asking grantseekers to take the argument full circle and go beyond, "We will do this cool program" to, "and these people will be served in *this* way and a year from now the community will look different in *this* way."

Every proposal has to be submitted with the thought that it might actually be funded. Projects with unclear or vague outcomes should never make it to the mailbox.

Different Types of Outcome Statements

The proposal writer can use various types of outcome statements to describe the purpose of a project. Jane Reisman and Judith Clegg, authors of *Outcomes for Success* (2), one of the most widely used texts for designing outcome evaluations, describe these as follows:

- **Change statements** include the increase, maintenance, or decrease in a behavior, skill, knowledge, or attitude.

  Example: increase immunization among young children

- **Target statements** state specific levels of achievement.

  Example: immunize 80 percent of the two-year-old children in the community according to recommended public health schedules

- **Benchmark statements** include comparative targets, generally related to other time periods or organizations.

Figure 7-2: Three Types of Outcome Statements

The change or desired effect in what for whom (*outcome change statement*).

   Example: Increase reading skills of first grade students in XYZ school

The amount of change for whom in what (*target outcome statement*).

   Example: Increase by 20 percent all first grade students' reading comprehension skills in XYZ school.

The amount of change for whom in what against what standard (*benchmark statement*)

   Example: Increase by 20 percent all first graders' reading comprehension skills in XYZ school compared to their scores on district tests on x date.

Example: increase the current 70 percent immunization rate for children 0 to 24 months to 90 percent by a specified year. (1)

Figure 7-2 shows how an outcome can shift from a *change* to a *target* to a *benchmark* statement by adding increasing amounts of specificity.

Outcomes versus Outputs

One word of caution: A number of grantmakers will ask for *outcomes* (i.e., purposes that result in improvements that can be measured), when what they really want is *outputs* (i.e., purposes that can be counted). For example, if they ask for you to specify the **number** of participants that will be able to do something as a result of your program, they likely want *outputs*. On the other hand, if they request that you say **how well** the participants will perform, they are more interested in *outcomes*. This distinction is important for two reasons: One, it will dictate the approach you use in designing the project's evaluation. Two, it will influence reviewers' judgment about how close your project matches the funder's interests. It is up to you to match the way that you describe your project's purposes to what the funding source requires and expects.

Tools for Designing Outcome Statements

Reisman and Clegg suggest applying a "so-that chain" to identify appropriate project or program outcomes as seen from the perspective of those other than the applicant. When applied to the previous example, it might look like this:

Train parents to use checklists . . . . so that

Parents will get involved in monitoring their children's reading performances . . . . so that

Parents will emphasize the importance of reading to their children . . . . so that

Children's reading skills will improve . . . . so that

Children will be more successful in school . . . . so that

Children will stay in school and complete their education . . . . so that

Children will be happier, more self-sufficient, more responsible adults.

This example is also helpful to the novice grantwriter who struggles to identify what is a *goal* versus what is an *outcome* versus what is an *objective*. The first four statements in the example suggest themselves as the basis for *objectives*. The statement, "children will be more successful in school," can serve as the basis for an *outcome* (although it will need to be worded in more measurable terms). Either of the last two statements might serve as a *goal* as both let the reader know what the ultimate purpose of this program is and how the results will benefit society.

Another useful tool for writing outcomes is commonly called a *program logic model*. The theory behind this model is generally credited to Joseph Wholey and others in the *Handbook of Practical Program Evaluation* (3). This model, outlined in Table 7-1, is useful to any proposal writer as a disciplined way to clarify the essential *inputs, activities, outputs, outcomes,* and *goals* of the effort for which you are seeking funds.

Filling out the logic model early in the process also helps pinpoint ways to strengthen your proposal that you might not otherwise think about. In identifying the resources or inputs for a goal, an agency might realize it has facilities and equipment, well-trained staff, a big pool of volunteers and a strong board. This sets them apart from another group which has an idea, but no infrastructure yet.

TIPS FOR WRITING PURPOSE STATEMENTS

- **Write purpose statements that relate to the priorities of the funder.** Use terms that clearly signal your understanding of the grantmaker's interests.

- **Select purposes that, if implemented, will obviously help achieve the applicant organization's mission.** A project whose outcomes seem totally irrelevant to the stated mission of the agency is a tip-off to funders that the grantwriter is simply "chasing money."

- **Focus on meaningful outcome statements.** Explain what will happen as a result of this

Table 7-1: A Program Logic Model				
Resources	**Activities**	**Outputs**	**Outcomes**	**Goals**
Program inputs	The methods used to carry out the specific program	Units of service or product. How many, how often, over what duration	Short-, intermediate- or long-term changes anticipated in those being served by your program	Ultimate impact(s) expected to occur, usually beyond the time of one grant
Examples: Staff, money, clients	Examples: Service delivery, steps in research, events, processes	Examples: Number of clients served in various types of training	Examples: Increased knowledge, improved performance	Examples: healthier community, problem prevention

project that will really make a difference. This is particularly important in proposals to private foundations and corporations in which the outcomes need to be described succinctly.

- **Make certain that your purposes and your needs statement tie to each other.** Proposal writers are often bewildered about which should come first—the statement of the need or the description of the project's purpose. Funders differ on the best sequence of these two elements. But, however presented, the two must reinforce each other.

- **Select purposes that are realistic.** Remember, your purpose statements are what you promise the funder you will accomplish in return for the money. They are what the grantmaker will expect you to evaluate and report. Include only those that you can really accomplish. Don't promise what you cannot deliver. And review your purpose component again after you've completed the procedures, evaluation, and budget components. If the latter are not of sufficient scale to accomplish the original purpose, revise it and scale it down.

- **Write purposes clearly.** Don't get lost in verbiage. Present them early on a page and make them stand out (use bold face type or bullets or indentations). This is ***extremely important***. Reviewers have only a few moments to decide if your request matches their interests. Make your purpose(s) explicit early in the application. Reviewers should not have to hunt through the proposal to puzzle out your intentions.

- **Do not confuse *purposes* with *procedures*.** Some proposal writers confuse their project's ends and means and write purpose statements that describe the *activities* that will take place, rather than the *results* that can be expected from those tasks. Unless the activities *themselves* are the purpose of the proposal (such as an effort to develop innovative processes of some kind), always focus the purpose statements on *what* you intend to achieve, not *how* you plan to get there.

- **Write purposes that can be evaluated.** If there is no way to judge whether your efforts are responsible for a promised change, then revise the purpose section until you have something measurable. For example, you don't want to promise that the outcome of your project will be that young people never join gangs, because there are far too many factors influencing that decision for you to affect with a single project. But it is possible for you to propose a project that would improve a young person's school attendance and their participation in healthy after-school activities and would change what they say about the desirability of joining gangs.

- **Choose purposes for which you will have access to the information needed to evaluate success.** It is critical that the purpose and evaluation components of a proposal mesh. If all information about clients is confidential, do not write purposes that rely on access to patient records as the only means to determine if the purpose was accomplished.

- **Include purpose statements that adequately justify how you plan to spend the project's budget.** One proposal presented its purpose as launching a new type of reading program, but planned to spend over half of the budget to buy new computers and software. The grantmaker decided, understandably, that the real purpose of the request was to upgrade the school's equipment and rejected it.

Not every purpose statement must be written as goals, objectives, and/or outcomes. Government agencies, foundations, and corporations often make grants in response to proposals that are not presented in the formal "outcome" format. For example, the following purpose statement was found in a proposal recently funded by a major corporation, which had also supported the applicant in the past:

> As one of our corporate friends, you know that we have had an enormous impact on environmental policy in the United States. Further, our mediation work over the last decade has helped establish a cost effective alternative to the courts for resolving environmental disputes. It is now time for us to expand our activities into Eastern Europe, where the rapid growth in entrepreneurism is leading to significant environmental concerns. We are asking for a grant of $XXXX to help us initiate a center in Belgrade.

One might conclude from this statement that the corporation did not care about the specificity of outcome statements. *Wrong!* The corporation and the applicant had met several times to discuss the request. The proposal was simply the necessary paperwork to authorize a check and was never intended as a competitive document. The corporation also negotiated a written *memorandum of understanding* with the nonprofit as part of the grants process. This document spelled out the specific parameters for the use of the grant funds and specified what was to be measured in judging the project's success. This approach is often used by private foundations and corporations to clarify intended uses of a grant.

However, even if the grantmaker doesn't require specific outcomes, it is the funded project that suffers most if a project's purposes are poorly defined. Some reasons are:

- **Unclear outcomes must be clarified before the program can be implemented.** The staff may flounder through several months of operation arguing points that should have been settled when the proposal was developed.

- **The applicant and the donor may end up with very different perceptions of what the funds were intended to achieve.** Not only might this end opportunities for further grants from this source, but it could really hurt the reputation of the organization with other grantmakers.

- **The budget or the timeline for the project may turn out to be unrealistic.**

- **Important partners for the project may become frustrated** at the confusion and withdraw from future collaboration.

- **The project may become embroiled in a political fight with its constituents** because of a lack of agreement on what the funds were intended to achieve.

PURPOSE STATEMENTS FOR RESEARCH PROPOSALS

Typically, purpose statements in research proposals have at least three major components: *Goals, objectives,* and *hypotheses* or *research questions.*

The first two are the same as for a project proposal, but the third is unique to research.

- **Goals.** Broad statements that orient the reader to the overall purpose(s) of the project and its intended benefits.

  Example: This 3-year project will examine methods to help children learn better.

- **Objectives or aims.** More specific statements that operationalize the project's focus.

  Example: To explore the relationship between physical exercise and children's attentiveness in school.

- **Hypotheses or research questions.** A description of the specific ideas to be examined. Normally, these are framed as *hypotheses* if the research is to be quantitative, or as *research questions* if it is a qualitative study.

  Example: Children who engage in a 10-minute exercise program at the beginning of each school day will be more attentive in class.

Some funding sources ask that the goals and objectives be included in the proposal's introduction, and the research questions or hypotheses be included in the research methodology section. Be certain to secure the in-advance instructions for the funding source(s) you'll be approaching with your research proposal. Follow the directions explicitly.

TIPS FOR PURPOSE STATEMENTS IN RESEARCH PROPOSALS

The Internet provides a wealth of resources on how to write purpose statements in research proposals. Some of the most useful are listed at the end of Chapter 5.

Other advice from experienced researchers or reviewers includes:

- **Keep your project feasible.** An overly ambitious proposal leads reviewers to question whether the project has been thoroughly thought out.

The most successful applications typically have two to four specific objectives.

- **Realize your audience is diverse.** Reviewers may be experts in your field, but not in your topic, so explain your project's purpose clearly and use the background and/or literature review section to substantiate what contribution your project will make to a specific body of knowledge. Do so without jargon.

- **Present your goals, objectives, questions, and hypotheses as early in the proposal as possible.** Use bold face or italicized type to highlight them. Reviewers should never have to hunt through pages of gray text to try to determine what you're proposing to do.

- **Emphasize** *why* **you want to investigate these aims.** Tell why the outcome of your research is important. What is the larger context of scientific knowledge? How will your work contribute?

- **Describe the goals, objectives, and questions/ hypotheses in a logical sequence.** Some writers prefer to simply provide a sequential listing of the goal followed by relevant aims/objectives followed by relevant hypotheses. Others prefer to have a paragraph or so of discussion after each aim/objective that speaks to how this relates to the goal and why it is important.

CHAPTER REFERENCES

1. Jane Reisman and Judith Clegg. *Outcomes for Success!* © 2000 The Evaluation Forum: Seattle, WA, p. 18.

2. Reisman and Clegg, p. 14.

3. Joseph Wholey, Harry Hatry, and Kathryn Newcomer (Eds.). *Handbook of Practical Program Evaluation*, San Francisco: Jossey-Bass Publishers, 1994.

Chapter 8

Writing the Statement of Need

This chapter discusses the preparation of the statement of need and its role in the proposal, and provides examples from successful applications.

Ask a room full of grantseekers to draft a sample grant application form, and they will usually generate the standard list of questions posed by grantors. But one question they often neglect to include is "What's the problem?" They are so involved in their work that the problem seems obvious, and it doesn't occur to them that someone else might not understand the issues. That's why funders ask applicants to state clearly what external problem or need the grant will address. This is called the *Statement of Need*, *Need Statement*, or *Problem Statement*.

The statement of need is a pivotal element in a proposal, because it sets the stage for the rest of the document. Your response to every other question hinges on how you define the problem. The scope of work, methodology, evaluation, even the budget must reflect—indeed parallel—your statement of the problem.

PURPOSE OF STATEMENT OF NEED

The needs statement identifies the problem and its causes, clarifying the connections among the problem, its causes, and your proposed solution. It establishes the rationale for the proposed activity and ties a need in the community to a need for the funder's involvement. This section of the proposal demonstrates:

- A thorough understanding of the problem the project intends to explore, address, or resolve.

- The importance of this problem, not only to the project participants, but to the larger society.

- A critical analysis of the literature in the field and how this project will fill some significant gap.

- The timeliness of the project (why it should be funded now).

- How your work relates to that of similar organizations in your community or your field.

- The innovative nature of the effort, at least locally. If the project is, in fact, a duplication, then provide a rationale as to why additional resources should be allocated to the problem.

- The potential for replication or application by others. Will the result of your project help resolve other similar or related problems?

- The beginning rationale for the procedures, approach, and plan of action to be discussed in the next section of the proposal.

- Why you care about the problem, including the relationship of the problem and its proposed solution to the interests and capabilities of your organization. Research proposals especially are expected to describe how the current project will build on and extend your (or others') previous investigations.

- How the need you intend to resolve addresses the funder's goals.

A standard application form required by foundations used to confuse conscientious grantwriters by asking the following question. "Why are you asking us to fund this project?" On the face of it, that seems like a simple question. But savvy applicants realized that question could be construed three ways:

1. **Why** are you asking us to fund this project? (i.e., why is this issue more critical than all the other issues we're asked to support?)

2. Why are you asking **us** to fund this project? (i.e., how did you ascertain that our foundation was the most appropriate source to approach to help solve this problem?)

3. Why are you asking us to fund **this** project? (i.e., of all the things your organization does, what makes this the effort for which you chose to ask for help?)

These are all important questions, and the funders probably wanted to know the answers to all three, but alas, they afforded applicants only three inches on the form. (And at least one of those funders didn't allow phone calls for clarification.)

But if an organization has carefully assessed the need for the proposed work, it should be able to respond to all three questions within three inches.

FACTORS AFFECTING THE STATEMENT OF NEED

Significance

Even if you have already shown that the project relates to the general interests of the funding source, you must demonstrate that the specific problem or need you are addressing is of special importance to the broader community. In this competitive landscape, grantseekers who can position their issue as critical and timely—without diminishing the important work of others—will look especially appealing. Be sure to include answers to the following questions:

- Why is this problem more urgent or important than others under consideration?

- Why is our proposed solution more compelling than others?

Suitability

You must emphasize why this specific need is of unique or direct importance to the particular funding source. By solving this need, will you: Help them resolve a legislative mandate? Initiate an essential service in a community in which they already have major operations? Allow them to use their funds to leverage support from others? You must also make it clear why your organization is uniquely suited to tackle this problem. Make connections with your background, your familiarity with the issue, and your capacity to affect the issue.

Homework

The discussion of related research or prior experience (with both the problem and your proposed solution) bears the major burden for establishing your overall scholarship in and knowledge of the field. Reviewers for the Department of Defense say that fully one-third of the proposals they have received show that the writers had never bothered to check what work had already been done. Also, make sure that any statistics you cite are current and accurate.

Analysis

Funders want you to demonstrate that you have critically analyzed the appropriate literature and that your analysis has shaped your project. Do not simply include a bibliography. How you interpret the information cited and relate it to your work establishes your professional competence. You will also want to demonstrate that you have compared the relative merits of various methods for solving the problem and arrived at your approach only after careful analysis of possible solutions.

Competition

Overeager grantseekers sometimes aver that they are the only entity in their geographic area doing what they do. This is dangerous, since grantors may receive several proposals in the same cycle saying the same thing—a clear sign that the groups are not aware of one another and/or are not working together to solve the problem. Applicants should acknowledge the existence of other groups and show how they are distinct from them, show how they are cooperating with them, and prove that the problem is big enough or complex enough to require the efforts of several groups to solve it.

If numerous organizations or institutions are dealing with the issue, explain how your proposal complements but does not duplicate the efforts of others. When distinguishing your work from others', consider:

- Geographic scope (each group may serve a different neighborhood or county).

- Profile of participants (age, ethnicity, gender, sexual preference, ability).

- Methodology (one group specializes in prevention education, one in crisis intervention, and one in advocacy, all around the same issue).

- Partnerships (one group may be new and in a position to forge new relationships, while another may have developed trusting collaborations with stakeholders over many years).

- Amount of experience (of the organization or the leaders, either in the field or with this constituency).

- Whether work is being done by professional staff or volunteers.

- Whether the solution is stop-gap or long-term (emergency shelter or permanent housing).

- Whether you offer services to people or organize them to affect systemic change.

Feasibility

Statement of the problem must be sufficiently focused to assure reviewers that there is hope for a solution, given the time and resources requested in the proposal. Limiting the scope of the project to a manageable level demonstrates the experience and sincerity of the applicant. Proposing resolution of a problem that is obviously too complex or expensive for the resources sought is the sign of either a novice or someone willing to promise anything in order to get funded.

Data

Statistics on their own do not constitute a need. But it's difficult to corroborate need without them. Include sufficient statistical data to substantiate your case, describe the importance of the population to be served or studied and predict the contribution of the project's outcomes. But don't rely on charts, tables, or graphs to tell your story. A strong proposal will use both hard data (statistics) and soft data (anecdotes or quotes) to paint a vivid picture for the funder.

Assessment

If the problem was brought to light through a needs assessment conducted by you or others, be sure to mention this. If the results are lengthy, include a synopsis of them and offer to send the entire report separately.

Competence

Even if not instructed to do so on the application form, whenever possible, underscore your competence and prior experience in this section. You might cite relevant research or projects previously conducted by you or others in your organization, or refer to your roles in other programs which led you to understand the importance of the problem you are currently addressing.

Checklist 8-1. Questions to Answer in Your Statement of Need

❑ What is the problem?

❑ Who is affected by it?

❑ What is the impact of it?

❑ What are the implications to the community?

❑ Why does this situation exist (root causes)?

❑ What has been your organization's experience with it?

❑ What does external research reveal?

❑ Who else is working on it?

❑ What barriers have they encountered?

❑ What other challenges do you anticipate?

❑ What responses have been considered?

❑ What models or research have been tried elsewhere?

❑ What is your organization's experience with this response?

Pitfalls to Avoid

- **Don't paint a picture so bleak that the grantor feels the problem is insurmountable.** Make sure that the scope of the problem you describe relates to the scale of what you propose. For example, if you describe a problem that is truly monumental in scope, such as global warming or AIDS, narrow the discussion to a more manageable scope by discussing the local situation and whether an investment in local efforts could make an impact.

- **Don't present the lack of your solution as the problem.** Imagine a proposal that suggests, "There is no place for senior citizens to gather in our community. Therefore, we need money to create a senior center." A stronger argument could be made by stating that seniors in this community are experiencing declining physical and mental health due to poor nutrition and a sense of isolation, both of which could be addressed with the inception of a senior center that will offer healthy, inexpensive meals and social interaction.

- **Don't attribute the need to the applicant organization.** Instead, refer to the constituency the organization serves. Too many proposals use the words, "we need" instead of saying, "the community needs" or "the people we serve need." Eliminate the words "we need" from your grantseeking vocabulary.

CASE STUDIES OF SUCCESSFUL STATEMENTS OF NEED

Case Study 1

This case study represents an excerpt from a statement of need in a proposal submitted by a university to create a demonstration project providing services and training to potential female school administrators. It shows how the proposal can:

- Quickly summarize the problem being addressed and thus orient the reviewer to a more detailed discussion.

- Demonstrate familiarity with prior research.

- Give credibility to the problem by indicating that prior work on it has been documented.

- Include statistical data without interrupting the flow of the narrative.

- Give legitimacy to the procedures that will subsequently be proposed by showing that their lack of availability has been recognized as part of the problem.

- Establish the experience of the applicant by citing prior research of the principal investigator and other project staff.

Women have always been under-represented in school administration although they have predominated as teachers since the Civil War. This has been documented nationally and in our state. (1) Furthermore, women's status in educational administration has declined. (2) Three major reasons for women's under-representation in school management have been documented: a) because it is a male sex-typed occupational role, women have not aspired to be administrators, and men believe it is inappropriate for women to enter these roles; b) employed female certificated personnel have less advanced training than employed male certificated personnel, (3) and when women enter graduate programs in education they typically do not enter programs in administration, (4) and, finally; c) there are formal and informal processes of grooming, recruitment, and administrative selection at the local school level perpetuating sex inequity and sex-segregated jobs. (5)

Limited sex role definitions, lack of advanced training, and discriminatory recruitment and selection processes interact in perpetuating women's under-representation in administration. To actually achieve sex equity in school management it will be necessary to find simultaneous solutions to these problems.

1. See (name of project director), 2000, for reports of a study of school administrators in the state and (name of a project staff member) et al., 2000, for theoretical discussion of sex segregation and sex role socialization.

2. See Table 1, Appendix A.

3. See Table 2, Appendix A.

4. During 2000–2001, 181 males and 8 females received degrees in educational administration from (name of submitting university).

5. See Table 3, Appendix A.

Case Study 2

This case study is taken from an application for a research proposal submitted by a state agency to a federal funding source to evaluate the comparative effectiveness of different types of service and income maintenance programs. The short excerpt from the justification section of the application is included to show an approach for tying the statement of need at the local level to an interest of the funder itself.

The national investment in social welfare demonstration projects continues to expand, yet the consequences these projects have on the level of client and family functioning have been only partially evaluated. Without careful assessment, the relative merits of any given project will be lost or incorrectly estimated, while errors may be repeated if the project serves as a prototype.

A favorable set of conditions allowing a careful assessment has arisen in a demonstration project jointly sponsored by the 1115 Demonstration Project Section of the Bureau of Family Services, the Office of Special Services (Title V) of the Bureau of Family Services, and the Mississippi Department of Public Welfare.

The Mississippi Department of Public Welfare has agreed to the creation of four groups of AFDC clients who will receive various combinations of increased services and/or increased financial assistance.

Case Study 3

As noted earlier, most projects address problems that are a subset of a much broader area of concern. This excerpt, taken from an applicant for entomological research submitted to the National Science Foundation, provides an illustration of:

- How to briefly describe the scope and significance of the larger area of interest.

- How to delimit the specific topic that is to be the focus of the project and show its possible contributions.

The economic cost and environmental destructiveness of scolytid bark beetle outbreaks in the coniferous forests of the western and southern United States are too well known to need documentation here and the consequent importance of bark beetle control is clear. For over a decade the major effort has been in pheromone research.

The proposal then goes on to discuss some important prior research on bark beetle pheromones and the potential economic impact of this line of inquiry. It then continues:

However, there are still basic questions about the natural release of bark beetle pheromones which must be answered.

Following this, the writer identifies several problems that remain unsolved and quickly focuses on the specific set of issues that will be addressed in the proposed research. The section ends with a summary of how this project may affect future developmental efforts aimed at control of the bark beetle. Throughout the section, frequent references are made to the researcher's prior study in this field and to new products and control methodology that have resulted.

Case Study 4

In particularly fortuitous circumstances, an applicant can use the calamities facing other organizations as the rationale for expanding its own services. The following example is from a proposal to a private foundation. The request for funds followed hard on the heels of extensive media coverage of the terrible financial plight of major arts organizations in the area, a problem which had been documented by a task force appointed by a local big city mayor. Communities in the area had subsequently been mobilized to create a pool of funds, called the Arts Stabilization Program, for which organizations could qualify through better management and partial elimination of deficits.

The short proposal started off by reminding the foundation that the mission of the applicant was to recruit volunteer business consultants to help organizations resolve management problems, improve administrative procedures, plan for the future, and get maximum use from limited financial resources. The application then explained:

Our organization is now taking on an expanded role by providing technical assistance to arts organizations which will participate in the Arts Stabilization Program, an outgrowth of the mayor's task force on the arts.

After describing the types of new services to be provided, the proposal continued:

This added responsibility, along with increased demand for our services from smaller arts groups, necessitated that we increase the director position from half-time to full-time. Obviously, this has increased the budget and therefore the need for annual operating support.

Had the foundation not already been familiar with the local arts crisis, the applicant would undoubtedly have included as attachments (and briefly referenced in the needs statement) the most compelling of the newspaper stories.

SUMMARY

It may be helpful to conceptualize the *outcome* portion of the proposal as answering the question, "What should be done?" Locally, the *statement of need* or statement of the problem then answers the question, "Why?" It thus lays the groundwork for the next question, "How?" which will be described in the proposal's next section, the procedure or approach, which is covered in Chapter 9.

Chapter 9

Procedures

This chapter discusses elements typically found in the procedures component of proposals, including replication and dissemination. It covers how these vary in different kinds of applications and provides some general guidelines on writing and format.

The *procedures* section (also called the *approach* or *plan of action*) is typically the longest part of a proposal. It is usually the part applicants are most excited about crafting because it's where you get to describe what you want to do with the money. This section must tell how the project will be carried out and present the rationale for the majority of the budget. It must convince the funding source that you really know how to achieve the outcomes and solve the problems that have been described earlier. And, while a proposal may sometimes get by with imprecise objectives, it is very hard to hide inexperience or incompetence when designing and describing methodology.

COMMON PROBLEMS TO AVOID

Problem 1: The procedures do not match the outcomes.

This is the most common mistake, made in at least three different ways. One is a "sin of omission," where the procedures necessary to accomplish the stated objectives are not described sufficiently. Another is a "sin of commission," where the stated procedures do not correlate to or assure the promised outcomes. The third is procedures that are not parallel in scope to the outcomes. Examples of each are illustrated below.

- **Omission.** A nonprofit promised that its proposed program would prevent teenagers from joining gangs, but described only a drop-in center, without explaining exactly which activities they would sponsor to achieve that result. The proposal didn't address the fact that, even if the target population is small, the problem is complex and difficult and cannot be resolved with the initiation of one program.

- **Commission.** A university proposed a program to encourage public school personnel to become self-sufficient in conducting classroom evaluations. Yet, the suggested procedures called for producing courses, materials, and models that would always require the involvement of university faculty as trainers or consultants. The funding source pointed out that the outcomes and the procedures were mutually contradictory: One proposed to create independence, but the other simply called for a new form of long-term dependency.

- **Scope.** The procedures of one organization outlined how it would provide health care to thousands of low-income residents, but the outcomes promised an impact on a tiny segment of that population concerning one specific malady. Another group purported to reduce child abuse in an entire state by producing a video on child abuse prevention.

Problem 2: The proposal does not actually include procedures or a plan of action.

This mistake is most commonly found in applications that have described the initiation of some new type of service in the outcomes section of the proposal, rather than stated outcomes that tell the intended results of the service.

Example: An application to a private foundation said that the purpose of the project was to open a new food bank. The rest of the proposal was then devoted to justifying why hunger is a social problem and why more food banks are needed. It provided no clues about where the food bank would be sited, how the facility would be provided, what population it would try to serve, how the availability of the food would be publicized, how the actual food to be distributed would be obtained, how many people would be needed to operate the food bank and so forth.

Problem 3: The procedures do not match the objectives and needs regarding innovation and scope.

Countless proposals maintain that their approach is unique or innovative, with no evidence to support that claim. Funders usually assume that the applicant was too naïve or too lazy to check the literature or research what has worked for others.

Example: A corporation received an application from a large national group to underwrite a conference aimed at solving the problem of the lack of communication among scientists involved in acid rain research. The group devoted several pages to justifying why acid rain was such a significant issue. But it provided no justification as to why communications among scientists was the most important aspect of this problem or why a conference could be expected to make any lasting impact on the problem's resolution.

Problem 4: Only a tenuous connection is made between the need and the proposed procedures.

This practice surfaces often in capital campaigns, where requested funds will pay for a building or equipment. The statement of need describes a gap in services, but the procedures section spells out plans to build or buy something, without explaining how that will address the gap in service. Later, the outcomes and evaluation sections promise only the completion of the purchase or construction. You must relate the planned effort to the stated problem, showing how it will meet a community need, not an internal need.

Problem 5: The procedures have no sound rationale.

Many organizations seek grant funding simply to continue their current activities, without demonstrating why their particular approach was chosen above others. Justify your choices. Grantors expect applicants to explain why they have selected the particular approach found in the procedures. This is because donors know that a problem can reasonably be addressed many ways. You must convince them that you have selected the best one and justify your choice.

One method is to cite other projects that have successfully used similar procedures. Another is to cite expert testimony, such as research findings or articles by authoritative figures, which suggest that your approach is likely to be effective. A third possibility is to convene all the organizations in your community who do similar work to discuss what methodology each is using. Describe how, after reviewing the relative merits and challenges of each approach, the group concluded that the need in the community justifies several approaches, or that because of certain circumstances in your community or certain characteristics of the population served, the proposed approach is the most appropriate.

Problem 6: The procedures are not demonstrated to be feasible.

A number of studies have looked at reasons why proposals are not approved. Many have found that a lack of feasibility is one of the most important. Clues that reviewers look for when judging this include:

- Evidence that you know of other studies or projects where similar procedures have been used and are able to cite examples suggesting that the procedures will likely achieve the intended results.

- The care with which the procedures are separated into distinct and manageable activities.

- Documentation that the writer has thought through an effective time schedule and has sequenced the activities into logical and complementary phases.

- Evidence that the writer is aware of any potential problem areas with the suggested procedures and has some plan in mind for either correcting or dealing with them.

Problem 7: The procedures focus on an internal benefit, not an external one.

While the proposal pledges to address a community need, the procedures section details activities that meet a need of the applicant organization.

PROCEDURES IN A NONRESEARCH PROPOSAL

The information that private funders want about procedures is similar to that desired by government grantmakers, but in much less detail. However, both expect that the elements for a training,

service, demonstration, or development project will differ from elements included in a research proposal.

Figure 9-1 indicates the broad topics commonly found in proposals for demonstration, development, service provision, or training. Specific content and order should be dictated by directions from the funder.

Because procedures vary so widely from project to project, it is impossible to provide a definitive list of what to include or avoid in every application. However, the following suggestions cover several issues typically of concern to novice writers when they attempt to present their project's procedures.

Introduction

The procedures component will likely be the longest portion of an application, including many separate kinds of information and involving technical and sometimes complex material. Make it easy for the reviewer to see how this component is structured. The writer of a proposal is essentially telling a story and, like any good author, should pay attention to both the flow of the narrative and the plot construction. However, unlike the storyteller, the proposal writer does not want to leave the reader guessing about what will come next. So begin with an introductory subsection to set the stage.

In addition to providing a sort of outline, the introduction can play the following roles:

- Introduce the reviewer to the overall approach to be used in the project and provide a brief justification for it.

- Alert the reader to the specific tactics to be used. It is important to provide this kind of clue early in the procedures section. Otherwise, the reader may gain an initially negative or inaccurate reaction (which is difficult to overcome) because a superficial reading did not clearly signal the type of activity involved.

- Call attention to any innovative material or methods.

Figure 9-1: Elements in the Procedures Section of a Nonresearch Proposal

Introduction
Briefly summarize project approach and indicate why it was selected. Demonstrate the significance, innovation, appropriateness, and feasibility of the proposed idea.

Approach
Describe how you will achieve the objectives and address the problem described earlier, including services to be provided, and products to be produced. Who else agrees this is the best way to address the problem?

Participants
List the individuals or groups who will participate or be served, including how they will be enlisted and selected. Especially private funders will want to see evidence of community or participant involvement.

Work Plan
Include a specific plan of action with a detailed timeline, organized by sequential phases or by task categories, such as site selection, participant selection, material development, field testing, and major milestones or benchmarks. If requested, detail who will be responsible for which activities of the timeline.

Administration
Provide a description of the roles and responsibilities of project staff, consultants, advisors, and cooperating agencies. Include their experience and any unique qualifications. Show how the management of this project relates to the governance and administrative structure of the applicant organization.

Accomplishments to Date
Show the funder how your (or others') prior work led to this proposed idea and how this project will enhance previous work. Explain how lessons learned have improved these procedures.

Deliverables
List the specific products and benefits expected from the project.

Replication
Share what elements of the project might be replicable by others, and what types of organizations or communities might benefit most from its generalizability.

Dissemination
State how you intend to share the results of this work with others who could benefit from it, and what types of stakeholder groups that might include.

Source: *Getting Funded: The Complete Guide to Writing Grant Proposals* by Mary Hall and Susan Howlett. Available from Portland State University, Continuing Education Press, www.cep.pdx.edu.

- Summarize the theoretical base for the procedures and demonstrate how these will result in products or knowledge of utility and significance to others.

Approach

This is the most important part of the procedures section: It is where you describe the specific program, what methods you will use, the population to be served, the specific activities to be completed, and a rationale which justifies these choices. Begin by describing the specific services to be provided or the materials to be developed. Then proceed to a description of the techniques to be used in the work. To avoid common pitfalls of this subsection:

- Include evidence that establishes the effectiveness of the proposed approach.

- Avoid calling your approach innovative unless you are absolutely sure it has not been tried elsewhere.

- Keep the approach focused on external needs and benefits, not organizational ones.

You must describe how unexpected events or results will be treated. One paradox of project development is the necessity to plan for the unanticipated. For example, your initial participants may unexpectedly withdraw from the project, or a variable that was expected to be important to the research may prove to have limited utility, or materials that are developed may not have the intended results.

Unless the writer has tried to predict each point in the procedures where a major problem might occur, insufficient time or resources may be requested to correct the difficulty. And unless the writer flags potential difficulties and acknowledges the possible need for corrective action, the reviewer may get an impression that the grantseekers are inexperienced or their planning is sloppy. If you do not indicate your plans to revise the procedures based on the results of certain project activities, the funded program may be restricted to

continuing activities that are no longer appropriate or are clearly unworkable.

To avoid having to repeatedly seek approval from the funder for modifications in project operation, suggest one or more of the following possibilities in the application:

- Field-tests for all unproven procedures and materials, and activities providing for necessary revision or refinement.

- Activities in sequential phases with a period allowed at the end of each element for necessary modifications in the remaining plan of action.

- Periodic consultation with the funder to discuss necessary changes. Sometimes a project can avoid unnecessary hold-ups by including checkpoints in the application and indicating that consultations will generally be limited to these times.

- The scheduling of checkpoints when the project staff intend to evaluate data and make decisions about necessary modifications.

Participants

The participants subsection should specify the demographic profile of those to be affected by the project or program, whether they be clients, audience, students, residents, or fish. It should also describe how they will be located, recruited, screened, and involved. Next, it should detail how they will be served or affected by the project. How long will they be affiliated with you, to what degree will they be involved, and will they be charged for participating, participate voluntarily, or be paid? If there are issues that might be raised related to language or ability, what will you do to accommodate them?

Work Plan or Timelines

The major purpose of this subsection is to indicate the dates on which major accomplishments and products will be completed and to show the reviewer how the activities will be spread through the project period. In many proposals, the specific activities needed to implement the procedures, and their planned sequence, will have been included in the approach subsection. Even so, it is a good idea to summarize these in a separate subsection, clearly identified by a label such as "Work Plan" or "Project Timelines." Use charts, graphs or other types of diagrams to present your timelines for key activities. Unless the project is very short or has only a few activities, the reviewer may become lost if this discussion is presented only in narrative form.

There are many techniques to choose from in presenting your work plan, including Gantt Charts, PERT (Program Evaluation Review Technique), the Critical Path Method (CPM), or simple time charts. Examples of three of these methods are displayed in Figures 9-2, 9-3, and 9-4.

You should adapt these methods to your particular needs. Gantt Charts are most useful for depicting dates in relation to activities, while PERT and CPM are most useful for showing the intended interrelationships among events. Use some type of work sheet to develop the information, then summarize it in a timeline in your proposal. In doing this, consider information such as:

- The specific activities that must be carried out.

- The amount of time each will take.

- The order in which the activities must be accomplished.

- The amount of staff and consultant help that can reasonably be expected for each activity.

- The amount of "down time" that can be anticipated (such as holidays, vacations, sick leave, or delays caused by collaborators).

One sure sign of inexperience is promising too much work in too little time. For example, proposals often suggest that new staff will be hired as soon as the grant is awarded, when it takes a month or two to post and fill a new position. Have your timelines checked by a dispassionate colleague to ensure they are realistic.

If, after considering all of these issues, you feel that the projected timeline will exceed the anticipated grant period, you should consider modifying your procedures. If this seems impossible, you may want to go back and scale down the entire project—especially limiting promised outcomes.

Administration

This subsection may include answers to these questions:

- How will the project be administered?

- What are the key project positions? What are their roles?

- How are other project personnel to be utilized?

- How will project personnel be selected? What criteria will be used?

- How does the project relate to other units in your organization? What is the chain of command?

- Are other agencies involved in the project and, if so, what are their roles?

- What are the roles of any consultants and advisory bodies? How will these individuals be selected? What criteria will be used? How will participation be secured?

- Do you have the technology necessary to support this project? Are personnel trained to use it optimally?

In many proposals, this discussion is combined with the subsection on personnel. In others, the personnel subsection may be used solely to include the résumés of staff who are known at the time the proposal is submitted. Wherever presented, the information should serve four purposes:

1. To lay out the administrative rules for the project and thus avoid confusion and misunderstandings.

2. To explain clearly who will be responsible for the project and its various activities.

3. To document that you have competent people in charge of the project.

4. To justify your budget requests.

Figure 9-2: Example of a Gantt Chart

Event	Phase I		Phase II									
	Nov	Dec	Jan	Feb	Mar	Apr	May	Jun	Jul	Aug	Sep	Oct

1.
Sites selected — ① (Dec)

2.
Research design refined — ② (Jan)

3.
Development activities refined — ③ (Jan)

4.
1st quarterly report — ④ (Feb)

5.
2nd quarterly report — ⑤ (May)

6.
3rd quarterly report — ⑥ (Jun)

7.
Research activities plan for Year 3 — 7a (Jul) outline — 7b (Sep) final

8.
Development activities plan for Year 3 — 8a (Jul) outline — 8b (Sep) final

9.
Report of preliminary data analysis — 9a (Jul) outline — 9b (Sep) draft — 9c (Oct) final

Figure 9-3: Example of a PERT Chart

Program Schedule (dates will be adjusted according to project start date)

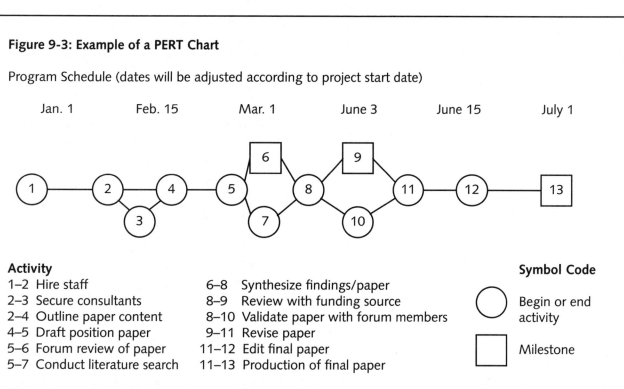

| Jan. 1 | Feb. 15 | Mar. 1 | June 3 | June 15 | July 1 |

Activity

1–2 Hire staff	6–8 Synthesize findings/paper
2–3 Secure consultants	8–9 Review with funding source
2–4 Outline paper content	8–10 Validate paper with forum members
4–5 Draft position paper	9–11 Revise paper
5–6 Forum review of paper	11–12 Edit final paper
5–7 Conduct literature search	11–13 Production of final paper

Symbol Code

○ Begin or end activity

□ Milestone

This chart was adapted from a much more elaborate PERT diagram included in a project whose purpose was to prepare position papers outlining needed research in a field. The writers included a diagram of this type for each major phase of the project. This example deals with one such phase.

Figure 9-4: Example of a Simple Time Schedule

Activity*	Project Months				
	July	August	September	October	November
Phase I	▓▓▓▓				
Phase II		▓▓▓▓			
Phase III			▓▓▓▓▓▓▓▓▓		
Phase IV					▓▓▓▓

*The activities which constitute each phase were described earlier in the proposal. This type of chart is suitable only for providing a quick overview of major project elements

This last point is very important. For example, if funds are to be included for a significant number of consultants, their roles in the project and their contributions to its success must be documented. Money may also be needed to pay travel and per diem expenses of advisory board members or to cover the cost of staff services to such groups. The importance of these individuals to the project must be explained.

Accomplishments to Date

For any proposal which builds on your earlier work or on related projects undertaken by your organization, mention this somewhere in the application in a clearly labeled subsection, possibly Qualifications. The purpose is:

- To show how the current project will build on past efforts.

- To demonstrate your prior experience and capability.

- To provide the funding source with details on other external funds which you've received to solve this same or a similar problem.

The last point is very important to many funders who, without this detail, may feel that they are being asked to support work that has already been paid for by another public or tax-exempt source.

Deliverables

Not all projects will generate *deliverables*, which are tangible products created during the course of the grant period. But if you do intend to develop such a product, include a description near the end of the procedures section. Examples include manuals, curricula, videotapes, reports, teaching tools or methods, service delivery models, mobile displays, scripts, and research papers.

Replication

Many grantors view the projects they fund as demonstration projects. They hope that if the proposed idea works well in one community, it may solve similar problems in other contexts. If you feel that your solution would work elsewhere, include a subsection on replication, responding to the following questions:

- **What elements of the plan are generalizable?** If your sexual assault program depends on the cooperation of police, the county health department, the local child protection agency, and clergy, it's safe to assume that all but the most remote communities likely have similar entities that could imitate your model.

- **What products will you create that could be used by others?** Perhaps your project will result in the creation of prevention education print and video materials, or a school-based curriculum, or the design of a crisis intervention phone system that others could copy or purchase.

- **Who else do you think could benefit from your experience?** Perhaps you belong to a regional or national network of sexual assault responders who could learn from your project. Municipalities you work with may want to adopt pieces of your plan.

Dissemination

Grantors also want to know that the lessons you learn might be shared with others, possibly affecting the standard practices in your field. Once you have results or findings, to whom will you disseminate that information? Here are some possibilities:

- Project participants.

- Your board, appropriate staff, advisors, and key volunteers.

- Financial supporters including individuals, and public- and private-sector funders.

- Cooperating agencies.

- Local umbrella groups such as United Way, an arts or church council, or an environmental coalition.

- Professional associations, networks, or clearing-houses in your field.

- Policy makers and advocates (elected officials, lobbyists, coalition members).

- The broader community.

Mechanisms for sharing the information include:

- Your organization's or department's newsletter.

- Your annual report.

- Your Web site.

- A written or electronic communiqué to colleagues in related professional associations.

- Letters (to funders, participants, etc.).

- A gathering where you share findings with supporters (luncheon, focus group, forum).

- An article in an industry magazine or scholarly journal.

- A news release to local, regional, or national media, as appropriate.

- A presentation at a conference.

As you present your findings, be sure to acknowledge the grantors.

LENGTH AND FORMAT

As mentioned earlier, private foundations and corporations want about the same type of procedural information as government funders; they just want less of it. Most federal applications, for example, suggest that the narrative in the procedures section not exceed 20 pages; foundations and corporations usually ask for no more than two pages.

The writer thus needs to be creative in getting a great deal of information across concisely. The following example was taken from an application to a foundation for a capital grant. After an opening section which explained the nature of the applicant's services and why a new facility was needed for its expansion, the organization included a chart, shown in Figure 9-5.

It then included a one-page chart outlining the major milestones for completing its fundraising, site selection, design, construction, moving, and a celebratory event. This was followed by a very short description of which staff would be involved

---

Figure 9-5. Example of Chart Used for Concise Presentation

Problem: Old Facility	**Solution: New Facility**
• Old building.	• Newer building.
• Not near highway.	• Central to county, near freeway access.
• Poor general visibility.	• Good corner visibility.
• Inadequate parking.	• 40-car parking lot.
• Mechanical and electrical system outdated.	• New or improved system part of the remodel.
• No inside van loading or parking.	• Space for eight vans and for van loading.
• Small, poorly divided office space.	• Office division based on program requirements.
• Lack of good meeting space for training and volunteers.	• Spaces designed for small and large groups for volunteers and classes.

(and to what degree) during each of these phases. The grant was approved and the building completed below budget.

PROCEDURES IN A RESEARCH PROPOSAL

The elements of the procedures section of a research proposal vary slightly from other types of requests. See Figure 9-6 for a list of possible topics.

Introduction

This subsection should prepare the reviewer for the type of methodology to be used in the project (e.g., survey, experiments, or longitudinal, formulative, or case studies) and explain why this approach was chosen. It should call attention to any innovative or unique aspects of the design and methods and how these improve on previous approaches. This subsection may also summarize prior related work of the principal investigator and indicate how the current project will build on or extend these efforts.

Population

Once you have offered a specific description of the population to be studied, describe how the subjects will be chosen, including assignment to treatment group, if appropriate. Specify the method you will use to secure their cooperation and participation and whether they will be paid for their involvement.

You must provide evidence that such groups are likely to cooperate with your project. For example, education grantmakers are well aware that many public school personnel will no longer volunteer as unpaid subjects for university-based research efforts—particularly those that are likely to interfere with classroom instruction or require extensive after-school time. These funders are no longer willing to gamble that you will be able to locate desirable subjects after the award is made. They require documentation in the proposal that such individuals have already been contacted and

have agreed to assume the necessary roles. This same point applies to other groups who feel that they have either been "over studied" in the past or exploited by unsympathetic or irresponsible investigators. The same is true for participation in the project by other agencies: Get formal agreements in hand before submitting your application.

Proposals dealing with animal subjects should be certain to conform to all professional and federal requirements for subject acquisition, breeding, care, feeding, disease control, and so forth. This process can be extremely complex and expensive. Compliance with requirements governing the qualifications of personnel dealing with animals should also be documented. Your administrative officers should be consulted on the amount of detail necessary to demonstrate that your organization has met federal requirements on registration and/or accreditation to use laboratory animals.

Federal agencies will expect you to describe how you will ensure adequate representation of women and minorities, particularly for experimental projects.

Finally, you should be aware of federal and state regulations governing privacy and protection of human subjects and those involving the use of minor children as research subjects. Evidence that you intend to comply with such requirements and the procedures you will use for doing so should be included in the application.

Design and Methodology

The narrative should describe the specific research to be conducted and the way in which it will be carried out. Usually, this includes a discussion of the theoretical base for the research (with appropriate citations to other studies), identification of research variables, elaboration of research questions and hypotheses, and the specific activities to test these. You may also want to identify any problems anticipated with the design or methods and describe what you intend to do to treat them. Unless they are mentioned elsewhere, this subsection should also discuss how you plan to evaluate project results, how they may be generalized, and how you intend to disseminate them.

Figure 9-6: Elements in the Procedures Section of a Research Proposal

Introduction
Briefly describe what type of methodology will be used and why it was chosen. Describe any ways in which it is innovative or unique and how it relates to any prior work by the principal investigator.

Population
Provide a clear description of the population to be studied and include relevant details on sampling procedures, subject or site selection, and securing participation. Identify any potential hazards to the population or staff and methods for coping with these. Address government requirements relating to human subjects or vertebrate animals.

Design and Methodology
Describe the specific research to be conducted and the way in which it will be carried out. Include the conceptual and theoretical base for the project, the research hypotheses or questions to be addressed, and the specific variables to be considered. Include plans for evaluation and dissemination of project results. Offer predictions about how the results may be generalized.

Instrumentation, Data Collection, and Analysis
Furnish the specific measures and procedures chosen to collect data, including details on establishing validity and reliability, particularly for new instruments. Define the methodology and criteria to be used in analyzing and judging the resulting data, justifying these choices, and indicating innovation.

Work Plan
Prepare a detailed work plan with sequential project activities and indications of who will do what.

Administration and Personnel
Discuss how the project will be managed and governed. Describe the roles, responsibilities, and background of project staff, consultants, and cooperating groups or agencies, including how much time each will devote to the project.

Accomplishments to Date
Share a summary of results of previous work, especially that which was funded by this particular funder, including related research by the applicant, and how the current project will extend those efforts.

Instrumentation, Data Collection, and Analysis

Funders of research projects may also ask for more detail on instrumentation, data collection, and analysis. Depending on the length and complexity of your description of these topics, they may be addressed in a single subsection or in separate ones. You should include an appropriate level of detail on issues such as:

- Variables to be addressed or types of specific information to be obtained (unless adequately covered elsewhere).

- Specific instrumentation for collecting the necessary data.

- Description of the background and content of any measures not well known to typical reviewers.

- Psychometric data supporting each measure and other evidence justifying suitability, technical soundness, and comprehensiveness.

- Sources from which specific information will be obtained.

- Methods of data collection.

- Rationale for data collection methods and how that is consistent with your objectives.

- Data collection schedules.

- Data preparation and storage.

- Data retrieval methods.

- Data analysis (including units of analysis, data analysis models, and justification of these choices).

- How you will ensure that the data is complete, recorded accurately, and transcribed correctly for analysis (including procedures for obtaining a high response rate from study participants, and for editing and preparing data for analysis).

- Data reporting (including report audiences, types of reports, and reporting schedule).

- Data use and application.

Identify any audience that must review and approve your data collection instruments or procedures. Identify the amount of time estimated for this review, which can be surprisingly long, and describe how modifications will be made, if necessary. Remember that all federally funded projects involving the administration of instruments to large groups of subjects must have prior clearance. Further details on this should be sought from the appropriate federal agency.

Work Plan or Timeline

In research, the project timeline and the work plan may be longer than in nonresearch projects, necessitating multiyear timelines. Build in checkpoints along the way at which you and the funder can assess progress and make any necessary adjustments.

Administration and Personnel

Describe the intended management of the project and the roles and responsibilities of project staff, consultants, and other groups or agencies involved. Research proposals depend more heavily than others on the background, experience, and reputation of the principal investigators and other key personnel. Mentioning collaborations or cooperation with particular institutions which would make your research project more appealing (such as a prestigious university, laboratory, or libraries) helps strengthen this subsection.

Accomplishments to Date

Especially in research, if your proposed project builds on the previous work of the principal investigator or others in your institution, be sure to describe that work, why it was significant, and how this project will enhance or contribute to that.

Use appropriate charts or tables for summarizing the narrative if the discussion is at all complex. Tables 9-1 and 9-2 provide some examples:

Table 9-1. Example of Table Displaying Data Collection Design

Instrumentation for Implementation: School Staff Reactions

Construct	Variable	Instrument Type	Source
Commitment	1. Self-reported level of personal commitment to the implementation process	Questionnaire	Principal
	2. Staff-reported level of commitment of the staff in general to implementation	Questionnaire	Principal
Resistance/support	1. Self-reported level of resistance/ support	Questionnaire	Principal
	2. Locus of resistance/support	Questionnaire/ interview	Principal district liaison
Influence/power	3. Perceived level of personal influence upon the implementation system and process	Questionnaire	Principal teacher
	4. Perceived level of referent group influence upon the implementation system and process	Questionnaire	Principal teacher
Satisfaction with process	5. Self-reported level of satisfaction with the implementation system	Questionnaire	Principal teacher
	6. Self-reported level of satisfaction with the implementation process	Questionnaire	Principal teacher

Table 9-2. Example of Display on Data Analysis

Types of Hypotheses and Related Data Analysis Procedures

Type of Hypothesis	Type of Analysis	Unit of Analysis	Data Analysis Model
Relationships between variables (e.g., task orientation is positively related to achievement)	Cross-sectional analysis Cross-lagged panel analysis	Generally corresponding to unit of observation for the related variables (see Instrumentation Section)	Correlational techniques (e.g., zero-order correlation, canonical correlations)
Comparison of states of affairs (e.g., student involvement will increase)	Longitudinal analysis	Generally corresponding to unit of observation for the related variables (see Instrumentation Section)	Descriptive statistics, time series, f and t tests
Path/amount of influence among variables (e.g., student achievement is influenced by programmatic functions, climate, and student backgrounds)	Cross-sectional analysis Cross-lagged analysis	Generally corresponding to unit of observation for the related variables (see Instrumentation Section)	Generalized regression analysis

Chapter 10

Evaluation

This chapter examines why a well-thought-out evaluation component is essential to a successful proposal. It looks at examples of what grantmakers ask to be included and describes methods for developing an evaluation plan, including what information on evaluation is usually included in a proposal. It ends with a checklist for judging the adequacy of an evaluation design.

WHAT IS EVALUATION?

Many folks roll their eyes when they reach the step of deciding what to say in a proposal about evaluation. In their minds, evaluation means some type of complex experimental design with treatment and control groups requiring sophisticated data analyses and reams of reports. While there are some types of projects where that approach may be appropriate, **there is no single best way to do evaluation.** There are many models and techniques available now that are viewed as perfectly legitimate by most funding sources.

So, just what is evaluation? The *W. K. Kellogg Foundation Evaluation Handbook* (which can be downloaded without charge from the Web site http://www.wkkf.org) defines evaluation as the "consistent, ongoing collection and analysis of information for use in decision making." (1) Or, to put it another way, evaluation is a systematic way of providing responses to the key questions that you and others want to ask about your funded project.

WHY DO EVALUATION?

The most obvious answer from the perspective of the proposal writer is: **Most funding sources now require some type of evaluation component in the projects they fund.** But there are at least two other key benefits to doing evaluation, whether required or not:

- Evaluation can help determine if the various parts of your project are working as envisioned and if they are not, allow you time to take corrective action before all of the grant funds are gone.

- A properly designed evaluation can help generate information about the results you have achieved that will be critical to your future funding appeals.

WHAT DO GRANTMAKERS WANT?

Just a few years ago, one could confidently predict that government agencies would always require much more extensive evaluation designs than private foundations or corporations. That is no longer true. So, let's look at some of the evaluation requirements in a variety of public and private grant sources.

Example 1: Please describe any evaluation efforts that you will undertake to determine that your objectives and outcomes are being achieved. Briefly describe the indicators that will be used to monitor progress. How will you use the information you gather to make your organization more effective? What are the challenges and obstacles you face in evaluating the effectiveness of your work? If you do not currently undertake formal evaluations, how do you measure success?
Application Guidelines from Wilburforce Foundation, a grantmaker in the environmental field. (2)

Example 2: The proposed project must demonstrate an evaluation component that will present clear educational outcomes to be discussed in the final project report.
Application Guidelines from Toshiba America Foundation. (3)

Example 3: A good evaluation plan appropriate to the scale of the project will provide information as the project is developing and will determine how effectively the project has achieved its goals. The effects of formative evaluation should be described. Also include how you intend to evaluate the final project and how you will determine whether this project met your scientific and pedagogical expectations. Discuss how you plan to collect and analyze data on the project's impact.
A Guide For Proposal Writing from the National Science Foundation. (4)

Example 4: Describe objectives, how project results will be measured, and who will be responsible for providing financial and quarterly information.
Application Guidelines from the Department of Labor's Employment and Training Administration grants program for small faith-based and community-based nonprofit organizations. (5)

Example 5: Briefly describe your plan for evaluating the success of the project or for your organization's work. What questions will be addressed? Who will be involved in evaluating this work—staff, board, constituents, community, consultants? How will the evaluation results be used?
Common Grant Application from the National Network of Grantmakers. (6)

While the specifics of what each funder requests in an application may differ, a careful reading will show some common themes. Most grantmakers want an evaluation plan, that, at a minimum:

- **Tells how you will judge the effectiveness of the project in achieving its stated goals, outcomes, and/or objectives** *as the project is being implemented.*

- **Describes how you will measure and report on what was achieved** *by the project's end.*

The first type of evaluation is typically called *formative* because it produces information that is helpful to you as the program is being implemented. The second type of evaluation is called *summative* as it is used to judge the success at the end of the project.

An increasing number of funders ask for a plan that also helps evaluate what has changed in the lives of individuals, families, organizations, or the community as a result of this program. This third type of evaluation is also a type of summative evaluation, but is often called an *impact evaluation* or *outcome evaluation.* Its purpose is to provide the data to assess the larger consequences of what you've achieved.

A PROCESS FOR PLANNING EVALUATION

Some common steps in developing an evaluation plan are outlined in Figure 10-1.

Step 1: Deciding What to Evaluate

First, decide what you want to evaluate. If you have clearly defined your goals, outcomes, and

---

Figure 10-1. Four Steps for Designing an Evaluation Plan

1. **Decide what to evaluate.**

- Determine main purpose(s) of and audience for the evaluation.*

- Identify what questions to ask.*

- Set performance targets if appropriate.*

- Decide from whom evaluation data will be collected and make sure you will have access to them and their information.

2. **Determine what information is needed and how to collect it.**

- Identify the specific information needed to answer the evaluation questions of the different audiences.

- Select general methodological approaches.*

- Clarify from which populations or source the information will be gathered.

- Select data collection techniques and determine what clearances and permissions will be needed.*

- Establish data collection timeline.

3. **Decide how you will analyze and report the data.**

- Select appropriate methodologies for analysis and synthesis.

- Determine what reports to produce for which audiences and decision makers.*

- Determine what reports to provide to funding source and when.*

- Lay out data analysis/reporting timeline.

4. **Identify resources.**

- Determine who will play what roles in performing the evaluation.*

- Identify how much evaluation activities will cost and include this in appropriate places in the proposal budget.*

*Normally emphasized in the evaluation component of a proposal.

---

objectives, this is much easier to do. Consider whether you'll have access to the information you'll need to judge success. For example, in many settings patient records are confidential, so you do not want to evaluate questions that can be answered only with data from such records.

As mentioned in Chapter 7, the program logic model is a useful tool for defining both your outcomes and choosing which things to evaluate.

Many grantmakers now want a program logic model in the proposal. For example, United Way of America adopted this model as its recommended approach to human service evaluation in 1995.(7) Table 10-1 reviews its major elements.

A further look at these elements will show how they will result in the information needed to answer the grantmakers' three key questions that were mentioned at the beginning of this chapter.

Table 10-1. A Program Logic Model

Resources	Activities	Outputs	Outcomes	Goals
Program Inputs	The methods used to carry out the specific program.	Units of service or product. How many, how often, over what duration.	Short-, intermediate- or long-term changes anticipated in those being served by your program.	Ultimate impact(s) expected to occur, usually beyond the time of one grant.
Examples: Staff, money, clients	Examples: Service delivery, steps in research, events, processes.	Examples: Number of clients served in various types of training.	Examples: Increased knowledge, improved performance.	Examples: healthier community, problem prevention.

- **Evaluating activities** can help you tell how well the project is going as it's being implemented and help you choose the specific processes or events to monitor.

- **Evaluating outputs** can help you answer questions about those aspects of the project that can be counted. By thinking about outputs, you can also clarify the performance targets that will mean your project succeeded. This is critical information for those funding sources that want number-based reports.

- **Evaluating outcomes** can help you complete your "so that" statements and provide data about the consequences of your project's results. Thinking through the short-, intermediate- and long-term outcomes of your project can also help you refine its real purposes.

- **Detailing the resources** is useful in budget planning. If you display the program logic model in your proposal, it supports your budget.

- **Defining the ultimate goals** for your project helps you clarify the major problem area you're trying to address, why it matters, and to whom. This produces insights helpful to your justification of the need for your project.

Few projects will be large enough or complex enough to require extensive evaluation of all five of the above elements. But, using the program logic model as a tool of analysis will help you uncover your options. You can then choose the specific things to evaluate that are most important to the funder and you.

The program logic model can also be modified as necessary to fit your particular project. An example of a variation to the model (see Table 10-2) was provided by the Wilburforce Foundation from one of its grantee's request for a grant to build more diversified sources of income.

Table 10-2 also illustrates an effective way to display important information about your evaluation design in a proposal. More resources on how to develop a program logic model and other aspects of evaluation are listed in Attachment 10-1 at the end of this chapter.

Step 2: Deciding What Information to Collect and How

Now you must decide, specifically, the information needed to answer your evaluation questions, who will be evaluated, and the methods you will use to gather the data. This is a critical step in planning

Table 10-2. Example of a Program Evaluation Model				
	Goals	**Objectives**	**Activities & Outputs**	**Outcomes & Evaluation**
Questions	What are you trying to accomplish?	What are the anticipated results of your work to which you plan to hold yourself accountable?	What work will you undertake to meet your goals and what level?	How will you know your goals and objectives have been achieved? What indicators will you use to measure success?
Examples of answers	Increase the capacity of our organization to sustain its wilderness protection campaign by improving its fundraising program.	Decrease reliance on foundation support as a percent of total revenue; increase number of board members both giving and raising funds; increase individual giving.	Hire development director to enhance individual fundraising; launch direct mail campaign to seek new donors; conduct phone campaign to renew existing donors.	Percentage of revenue from foundations decreases over time; increase in number of board members asking and giving; number of donors and dollars increased; monitor change in renewal rate.

Source: The Wilburforce Foundation (8)

your evaluation for two reasons: It is where you decide how to make the evaluation operational and it is those decisions that will have the most impact on your budget.

Five Key Decisions

1. **How specific are the questions you need to ask to satisfy the overall purposes of the evaluation?** Consider these two examples:

   Example 1: The goal of the project is to reduce the number of teenage pregnancies in a community. The evaluation is designed simply to collect data on teenage pregnancy rates at the start, middle, and end of the project. That data is already available from the county health department, so there is little additional cost to the project.

   Example 2: While the goal of the project is the same, the evaluation is designed to determine which activities are the most effective in reducing teenage pregnancy. This evaluation

design must specify what questions to ask about each activity. This will require a multi-faceted and more expensive approach to collecting the necessary data.

2. **What general methodological approach (i.e., what evaluation design) will you use?** Jane Reisman and Judith Clegg in *Outcomes for Success!* (9) provide a useful summary of major types of evaluation designs and their relative costs (see Table 10-3).

   In selecting your evaluation design, you must also consider the amount of time that each methodology will require, its suitability to those from whom you will be collecting data, how often you'll be able to contact those individuals, and when those contacts are likely to occur. For example, if your organization has no way to stay in contact with individuals who have successfully completed a program, do not select an evaluation design that requires you to collect post-program data.

Table 10-3. Various Types of Evaluation Designs and the Level of Resources Each Requires

Type of design	Indicators	Resource intensity
Customer feedback surveys	Participants' reports of satisfaction with services they received (e.g., quality, access, friendliness, impact).	Low
Post-program measures	Use of evauation tools to describe outcomes (e.g., behavior, attitudes, experiences, or knowledge) *following* a program.	Low
Pre- and post-program measures	Describes participants' scores on expected outcome variables (e.g., behavior, attitudes, experiences, or knowledge) *prior to* a program as well as *following* completion of the program.	Moderate
Pre- and post-program measures with a comparison group	Same as described above, but with the added component of collecting similar scores for a *comparison group*.	High
Post-program measures and benchmarks	Same as post-program measure approach, except similar scores are also collected from partner organizations or other targets selected for *benchmark* comparisons.	High
Pre- and post-program measures and long-term, post-program measures	Same as pre- and post-program measure approach, with additional s*cores obtained again at a later point in time* (e.g., six months, one year, two years).	High

3. **Will you create your own data collection methods or use existing instruments?** The Internet is a terrific way to identify available resources. Many federal agency Web sites now include inventories of data collection instruments used in projects they've funded previously—for example, the Juvenile Justice Evaluation Center Online at the Department of Justice available at http://www.jrsa.org/jjec/resources/instruments.html. Many universities have excellent on-line resources—for example, the Center for Evaluation, Research and Public Service at the University of Idaho available from http://www.uidaho.edu/ed/cerps. This Web site includes links to many other on-line resources for evaluation, assessment, measure-ment, research methods, and reporting, among other topics.

4. **Will you collect evaluation data from cooperating agencies or partners?** This is an increasingly important decision because so many funders are interested in collaborations and sustainability. For example, an agency wishing to launch a new program brought in representatives from other area agencies that served the same constituency to help corroborate the need and design the program. A year after the program started, the other agencies were invited back to discuss what changes they had seen. Their insights helped alter future projects and methods.

5. **Can you get the clearances and permissions needed to collect your information?** This is a topic that most funding sources want referenced somewhere in the proposal. They get very nervous if they receive a proposal involving human or animal subjects without evidence the applicant is aware of, and fully in compliance with, federal, state, and local regulations. These requirements may have been specified in the grant announcement, be imbedded in state law, or be part of your organization's processes. Increasingly, funding sources also want information on how you will ensure there is adequate representation of minorities and females in your study population. Federal agencies are particularly sensitive on this subject and expect it to be addressed explicitly in all research or experimental projects. The time needed to carry out the procedures required to protect human or animal subjects or to gain permission to study minor children and other vulnerable populations must be built into your evaluation timeline.

Step 3: How will you analyze and report the information?

Most funding sources want to know what evaluation reports will be generated, when, to which audiences, and for what kinds of decisions they will be used. Sorting all this out can be more complicated than first appears. Will you share the evaluation data with participants, cooperating agencies, others in your field? When will you provide evaluation data—periodically or only at the end of the grant?

Funders are especially interested in what evaluation reports you will be giving them. Some specify these reporting requirements in their guidelines. Others leave it to you to propose a reporting schedule. Few funders require much specificity on analysis techniques in a proposal, unless it is for a research project or highly experimental treatment program. But you still need to think about this while writing the proposal because it may affect your overall timeline and your budget.

Table 10-4 shows one method of plotting this out. In some proposals, this type of table might actually be included either in the narrative or as an attachment. In others, pertinent information from the plan can be put in the overall description of procedures and timeline.

Step 4: Determine Resources Needed for Evaluation

Normally, funding sources expect evaluation to cost five to ten percent of the total project budget. But there may be instances where the evaluation budget is legitimately much higher. Items that typically need to be considered are the costs of evaluation staff salary and benefits, consultants, travel, purchase of questionnaires or data-collection instruments, office supplies, printing and

Table 10-4. Planning Data Collection, Analysis, and Reporting					
Objective	**Design**	**Instrument**	**Schedule**	**Analysis**	**Reports**
By the end of the school year, the 4th graders in this program will have increased their reading scores by an average of 25%.	pretest/ post-test	Woodcock Reading Test	Sept. 15–18 May 12–16	Will compute t-test to see if growth was significant compared to the test's national norms.	June 1 to Principal, District Admin. June 15 to State Dept. of Education

duplication, equipment, analysis software, and others. Unless the funding source requires that the evaluation budget be displayed separately, these costs are usually folded into the overall budget in the application.

A key decision is whether to have the evaluation activities performed by staff in your organization, by consultants, or by a mix of the two. The Kellogg Foundation's *Evaluation Handbook* (10) has a useful, extensive discussion of how to make this decision, how to select a consultant, and how to develop the evaluation budget.

Table 10-5 provides an example of how to divide evaluation responsibilities between staff and consultants. This type of table is also a useful inclusion in a proposal, particularly where the costs of the evaluation may exceed ten percent of the total budget or where extensive use of consultants is required.

Other Frequently Asked Questions About Evaluation

- **Do all proposals require an evaluation component?** No. While the majority of funding sources do require some type of evaluation, for some types of projects (such as buildings, equipment or even general operating support), a report showing that the money was spent *correctly* is all the funder needs or expects. Funders seldom expect evaluation details in proposals for small amounts ($25,000 or less). Some very large foundations explicitly state that you should not include an evaluation plan and budget in the original proposal, as they will negotiate a plan and the funds to implement it soon after announcing an award.

- **Must all evaluations be complicated and expensive?** No. There has been a fundamental shift in the thinking about evaluation in the past 10 years or so. Grantmakers no longer expect that everyone will hire expensive evaluation consultants or that evaluation must be highly technical and complex. Most simply want to know if you've succeeded and, if not, what you have learned that is helpful. For example, a colleague

once told a wonderful story about a social service director who was in a tizzy about how to answer a request from a major donor about whether their program had actually helped the Native American fathers they were training in parenting skills. The director mentioned her dilemma on the last night of training, and a shy father in the back row quietly suggested, "With all due respect, ma'am, you could ask us."

- **How should we handle an evaluation component in a proposal for a prevention program?** Admittedly, projects whose success is judged by what *didn't* happen may feel they face a special challenge. So, how will you know it didn't happen? There is usually some type of indicator (such as dropout rate) and source of data (such as school attendance reports) you can use to measure progress and monitor your degree of success, even if it isn't required by the grantmaker. Selecting the indicator and citing your data source is a very simple and commonly used approach in evaluation. You may also want to learn which of your prevention activities worked the best. As the Native American father said, you can ask your participants.

- **How do you handle evaluation in proposals for fields like the arts?** All fields can be evaluated. Proposals for grants to fund general operations of organizations seldom need an evaluation component. But when you apply for funds to create some type of change or improvement (even in the arts), grantmakers expect you to measure and report on whether this goal was achieved. The arts, just like social programs, have services (performances) and clients (audiences). The key is to be careful how you describe the **purposes** of your request. If you say you will use the money to increase audiences, you must tell how you're going to measure this. If you promise to provide artistic programming that will educate young people, you need to define what you mean by "educate," as well as how you'll judge its accomplishment.

Table 10-5. Evaluation Responsibilities of the Project Staff and of an External Evaluator		
Task	**Project staff**	**Evaluator**
Coordination	Designate a person to coordinate the evaluation responsibilities for the program.	Designate an evaluation person as a primary contact for working with this program.
Evaluation Plan	Review the general evaluation plan and revise as necessary to fit the project. Return the revised plan to the external evaluator.	1. Prepare a general evaluation plan in cooperation with the project staff. 2. Revise and approve the project's revised evaluation plan.
Instrumentation	1. Reproduce required copies of all evaluation instruments. 2. Order required copies of standardized instruments and answer sheets. 3. Develop any local monitoring or evaluation instruments. 4. Obtain a review and approval for use of each proposed evaluation instrument.	1. Prepare a draft copy of all instruments to be used. 2. Provide the project with a specimen set of standardized instruments to be used together with cost information and an order blank. 3. Review any project-developed instruments if requested by the staff.
Data Collection	1. Schedule and administer all evaluation instruments identified in the evaluation plan. 2. Collect and code file data specified in the plan. 3. Code responses to all instruments where needed. 4. Mail a duplicate copy of all code sheets to the external evaluator for computer processing.	1. Provide the project with a schedule and design for data collection. 2. Provide written directions for administering nonstandardized evaluation instruments. 3. Prepare common codes and coding directions for all answer sheets and data collection forms.
Data Analysis	Identify if there is any special data analysis the staff would like to have run that has not already been included in the evaluation plan.	1. Verify the correct scoring and/or coding of all instruments. 2. Keypunch the data. 3. Provide scoring services. 4. Analyze the data.
Reporting	1. Identify the information needs of the people in the project if they have changed since the evaluation plan was prepared. 2. Review the draft evaluation report for any factual errors or misrepresentations. 3. Print the required number of evaluation reports and abstracts.	1. Prepare a draft copy of the evaluation report and give it to the project evaluation coordinator for review. 2. Prepare a final camera-ready copy of the evaluation report. 3. Prepare a camera-ready copy of an evaluation report abstract.

SOME FINAL COMMENTS

The number of proposals submitted to government and funding sources has grown exponentially, far outstripping the growth in available resources. There has also been an increased demand for accountability at all levels. The question is increasingly being asked whether anything worthwhile has resulted from the billions of dollars awarded as contracts or grants-in-aid each year. Grantmakers now look much harder at the quality of evaluation plans in applications and place greater emphasis on evaluations.

However, the best reason for doing a careful job of planning evaluation during the proposal stage is that evaluation is an essential element of competent management. Earlier in the book, reference was made to Alice's famous remark: "If you don't know where you are going, any road will take you there." Likewise, if you haven't planned a good evaluation, you may never know if you've arrived.

Table 10-6 provides a final checklist to help you judge the adequacy of an evaluation plan.

CHAPTER REFERENCES

1. *W. K. Kellogg Foundation Evaluation Handbook*, available at http://www.wkkf.org

2. *Application Guidelines 2002*, Wilburforce Foundation, 360l Fremont Avenue N. #304, Seattle, WA 98103, e-mail grants@wilburforce.org

3. 2002 *Application Guidelines for Grants for K–6 Science and Math Education*, Toshiba America Foundation, 1251 Avenue of the Americas, 41st Floor, New York, NY 10020.

4. *A Guide for Proposal Writing*, National Science Foundation, Directorate for Education and Human Resources, Division of Undergraduate Education, available at http://www.nsf.gov

5. *Grants for Small Faith-Based and Community-Based Nonprofit Organizations 2002*, Department of Labor, Employment and Training Administration, available at http://wdsc.doleta.gov/sga/sga

6. *Common Grant Application*, National Network of Grantmakers, 1717 Kettner Boulevard, #110, San Diego, CA 92101, available at http://www.nng.org

7. *Current United Way Approaches to Measuring Program Outcomes and Community Change*, United Way of America, Alexandria, VA. 1995.

8. *A Sample Program Evaluation Model*, p. 41, Wilburforce Foundation, Seattle, WA 2002.

9. Jane Reisman and Judith Clegg, *Outcomes for Success!* © 2000, The Evaluation Forum, Seattle, WA, p. 41.

10. *W. K. Kellogg Foundation Evaluation Handbook*, pp. 54–68, available at http://www.wkkf.org

Table 10-6. A Checklist for Judging the Adequacy of an Evaluation Design

Directions: For each question below, check whether the evaluation design has clearly met the criterion (Yes), has clearly not met the criterion (No), or cannot be clearly determined (?). Check NA if the criterion does not apply to the evaluation design being reviewed. Use the "Elaboration" column to provide further explanation for criterion where a "No" or a "?" has been checked. The word "program" will be used to mean the program, project, or product being evaluated.

Criterion	Criterion Met				Elaboration
	Y	N	?	NA	
I. Criteria regarding the adequacy of the evaluation conceptualization	Y	N	?	NA	
A. Conceptual clarity and adequacy					
1. Is an adequate description of the whole program presented?	❑	❑	❑	❑	
2. Is a clear description given of the part of the program being evaluated?	❑	❑	❑	❑	
3. Is a clear description of the evaluation approach given? (e.g., comparison group study, single group study, goal-free evaluation, formative, summative, etc.)	❑	❑	❑	❑	
4. Is the evaluation approach adequate and appropriate for evaluating the program?	❑	❑	❑	❑	
Based on the above, do you feel the evaluation is clearly and adequately conceived?	❑	❑	❑	❑	
B. Scope					
1. Are the intended outcomes or goals of the program clearly specified?	❑	❑	❑	❑	
2. Is the scope of the evaluation broad enough to gather information concerning all specified program outcomes?	❑	❑	❑	❑	
3. Are any likely unintended effects from the program described?	❑	❑	❑	❑	
4. Is the approach of the evaluation broad enough to include measuring these unintended effects?	❑	❑	❑	❑	
5. Is adequate cost information about the program included in the scope of the evaluation?	❑	❑	❑	❑	
Based on the above, do you feel the evaluation is adequate in scope?	❑	❑	❑	❑	
C. Relevance					
1. Are the audiences for the evaluation identified?	❑	❑	❑	❑	
2. Are the objectives of the evaluation explained?	❑	❑	❑	❑	

Table 10-6. A Checklist for Judging the Adequacy of an Evaluation Design (continued)

Criterion	Criterion Met				Elaboration
	Y	N	?	NA	
3. Are the objectives of the evaluation congruent with the information needs of the intended audiences?	❏	❏	❏	❏	
4. Does the information to be provided allow necessary decisions about the program or product to be made?	❏	❏	❏	❏	
Based on the above, do you feel the information provided is relevant to and adequately serves the needs of the intended audience?	❏	❏	❏	❏	
D. Flexibility					
1. Can the design be adapted easily to acommodate changes in plans?	❏	❏	❏	❏	
2. Are known constraints or parameters on the evaluation discussed thoroughly?	❏	❏	❏	❏	
3. Can useful information be obtained in the face of unforeseen constraints, e.g., non-cooperation of control groups?	❏	❏	❏	❏	
Based on the above, do you feel the evaluation study allows for new information needs to be met as they arise?	❏	❏	❏	❏	
E. Feasibility					
1. Are the evaluation resources (time, money, and personnel) adequate to carry out the projected activities?	❏	❏	❏	❏	
2. Are management plans specified for conducting the evaluation?	❏	❏	❏	❏	
3. Has adequate planning been done to support the feasibility of conducting complex activities?	❏	❏	❏	❏	
Based on the above, do you feel the evaluation can be carried out as planned?	❏	❏	❏	❏	

II. Criteria concerning the adequacy of the collection and processing of information

A. Reliability

Criterion	Y	N	?	NA	
1. Are data collection procedures described well and was care taken to assure minimal error?	❏	❏	❏	❏	
2. Are scoring or coding procedures objective?	❏	❏	❏	❏	
3. Are the evaluation instruments reliable? (i.e., is reliability information included?)	❏	❏	❏	❏	

Table 10-6. A Checklist for Judging the Adequacy of an Evaluation Design (continued)

Criterion	Criterion Met				Elaboration
	Y	N	?	NA	
Based on the above, do you feel that if the evaluation were conducted again the results would turn out the same?	☐	☐	☐	☐	
B. Objectivity					
1. Have attempts to control for bias in data collection and processing been described?	☐	☐	☐	☐	
2. Are sources of information clearly specified?	☐	☐	☐	☐	
3. Do the biases of the evaluators preclude an objective evaluation?	☐	☐	☐	☐	
Based on the above, do you feel adequate steps have been taken to ensure objectivity in the various aspects of the evaluation?	☐	☐	☐	☐	
C. Representativeness					
1. Are the data collection instruments valid?	☐	☐	☐	☐	
2. Are the data collection instruments appropriate for the purposes of this evaluation?	☐	☐	☐	☐	
3. Does the evaluation adequately address the questions it was intended to answer?	☐	☐	☐	☐	
Based on the above, do you feel the information collection and processing procedures ensure that the results accurately represent the program?	☐	☐	☐	☐	
D. Generalizability					
1. Are sampling techniques adequate to permit generalizations to the population of interest?	☐	☐	☐	☐	
2. Does the cultural context of data collection techniques affect generalization?	☐	☐	☐	☐	
3. Are the inferential statistics employed appropriate for the sample, data, and the questions to be answered?	☐	☐	☐	☐	
Based on the above, do you feel the information collected can be generalized when necessary?	☐	☐	☐	☐	

III. Criteria concerning the adequacy of the presentation and reporting of information

A. Timeliness

1. Have efficient reporting techniques been used to meet the needs of the clients?	☐	☐	☐	☐	

Table 10-6. A Checklist for Judging the Adequacy of an Evaluation Design (continued)

Criterion	Criterion Met				Elaboration
	Y	**N**	**?**	**NA**	
2. Does the time schedule for reporting meet the needs of the audience?	❑	❑	❑	❑	
Based on the above, do you feel the information is timely enough to be of use to the client?	❑	❑	❑	❑	
B. Pervasiveness					
1. Is information disseminated to all intended audiences?	❑	❑	❑	❑	
2. Are contractual constraints on dissemination of evaluation information observed?	❑	❑	❑	❑	
3. Are attempts being made to make the evaluation information available to relevant audiences beyond those specified in the contract?	❑	❑	❑	❑	
Based on the above, do you feel that information is being provided to all who need it?	❑	❑	❑	❑	
IV. General Criteria					
A. Ethical Considerations					
1. Do test administration procedures follow professional standards of ethics?	❑	❑	❑	❑	
2. Have protection of human subjects guidelines been followed?	❑	❑	❑	❑	
3. Has confidentiality of data been guaranteed?	❑	❑	❑	❑	
Based on the above, do you feel the evaluation study strictly follows professional standards of ethics?	❑	❑	❑	❑	
B. Protocol					
1. Are appropriate persons contacted in the appropriate sequence?	❑	❑	❑	❑	
2. Are departmental policies and procedures to be followed?	❑	❑	❑	❑	
Based on the above, do you feel appropriate protocol steps were planned?	❑	❑	❑	❑	

ATTACHMENT 10-1.

OTHER USEFUL RESOURCES ON PROJECT EVALUATION

James Connell, Anne Kubisch, Lisbeth Schorr, and Carol Weiss, *New Approaches to Evaluating Communities Initiatives: Concepts, Methods, and Contexts,* Washington, DC: The Aspen Institute, 1995.

A. Fink and J. Kosecoff, *How to Conduct Surveys: A Step-by-Step Guide,* Newbury Park, CA: Sage Publications, 1989.

Sandra Gray and Associates, *Evaluation with Power: A New Approach to Organizational Effectiveness, Empowerment, and Excellence,* San Francisco: Jossey-Bass Publishers, 1998.

Michael Patton, *Utilization-Focused Evaluation: The New Century Text, 3rd edition,* Beverly Hills, CA: Sage Publications, 1997.

Harold Williams, Arthur Webb, and William Phillips, *Outcome Funding: A New Approach to Targeted Grantmaking, 2nd edition,* Rensselaerville, NY: The Rensselaerville Institute, 1993.

Blaine Worthen, James Sanders and Jody Fitzpatrick, *Program Evaluation: Alternative Approaches and Practical Guidelines, 2nd edition,* White Plains, NY: Longman Inc., 1997.

Quick Guide for Grant Applications, National Cancer Institute. Available at http://deainfo.nci.nih.gov/extra/extdocs/gntapp.htm

Chapter 11

Qualifications and Personnel

This chapter discusses presentation of organizational capability to complete the project, including personnel, facilities, contractors, consortia, and other unique or special resources or organizational assets.

Grantors want assurances that if they fund a proposal, they can count on applicants to follow through on their promises. You can demonstrate evidence of your capability and credibility in several different sections of a proposal: organizational background, purpose, statement of need or procedures. But whether or not the application form contains a separate section called "Qualifications," include sufficient detail to help a reviewer understand your competitive advantage over others in tackling this problem.

QUALIFICATIONS HIGHLIGHTS

Factors highlighting your qualifications include:

- How your organization's history, mission, and prior experience uniquely qualify it to be selected for this project.

- What personnel (permanent, temporary, or consultants) will be needed for the project, their roles, relevant experience, and professional backgrounds. If not all staff have yet

been chosen, describe your planned selection process.

- Whether any services or activities will be subcontracted, why, and to whom. Again, a planned selection process should be included if subcontractors have not yet been identified.

- The facilities and equipment needed for the project, those already possessed by the organization, and plans for securing the remainder.

- The status of relationships that will enhance the project, such as advisory bodies, collaborators, elected officials, vendors, or consortium members.

- Shared belief in the project's importance by other stakeholders in the community, including other donors, volunteers, and contributors of in-kind goods or services.

- Internal systems for administering the funds, once granted.

- Resolution of unique or special administrative issues, such as who will retain copyright, patent, or ownership of items produced or purchased with grant funds.

- How the donor can be assured that the project has appropriate support in the community. This issue is of particular importance to private foundations and corporations. It can be dealt with through reference to appropriately constituted advisory boards, by some project funds being provided by community sources, or through letters of endorsement.

HISTORY AND ACCOMPLISHMENTS

Most funders like to know about an organization's history and track record. However, just having been around a long time does not necessarily make you qualified to manage your project, so make sure you can name some distinctions along with your history. These might include:

- **First or only.** Yours was the first agency of its kind in the community, region, or country or is the only one addressing this issue in this way.

- **Origins.** Your organization emerged due to a unique set of circumstances that make it distinct from others. Perhaps all the founders had family members with the same health challenge, which wasn't being addressed by established institutions. Maybe state legislation called for its creation.

- **Experience.** You have tried things related to this project, whether successful or not, which taught you lessons about how to improve your endeavors.

- **Past support.** You've garnered financial support from multiple types of sources, in-kind contributions of goods or services, or significant commitments of time or advice from volunteers or experts.

- **Partnerships.** You've invested the time necessary to build cooperative relationships with other stakeholders.

- **Reputation.** You've gained the respect of colleagues and associates.

LEADERSHIP

Depending on the priorities of the funder, emphasis on leadership may vary. Traditional funders may prefer organizations with history and accomplishments, with long-term staff and carefully built alliances. But newer foundations, especially those created by entrepreneurs, may be more impressed with a founder with a vision and a handful of well-placed board members. A giving circle type of private foundation may put more value on the governance model of a nonprofit than its history, or may be more impressed with a board made up of those being served than a board of wealthy civic leaders. The more you know about the funding source, the easier it will be to establish your credibility based on what they value.

Some funders ask pointed questions about the board of directors of nonprofit organizations (sometimes called trustees), such as:

- Have they crafted a long-range or strategic plan for the organization?

- Were they instrumental in determining that this project was a priority for the organization?

- Are they aware that this request is being submitted?

- Are they all donors to the organization? (Some funders insist that every board member be a financial contributor to qualify for funding.)

- Does the board reflect the community or constituency served?

- How often does the board meet and what percentage of the members attends those meetings?

- Are board members genuinely engaged in the organization's governance?

Many grantmakers have realized that the questions they pose in their application forms or RFPs help drive desired behavior. By requiring organizations to jump through certain hoops to garner support, they are helping strengthen the infrastructure of the organization and the project. While some applicants may view such questions as troublesome, the effort expended to answer them adequately helps make the organization more competitive and more qualified for funding from all types of supporters.

PERSONNEL

Review the instructions of the funding source to see what information is requested about personnel. Usually, these instructions are fairly general, so the Dos and Don'ts listed below may help.

Do's

- **Do** include the title, responsibilities, number, and percentage of time assigned to the project for each type of staff person. Sometimes this information can best be displayed in a table or organization chart.

- **Do** give the names and biographical sketches for key staff. Proposals for large or complex projects or research funding usually should include a full biography for the project director or principal investigator, including prior research and publications.

- **Do** tailor the biographies to emphasize experiences relevant to the project.

- **Do** briefly describe the selection process and criteria for key project positions unfilled at the time of application. This issue is discussed in more detail later.

- **Do** include ample justification for the use of consultants. Indicate the number and their responsibilities and explain why these roles will not be filled through regular appointments. Include a background sketch for consultants known at the time of application.

- **Do** mention the source of other compensation for key personnel who will not be assigned full time to the project. Donors are wary of projects headed by part-time individuals whose other sources of income are unknown.

- **Do** provide information on the sex, race, and ethnicity of key staff. Some federal funding

sources also require the age of the project director.

- **Do** give a brief overview of the organizational and management structure of the project, if this has not already been provided in the procedures component.

- **Do** include a description of the types of members who serve on advisory bodies and their roles.

- **Do** include, or be prepared to furnish, letters agreeing to participation from any consultants or significant advisors mentioned by name in the proposal.

Don'ts

- **Don't** include the names of well-known experts in the field and indicate that "they will be asked to participate once the project is funded."

- **Don't** pad biographies by multiple references to "manuscript in progress." This is an unfortunate but frequent ploy by young researchers. Other techniques helpful to those applying for their first research grants are discussed later.

- **Don't** request salaries for project directors that, when added to other sources of compensation, total more than 100 percent of normal pay, unless this is specified and explained in the proposal. Most federal agencies simply do not allow this and demand documentation of other sources of income for key project staff. Increasingly, private foundations and corporations are also asking for written verification on this issue. (Although this is a budget item, it is mentioned here because the problem usually starts when one is planning the personnel narrative in the proposal.)

- **Don't** inflate proposed salaries for upper-echelon staff. The IRS Form 990, which itemizes your organization's current salary levels, is public information, accessible on-line for funders to check.

A question frequently asked by novice proposal writers is: "How do I reconcile requirements for affirmative action procedures with requests from funding sources to include resumes for intended project staff?"

This question is a good one because it presumes that most organizations must follow some type of open competition for available posts. This competition may not have taken place by the time the proposal must be submitted.

There are at least two ways this problem has been handled by others. Examples are provided with the caveat that the advice of your local affirmative action officer should always be sought when planning projects involving the hiring of new staff.

1. **The project director or principal investigator can be named from among those in the organization who are expected to have some responsibility for the funded project anyway.** Organizations frequently overlook the fact that a senior member of the faculty or staff is expected to provide informal supervision for most projects, even though this person's salary is not charged to the project budget. By formally recognizing this already-presumed responsibility in the application and including a percentage of the person's time in the salary requests, the organization can avoid the problem of having to submit a proposal that includes none of the names or backgrounds of key personnel. To help share administrative duties, you may also choose to include a second leadership position (such as a co-director, assistant director, or senior research or development associate) to be hired once the funds are committed.

2. **An existing staff member can be designated as a temporary or acting project director.** The individual is presented as the one responsible for the project until staff are found who meet the qualifications listed in the application. In some cases, the continuation of the project past this initial phase may be contingent on the funding source approving the selection of the regular project director. The acting staff member may, at a later point, be moved to another position within the project or may be designated as the person in the organization to whom the regular

project director will report. In any case, the résumé and experience of this existing staff member can be included in the proposal to demonstrate personnel capability.

If an individual's hiring is contingent upon approval of the proposal, this should be clearly specified in the proposal. The proposal should also provide some evidence that this individual is willing to accept the position if the funds are received. The individual may also be employed as a consultant during the proposal's preparation to make certain that he or she can live with its contents once an award is made.

These same approaches may be adapted to the filling of project positions other than that of the director.

Whenever possible, however, the project planner should always attempt to identify as many of the project staff as possible prior to submitting the proposal. Not only will the funding source consider it a plus that the project will not be delayed by personnel searches, but the availability of existing capability in the organization and the demonstration of the organization's prior experience within the project field are all important selling points in an application.

Less Experienced Personnel

A second question frequently asked by beginners is, "How can I increase a project's competitiveness when my age, status in the organization, or lack of prior writings and project management may place me at a disadvantage?"

Again, there are several ways that this has been handled by others; but these ideas should be checked with key officials in the organization and scrutinized for their legality or applicability.

1. **Submit the proposal to a funding source that limits its awards to junior faculty members or beginning professionals.** Some federal agencies, foundations, and corporations have "small grants" or "young investigators" programs explicitly designed for those who are not yet ready to apply for funds in direct competition with senior individuals.

2. **Send the proposal to funding sources that are more interested in the quality of the idea and the application than they are in the prior reputation of project personnel.** All funding sources want some assurance that the project personnel are capable of doing what is proposed. But some are more likely than others to base their judgments on the application and their personal impressions of the quality of the director than to rely primarily on the extensiveness of prior activities.

3. **Ask a more experienced colleague to serve as project director or principal investigator, with the initiator of the idea taking a less senior position.** This is a time-honored approach used particularly in research applications originated by junior faculty members. And it is an accepted practice, as long as the person designated as project director has agreed to participate, is willing to assume the administrative and legal responsibilities, will actually play the role described in the application, and is not overburdened with other assignments. A variation on this approach is to have a more senior person serve as co-director or co-investigator.

4. **Have a more experienced person serve as an active consultant.** Again, as long as the person truly intends to play this role, most funding sources are willing to accept this practice.

5. **Beginning investigators can include a brief biographical sketch of those who currently serve or previously served on the person's doctoral committee or supervised subsequent postdoctoral research.** Reviewers can partially judge the likely capability of the applicant by the quality of the applicant's mentors. This same approach can help young applicants in other fields who may previously have worked under someone well known in the profession.

INFRASTRUCTURE

Funders need to see that the grantee is structurally able to support the proposed work. Things that might distinguish a strong organization from a less competitive one include:

- **Policies and procedures.** If issues emerge in the middle of the project, has the organization already created processes for resolving such issues or defined criteria, standards or best practices that will help? Is the chain of command clear? Who will speak to the press if the project makes the news? How will the project proceed in the event of a natural disaster or event such as an arson fire or theft or embezzlement of funds?

- **Accounting systems.** Organizations are sometimes unprepared to account for grant funds separately or don't have data management systems sophisticated enough to track expenditures as precisely as funders wish.

- **Evaluation systems.** Sometimes the very people who are delivering services as part of the project are reluctant to measure their work. Nonprofits, especially, need to assure funders that the process for gathering statistical results has been agreed to by all parties who must participate and that the proposed systems are feasible and cost effective.

- **Communications systems.** A plan for disseminating periodic reports to the funder, with anticipated dates, expected information, and methods for communicating (phone, mail, e-mail) will make an applicant look more desirable. Indicating where else the applicant plans to disseminate reports (collaborators, other funders, appropriate agencies, appropriate media) shows forethought.

- **Prior work.** If you're seeking grant money to expand your program, show the funder how solid the current program is. If you have curriculum developed or collaborators in place, you'll be more appealing than if you're starting from scratch. If you seek support to spread your prevention education program from regional to national, let them know you've already developed marketing materials and a geographic distribution map with contacts in your major markets.

With the emergence of new large foundations in the last decade, some nonprofits, lured by the promise of enormous grant awards, discovered that they were ill-equipped to absorb a large gift. Indeed, trying to administer programs that trebled the size of the organization resulted in unhealthy growth. Organizations must have a firm foundation beneath them to sustain the culture shift of a major new program or project, so if you're stable, let the funder know.

Facilities and Equipment

Expectations of Particular Funders

The facilities and equipment section of the application should be tailored to the specific requirements and needs of the project rather than simply lifted from previous proposals or taken from existing agency documents. The narrative should be made as readable as possible, with the reviewer directed quickly to the most important facts.

Carefully check the funding source's policies on purchase versus rental of equipment and also its approach to ownership of purchased equipment and materials after the project ends. The writer should then restate his or her interpretation of these in the proposal so that future conflicts can be avoided.

Provide an adequate description of the facilities and major equipment needed for the project and identify what the organization already has and what it is requesting funds to purchase, rent, or renovate. Wherever possible, the project planner should minimize extensive acquisition and try to build on existing capabilities. Otherwise, the funder may be negatively impressed by the amount of time that would be lost while arranging for the necessary facilities and equipment.

You should also justify facilities and equipment by showing how they will be used in the project, especially if they represent a significant part of the budget. Otherwise the funder may conclude that the project's real agenda is to acquire buildings and hardware needed by the organization. For example, a federal reviewer recalls doubting the necessity of an expensive recreational vehicle in an application proposing a wilderness-based environmental education program for urban youth and a state-of-the-art computer system for a preschool classroom.

Currently-Held Assets

Whenever possible, emphasize any unusual or outstanding facilities or equipment in the organization. These may include:

- Particularly well-stocked or planned laboratories.

- Exceptionally extensive or modern computer facilities.

- A large library or unusual materials collections.

- Sophisticated or hard-to-secure equipment.

- Ready access to other organizations with unusual capabilities.

- Outstanding materials-production capabilities.

- A complete range of advisory or consultative services (such as a survey research center or university-based evaluators).

- Sites for research owned by the applicant.

Shared Items

If facilities or equipment from other organizations are essential elements of the proposal, provide documentation that these will be made available.

Unusual Items

If any unusual or unproven facilities and equipment are to be used in the project, provide sufficient information to justify why they are being tried. Information should also be given on how they will be developed and/or evaluated and what provisions will be made if alternatives turn out to be necessary.

Renovation

Any extensive renovation of facilities, particularly for office space, should be justified by providing a comparison to the cost of renting such space from a commercial source. Funding agencies are well aware that grants have been used on occasion to finance improvements that were not relevant to project activities. Some funding sources may also insist that such renovation be paid for from the project's indirect costs. Others may require that the indirect cost rate be reduced if a direct cost is being requested, so that the changes can be made and paid for at the outset of the award.

Chapter 12

The Budget

This chapter discusses the importance of the budget in a proposal, provides suggestions on budget preparation, describes differences in budgets for public and private funding sources, and gives examples of budget formats.

ROLE OF THE BUDGET

Budgeting is simply the process of translating the project plan into fiscal terms. Because it is one of the last things to be prepared, the weary writer may be tempted to slap it together and hope that any obvious mistakes can be corrected during negotiations or taken care of through supplemental requests after the program is started. **Not so!**

The preparation of the budget is an important final check in clarifying the practicality of the proposed project. Its adequacy will be an important consideration to the funder in judging whether you have the necessary experience and managerial capability to complete the project successfully. Unless you prepare your budget carefully, understanding its relationship to the proposed plan of action, you will be unprepared to successfully answer funders' questions or engage in final fiscal negotiations. Mistakes made in preparation can result in your being committed professionally and legally to a project whose resources are totally inadequate.

If total projected costs exceed your options for funding, you must redesign the project by reducing the scope or utilizing less costly means. Only the foolhardy or irresponsible go forward with an application, knowing that the resources are inadequate to conduct the proposed scope of work. Most funders are distinctly hostile to organizations that later request substantive program modifications or ask for additional funds because original estimates were unrealistic.

As much care should be given to the budget as to the development of the rest of the application. Seasoned reviewers will often turn to the budget first, before reading the narrative, because they can tell so much about the applicant and the proposal by simply reading the story told by the numbers.

BEFORE YOU BEGIN

Before you can frame your budget, you must learn the ground rules that apply to your own organization or institution and the funder. Best to look internally first, then make sure you understand the expectations of the grantmaker before finalizing your project or program budget.

Internal Ground Rules

If you are part of a sophisticated institution with a history of grantseeking and extensive infrastructure, there will likely be staff who specialize in the fiscal aspects of externally funded projects. If not, ask your finance personnel or board treasurer if there are any guidelines you must follow. Find out your institution's policies about indirect costs (see below) and other budgeting issues. And check to see if your organization already has budget worksheets with itemized expense categories.

Your organization may also have a position on what types of contracts it is willing to sign, such as *fixed-price, cost-reimbursement, cost plus fixed-fee,* and *cost sharing.* For example, your organization may not be in a position to sign a contract that obligates you to pay all the expenses up-front and get reimbursed every few months or once a year. Similarly, signing some grant contracts might obligate your organization to incur additional expenses (e.g., an audit or handicapped access) which you are not allowed to include in your application budget.

External Ground Rules

Each funder has guidelines about what it will and will not fund. Secure a copy of the guidelines or the RFP to ascertain its preferences on the types of issues in Checklist 12-1.

As noted earlier, there is considerable difference between the amount of budgetary detail required in proposals to private sources and to government agencies. However, you will want to prepare a carefully planned budget for all projects, even if you do not submit this in writing to the potential funder. Not only can you expect to use the information during subsequent discussions, but you will need the budget for successful project management.

While the process of preparing budgets becomes easier as one becomes familiar with fiscal terms, learns what kind of information is needed, and begins to develop "rules of thumb" about probable costs of certain kinds of activities, each new initiative presents new challenges. The resource needs of each project are as unique as the proposed outcomes and planned methodology.

STEPS IN THE BUDGET DEVELOPMENT PROCESS

The complexity of the project, the procedures of your organization, and the instructions of the funding source will together determine the ease with which a budget is prepared. In any case, you will find that budgeting is essentially a three-step process, which will be covered in detail in the rest of this chapter:

Step 1: Identify the total costs of the project.

Step 2: Arrange items by category, by timeframe, and by anticipated source.

Step 3: Transfer your data into the format requested by the funder.

Step 1: Identify Total Costs

It is inadvisable for a single individual to frame the budget for any proposal. Include in the process those who will be pivotally involved in implementation, as well as those who must manage the funds. And as you discuss the need for particular elements, consider devising two budgets—one that represents your ideal and one with only the bare essentials.

To help in building the project budget, begin with a worksheet similar to those shown in Tables 12-1, 12-2, and 12-3. Such worksheets:

- Provide a way to structure the budget planning so that no probable expense is overlooked.

- Record how each item was computed so that you are prepared to discuss the possible impact of cuts proposed during negotiations.

- Aid the writer in determining whether each request is sufficiently justified in the proposal narrative.

- Provide an expenditure plan for use in actual project operation. This is particularly valuable if the proposal writer or budget developer will not be included in project management once the funds are received.

Checklist 12-1. Ground Rules Set by Funding Sources

❑ **Allowable costs.** Most public funders allow indirect costs, but private funders generally do not. Many will also not permit a project budget to include as direct costs items they assume to be the normal responsibility of the organization, such as the availability of a library or accounting services. (For more information on direct and indirect costs, see page 135.)

❑ **Percentage of project costs requested.** Will the funder entertain requests for the entire project cost or expect part of the funds to come from another source? Many foundations and corporations have fixed rules about providing only a certain percentage of a project budget (often 20 percent) which assures them there is shared ownership of your idea and they aren't the only ones invested in its success.

❑ **Matching funds.** Both government and private funders may ask for *matching funds*, where their award is contingent on the receipt of charitable contributions from other sources totaling the same amount. Matching funds can sometimes be provided through *in-kind contributions*—non-cash assistance offered through goods, services, equipment, space, advice, or other things that would otherwise constitute a hard cost of the project.

❑ **Changes.** What changes, if any, will be permitted in the budget once it is approved? Frequently, grantors will allow the transfer of up to 10 percent of one budget category (such as supplies and materials) to another (such as travel) without prior approval.

❑ **Contingencies.** While most funders expect a "Miscellaneous" line item to cover inconsequential or small unanticipated expenses, there are divergent positions on items labeled "Con-

tingency." Some want you to budget so carefully that there won't be surprises, some expect you to include a little leeway in your projections and others assume that costs will always end up higher than you predicted. Check to see what each grantor prefers.

❑ **Computing costs.** When responding to an RFP, the writer can estimate the acceptable budget range by computing the costs of the estimated staff time suggested by the funding source. In a solicitation from the National Science Foundation, for example, the RFP specified that the project would take an estimated "one person-year of effort." NSF used a general rule of thumb that this would cost about $60,000, a figure which became the average budget target for responding proposals.

❑ **Reviewers.** Find out who in the funding source will be reading the budget and whether it will accompany the narrative or be considered as a separate document. Many federal agencies have contracting officers who read only the budget, unless they initiate a special request to see the rest of the application. This may necessitate more detail in the budget showing how totals were calculated, or a separate column on the budget indicating page numbers of the narrative where the justification for each item is found.

❑ **Timing.** Make sure you can spend the money in the time required by the funder. One government agency was unable to award a grant to a nonprofit because the funder's monies had to be used by the end of the fiscal year, but the organization couldn't spend the money in that time due to permitting and construction timeframes.

Table 12-1. Example of Budget Justification Worksheet (by Cost Center)*

Cost Center / Item	Total	Requested from funding source	Local	Reference to Narrative	Justification or Explanation
Administration					
Advisory Board					
Salary	$3,000	–0–	$3,000	page 21, 22	5 members × $50 each for 12 meetings
Supplies	100	100	–0–	page 22	$20 each
Telephone					
(rental)	–0–	–0–	–0–		
(long distance)	600	600	–0–		$10 each for 12 months
Travel					
(in state)	1,800	1,800	–0–	page 23	$30/day × 5 members × 12 meetings
(out-of-state)	1,200	1,200	–0–	page 24	$600 for 2 members to attend national meeting
	6,700	3,700	3,000		
Project Director					
Salary	$24,000	$25,000	–0–	page 15, 17, 20	$2,000 × 12 months
Benefits	2,400	240	–0–	page 20	Institutional rate is 10% of salary
Supplies	480	480	–0–	page 17, 25	Agency requires $40 per person per month
Postage	240	240	–0–	page 17	Agency requires $20 per person per month
Telephone					
(rental)	240	240	–0–	page 17	1 instrument × $20 × 12 months
(long-distance)	1,200	1,200	–0–	page 15, 25, 30	$100/month × 12
	28,560	28,560	–0–		

*This shows examples for just two cost centers. The entire budget would require many pages. Advantages of this model are that it groups all planned expenditures for each cost center (i.e., administration) together and makes certain no needs are overlooked. However, it does not account for use of money over time and it does not organize expenditures by the categories normally required on most proposal budget forms.

Table 12-2. Example of Budget Justification Worksheet (by Activity)*

Page	Activity	Dates	Description	Amount	Explanation
13–17	Start-up	1/1–2/15	Salaries and wages	$5,000	Director—$3,000 (45 days)
					Asst.—$2,000 (45 days)
			Benefits	1,000	Figured 20%
			Supplies/materials	300	$150 each
			Travel/transportation	600	$200 in-state / $400 other
			Postage/shipping	100	$50 each
			Rent/comm./utilities	500	$100 each
			Other services	500	Consultants (5 × $100)
20–20	Literature search	2/15–4/1	Salaries and wages	3,000	2 Res. Assoc. × $1,500
			Benefits	600	Figured 20%
			Supplies/materials	1,000	Acquire library
			Travel/transportation	–0–	
			Postage/shipping	100	$50 each
			Rent/comm./utilities	200	$100 each
			Other services	600	Computer searches (6)

*This example shows cost estimates for just two activities. Again, many sheets would be needed for the complete proposal. This model has the advantage of tying specific costs to specific activities, and it does lend itself to estimating expenditures over time. However, it also has the disadvantage of not organizing the expenditures in the way normally requested in most proposal budget forms. For example, all salaries and wages for all activities would need to be totaled in order to build the type of information usually requested in the final proposal.

Major Budget Components

Indirect versus Direct Costs

As you list your budget categories, you will need to distinguish between direct costs and indirect costs. *Direct costs* are expenditures specifically attributable to this project or program. *Indirect costs* relate to the infrastructure necessary to support the project—facilities, personnel, materials, services—but are difficult to cost out separately for each application.

Direct Costs

The following direct costs listed in a project budget make up the customary expense categories:

- Personnel (salaries, wages, and benefits)

- Contract services

- Travel and per diem expenses

- Facilities

- Equipment

- Supplies and materials

- Program-related expenses

- Communications

Personnel. *Salaries* (monthly or yearly pay) and *wages* (hourly pay) should be computed for all personnel associated with the project. The budget display should also indicate the amount of time each individual will allocate to the project (shown as a percentage of total salary or as number of staff

Table 12-3. Example of Budget Justification Worksheet (by Time Period and Category)*

Description	Fiscal Year: Start Date: End Date:	Budget by Time Period				Total Budget
Personnel costs						
Salaries						
Personnel benefits						
Consultant claims						
Other personnel						
Travel & transportation						
Staff travel						
Consultants travel						
Other travel						
Postage & shipping						
Rent, comm. & utilities						
Facility rental						
Equipment rental						
Telephone						
Utilities						
Printing & duplication						
Printing						
Duplication						
Other services						
Data processing						
Subcontracts						
Conference expenses						
Other services						
Supplies & materials						
Office supplies						
Printed materials						
Other supplies						
Total direct costs						
Equipment purchases						
Indirect cost @ ___%						
Total costs						
Fee @ ___%						
Total costs and fee						

*This model has the advantage of collecting costs by the categories frequently found in required budget forms. It also allows their estimation by major time period (another kind of information usually requested by federal agencies). But it does not have the advantage of showing how the sums included in each category were computed, nor is it tied to costs of specific activities. It also does not include a reference to the page in the narrative where justification may be found. The form could be made more useful if it were completed separately for major cost centers (i.e., administration, training, materials development, evaluation, and so forth) and if additional columns were added to capture the other information discussed above.

days) and whether the amount is to be paid by the funding source, the applicant, or other donors to whom you are applying.

Salary/wage rates should be comparable to those regularly used by the organization. Grant funds should not be used to augment people's normal pay. However, provision should be made to cover anticipated promotional increases and inflation in multiyear budgets. If you need to ascertain prevailing pay rates, contact your United Way affiliate, a nearby university, the local school district, or your city or county government.

Inexperienced grantseekers often neglect to acknowledge that managing the program or project will require the time and expertise of individuals not directly involved in the project. For example, if a nonprofit is launching a new initiative, the budget should include a percentage of the executive director's time, the time spent by those who will supervise the service delivery staff, the time of the financial services and data entry staff, etc. This shows the funder that the organization realizes those elements are a cost of implementing the program. And even if the request does not include a commensurate amount of their pay, it should be reflected in the budget and marked as in-kind support or a cost absorbed by the organization.

In addition to including the salaries and wages of all regular project staff, the personnel category may also include funds for consultants and/or advisory board members. Consultants are usually hired as private contractors at a daily rate (which may be set by the funding source rather than the applicant). The daily rate should be mentioned somewhere in the narrative or referenced in the budget document itself.

Employee Benefits. Employee benefits differ with each organization. Included in this category might be retirement, social security, fringe benefits, unemployment taxes, and other payroll taxes. Usually these are computed by applying a certain fixed percentage against the salaries and wages of project staff. The applicant's business or finance staff can provide advice on the percentage to use in this computation and which types of positions to exempt from its application. You should also find out whether funds must be included to cover the fringe benefits of consultants and advisors. Normally this is not done, but policies vary.

Contract Services. This rather nebulous category will vary considerably from organization to organization and from one grantmaker to another. Services purchased on contract might include legal or financial help (bookkeeping or auditing), data management, computerized materials searches, statistical services, page costs for articles in journals, editing, photographic or design services, printing and publishing, and consultants or subcontractors. Table 12-4 offers a helpful framework for identifying contract costs.

Travel and Per Diem. This category covers costs associated with the travel and transportation of individuals connected with the project. Some funding sources require that amounts be estimated separately for project staff, consultants, and advisors. Others also require separate estimates of in-state costs and those associated with regional, national, or international travel. The *per diem* expenses (money for food and lodging, parking and other such items on a daily basis) should be included, as well as actual costs for air or ground transportation. It is quite permissible to include costs for travel to a national professional meeting in most grants—especially if you plan to report on the progress or results of the project. See Table 12-5 for a sample planning document.

Facilities. Office space and other facilities necessary for the project may be charged directly to the project or provided by the applicant organization, either as indirect costs or as costs the organization offers to absorb. If facilities are listed in the requested amount as indirect costs and any renovation is planned, a problem may arise during the project's operation. Indirect costs are usually released to the applicant by the funding source at the same rate as salaries and wages are paid out. For a 12-month project, for example, only 1/12th of the indirect costs is paid each month. If your organization insists on having "cash in hand" before renovation proceeds, it may be several months before sufficient monies are accumulated via receipt of indirect costs. You may thus want to consider inserting a direct cost for renovation or construction and reduce the indirect cost rate accordingly.

Table 12-4. Consultant Fees and Travel

Name, residence if known	Service to be performed	Consultant Fee			Per Diem			Travel	
		Days	Rate	Total	Days	Rate	Total	From–To	Total

Table 12-5. Staff Travel*

Destination	Purpose of Trips	Number of Trips	Trans-portation	Per Diem		
				Days	Rate	Total

*It is usually a good idea to check with a travel agency and find out whether carrier costs are expected to increase substantially during the project period. Some individuals also include an inflationary factor to guard against unanticipated increases. Remember, many funding sources require that all travel planned outside of the United States be cleared in advance with the project monitor.

A caution: If you are asking for funds for facility improvements or fixed assets (such as lights and sound equipment in a theatre or a room outfitted with a one-way mirror for research or focus groups), be sure to let the funder know whether you own the property, as some are reluctant to invest in capital improvements for property the applicant does not own.

Check all policies governing facilities. If space is to be rented, some federal agencies pay a flat amount regardless of the availability of local space at this rate. Also include any costs connected with the use of facilities for field-based research, training, gatherings, etc. If these are to be provided free of charge by the local organization or collaborating agencies, the costs of such services can also be estimated and included as a match.

Equipment. Equipment may include office desks, chairs, file systems, computer hardware and software, laboratory equipment, and research equipment. List all equipment necessary for the project and indicate whether it will be leased, purchased, or donated to the project by an external source or the applicant organization.

Supplies and Materials. Supplies and materials include all consumable office supplies, costs connected with duplicating and reproduction, and funds to acquire documents and other project materials.

Program-Related Expenses. This is a catch-all category for items necessary to the project that aren't really supplies or equipment. For example, an arts production may require costumes or music scores; an environmental education program may need topographic maps and specimens of flora and fauna; a child therapy program may require dollhouses and stuffed animals. Make sure that the procedures section delineates how such items will be used as the program takes shape.

Communications. This item could include telephone costs (purchase and installation of equipment, monthly service, long distance, teleconferencing), plus videoconferencing, satellite hookups, cable access, Internet access, and cell phones and service if essential to the project (such as a rural health delivery service). Reviewers will be skeptical of substantial long distance sums, which may signal an inexperienced applicant or a padded budget.

Indirect Costs

Examples of indirect costs (also called "overhead") include the applicant's business services (financial), central administration, legal services, library, and depreciation of buildings and equipment. To provide reimbursement for the project's access to such organizational resources, most government agencies allocate a lump sum which is usually computed using a fixed percent of the total budget. Normally, this percentage is negotiated annually between the applicant organization and the federal agency and remains the same for all projects submitted to that source. Indirect costs can represent from 10 to 200 percent of the amount requested for the actual work.

Foundations and other nongovernment funders seldom pay indirect costs. If they do, they usually limit them to 15 percent. In those cases, transfer funds for those items normally covered in indirect costs (rent, utilities, insurance, licenses and permits) into direct costs and show them as line-item expenses.

Overhead or Fees. As noted earlier, most funders recognize that there is a variety of services provided by the applicant that are difficult to cost on a project-by-project basis. The availability of a modern laboratory, top-of-the-line computer equipment, an outstanding library and effective organizational leadership are important to the success of any funded project. Yet because these facilities and personnel exist to serve the entire organization, it is almost impossible to determine their specific percentage of use or benefit to a single program.

To reimburse organizations for these generally available items, federal sources have adopted the policy of paying an indirect cost—a flat amount determined as a percentage of all or part of the project budget. Regulations governing these policies are periodically changed, so be certain that your business office or finance personnel have the latest version. Usually this percentage is negotiated by the applicant's business or research administrators annually and is simply applied to all proposals. In some cases, however, the funding source may require a different indirect cost rate, may pay no indirect costs at all, or may require a reduction in this rate as an aspect of cost sharing.

You should always consult with your administrative, business, or finance staff to determine the amount to include and its implication for other aspects of the budget. In addition to indirect costs, some organizations request a "fee" in their budgets. This amount is usually included to cover research and development activities which the organization conducts independently of any sponsored projects. Funders differ on whether they will honor this request. Finally, one should determine how to handle indirect costs or fees for subcontractors that will be involved in the project. Many funding sources will not cover requests for a second organization's overhead and will insist that this be deducted from the amount due the primary applicant.

Step 2: Arrange Budget Items

By Category

When arranging the line items in your budget, segment them into the broadest categories possible, as some funders limit movement from one category to another to 10 percent. More and more funders are asking for three broad categories: personnel, other expenses, and indirect costs. For those who do not allow indirect costs, the items traditionally included there would constitute a category labeled overhead expenses.

By Time

If you seek funding for more than one year, funders will want to see how much you plan to spend each year. They may match their payment schedule to your plan or they may reimburse your costs only as you incur them. As you craft your budget documents, display the expenses on an annualized basis.

If your proposal signals the launch of a new initiative, your costs may vary greatly from the first year (preparation) to the second year (launch) to the third (maintenance). For example, before

a church can house a new child care center in its basement, it will need to construct a fence, an outdoor play area, a stroller-accessible ramp, and sinks in each room. In its first phase of operation, expenses will be incurred that may never arise again: developing curriculum, determining policies, hiring staff, marketing to families, setting up systems, purchasing books, toys, and furniture. But the next year, expenses may look more routine: staff salaries and benefits, supplies, snack food, communications with parents, replacement or repair of used items.

By Source

You must demonstrate how much of the total project cost you anticipate funding yourself, how much you are asking of this funder and how much you seek from other sources. This can be accomplished by creating four columns: total, our funds, your funds, and others' funds. Funders will want to know who else is participating in the project, so whether you include a budget narrative or a footnote on the budget page, indicate who has already committed, and for how much, as well as who you intend to approach and for how much.

Step 3: Transfer your data into their format

Budget formats will vary depending on what each funder wants to know. As you frame your budget, collect all the information suggested by the worksheets in the tables in this chapter so that, as deadlines approach, you needn't struggle to tailor your numbers to the requested arrangement. Two common formats are illustrated in Tables 12-6 and 12-7.

Demonstrating In-Kind Donations

You may want to highlight how much support you have garnered from in-kind contributions. If entire line items on the budget are being contributed, put the in-kind items in bold or italics. However, if only part of a category is being covered, have two columns, one listing total program costs for each category and the other indicating how much is in-kind. The rule of thumb about valuing people's

Table 12-6. Model Format for Multi-Year Budget

Expenses	Year One				Year Two				Year Three			
	A	B	C	D	A	B	C	D	A	B	C	D
Personnel												
Salaries/wages	150,000		30,000	180,000	157,500		31,500	189,000	165,375		33,075	198,450
Benefits	60,000		12,000	72,000	63,000		12,600	75,600	66,150		13,230	79,380
Subtotal	210,000	0	42,000	252,000	220,500	0	44,100	264,600	231,525	0	46,305	277,830
Other Expenses												
Consultant & professional fees			15,000	15,000			5,000	5,000				0
Travel	5,000		5,000	10,000	5,250		2,000	7,250	5,513			5,512.5
Equipment	5,000		5,000	10,000	5,250			5,250	5,513			5,512.5
Supplies	2,000			2,000	2,100			2,100	2,205			2,205
Training	5,000		3,000	8,000	5,250		2,000	7,250	5,513		1,000	6,512.5
Printing/copying			2,000	2,000			1,000	1,000	0		1,000	1,000
Telephone	3,500			3,500	3,675			3,675	3,859			3,858.75
Postage	2,500		500	3,000	2,625		500	3,125	2,756		500	256.25
Rent & utilities	30,000			30,000	31,500			31,500	33,075			33,075
Program-specific property & equipment acquisition		20,000	20,000	40,000 0				0 0				0 0
In-kind expenses	13,000			13,000	13,650			13,650	14,333			14,332.5
Other expenses	12,000			12,000	12,600			12,600	13,230			13,230
Subtotal	78,000	20,000	50,500	148,500	81,900	0	10,500	92,400	85,995	0	2,500	88,495
Total project/ program expenses	288,000	20,000	92,500	400,500	302,400	0	54,600	357,000	317,520	0	48,805	366,325

A = Applicant organization
B = Requested from other funders
C = Requested from this funder
D = Total

Source: *Getting Funded: The Complete Guide to Writing Grant Proposals* by Mary Hall and Susan Howlett. Available from Portland State University, Continuing Education Press, www.cep.pdx.edu. Copyright © 2003. All rights reserved.

Table 12-7. Model Format for Standard Project Budget

Project/Program Budget

Organization Name: _____

Project/Program Revenue

Public $ _____
   Federal   _____
   State   _____
   Municipal   _____

      Subtotal   _____

Private
   Foundations   _____
   Corporations   _____
   Organizations   _____
   Federated Campaigns   _____
   Individuals   _____
   Earned Income   _____
   Interest Income   _____

      Subtotal   _____

   Total Income $ _____

Project/Program Expenses

Salaries   _____
Benefits & Taxes   _____

      Subtotal   _____

Facilities   _____
Equipment   _____
Supplies   _____
Travel & Per Diem   _____
Contract Services   _____
Communications   _____
Program-Related Expenses   _____

      Subtotal   _____

   Total Expenses $ _____

efforts on your behalf is this: If a person is contributing skill in his or her field (for example, a lawyer offering legal services), you can record the value as their hourly rate times the number of hours. If the same person helps to spread wood chips, you must calculate the value of their time at a base rate per hour for that type of work.

Demonstrating Other Support

Funders want to know who else is supporting the project for a number of reasons.

- They want to see that the applicant organization has made a commitment of some kind, whether in cash or in-kind.

- They want to know that others deem the work important, especially funders they view as obvious sponsors of such work.

- They want to make sure the other participants are entities with which they want to be associated.

- They want to see whether the support is predominantly government, foundation, or corporate.

- They want to see the level to which other partners have committed.

- They want to see whether they are being asked early or late in the process (some funders enjoy being leaders and some like to make the culminating gift.)

Be clear with each funder about which sources have committed, which have been approached, and which you intend to approach. Don't ever indicate that a funder has made a commitment without having something in writing. Grantmakers check with one another, and if they discover you haven't been truthful, your proposal will be automatically rejected, jeopardizing your prospects for future funding.

Demonstrating Potential Revenue

Your proposed budget needs to include projections for revenue as well as expenses. While few projects will have income from all these types of sources, your revenue section could include the following sources:

- **Public Funders:** Federal, state, county, borough, or municipal agencies.

- **Private Funders:** Foundations, corporations, and organizations. The corporations category should be itemized by type (e.g., event sponsorship, employer matching of employee gifts, in-kind contributions, or corporate cash contributions). Corporate foundation gifts could be listed under either foundations or corporations.

- **Individuals:** The individuals category should be itemized by the methods your organization will use to solicit gifts from individual donors (e.g., mail, phone, workplace campaigns, events, personal solicitations, etc.).

- **Earned Income:** Earned income should be itemized by the means generated: the sale of products associated with the grant (e.g., reports, manuals, curricula, videos), or fees for services associated with the project (e.g., fees from clients or conference or workshop registrations).

- **Interest Income:** Interest income should be itemized by the source (e.g., prior endowment gifts, reserves, a legal settlement).

OTHER FINANCIAL DOCUMENTS

Many funders will also ask for a copy of your organization's annual operating budget and the most recent audited financial statement.

Your Operating Budget

Figure 12-1 shows things reviewers may want to know.

If you think some items in your budget may raise questions for a reviewer, put an asterisk next to them and include an explanatory note at the bottom of the page. Some proposal applications allow a *budget narrative*, where an applicant can

Figure 12-1. What Funders Look for in Your Operating Budget

Human Resources

- Does the organization take good care of its people, which affects turnover and effectiveness?

- Do the salaries and benefits reflect the rest of the field?

- Is professional development (e.g., training or conferences) part of the budget?

- Does it pay for memberships in professional associations or subscriptions to professional journals?

- Does it spend enough money on retreats, celebrations, and appreciation for board, staff, and volunteers?

- Is donor cultivation and stewardship part of the budget?

Diverse Revenue Streams

- Is there a healthy balance of types of income?

    For decades, nonprofits (excluding government agencies) typically have received 4 percent of their contributed income from corporations, 6 percent from foundations, and 90 percent from individual donors. Since grantors know that grants are not meant to sustain organizations, a high percentage of income from grants will raise a red flag.

Fundraising

- Is the cost of fundraising included?

    Funders know it costs money to raise money, even if it's being done by volunteers.

Liquidity

- How much of your fund balance is cash or easily converted?

- How much is restricted funds or restricted assets?

Sustainability

- Are the growth patterns healthy and sustainable, or are there huge influxes of new staff or programming?

Reserves

- Has your organization prepared for unanticipated events by raising and holding part of a year's budget in reserve?

- Are you poised to survive the financial effects of a natural disaster, accident, economic downturn, sudden loss of government funding, or unexpected capital repairs.

- Are you in a position to seize an opportunity (e.g., to buy your building, absorb another organization, or respond to an emerging new constituency) if it presents itself?

Deficits

- If the current year's budget predicts a deficit, does your organization have a plan for overcoming it in the following year?

explain in text its rationale for particular financial decisions.

Audited Financial Statement

Funders often require the applicant's most recent *audited financial statement*. This document, the result of an external professional review of the organization's finances, often discloses information not clear from the budget, answering reviewers' questions about why and how the organization has made decisions and about the organization's financial health. If you haven't had an official audit and the cost of one is prohibitive for your organization, ask the funder if you may substitute a less expensive and less exhaustive document, such as a "compilation" or a "review."

OTHER BUDGET CONSIDERATIONS

How Much to Request

Grantseekers are often tempted to augment the budget, assuming the funder may award less than the requested amount. But even inexperienced reviewers can detect "padded" budgets, so keep the numbers as realistic as possible. Many a funder has awarded an applicant *more* than it requested because it asked for a modest amount and didn't appear greedy.

Unpracticed proposal writers frequently ask how to estimate whether the total budget amount is "realistic," given the resources available to the funding source. This is where the information-gathering discussed in Chapter 4 is particularly useful. If you have researched the funder well, you will know the total dollars available to them in this particular funding cycle, the minimum/maximum range of prior awards in this program field, and whether they've funded the types of things you've included in your budget.

Consider asking for no more than the funder's *average* grant amount on your initial approach to that funder. While records may document much higher grant amounts having been awarded, those recipients likely spent years building a relationship

and earning the trust of the grantor. When RFPs announce that applicants can request a maximum of $X,000, nearly every proposal requests the maximum award. Asking for a lower amount puts you at a psychological advantage in a competitive review. Asking for an unusual amount ($18,750 instead of $20,000) makes your request look more authentic and less capricious.

If you are approaching a particular funder for only a percentage of the project cost, make sure that the items requested reflect the values and priorities of the funder. For example, an arts commission does not want to see a performer's time listed as an in-kind contribution—it is a core value of the commission to pay artists what they're worth. Savvy proposal developers will not simply ask for $5,000 of the $20,000 project cost—they will choose an item in the budget that relates to the funder's guidelines and request funding for that discrete item. Some grantors will reject an entire proposal because the requested amount includes line items the guidelines strictly prohibit.

You may want to include a fallback position, as grantmakers will often fund a proposal for less than the requested amount. Don't assume that if you suggest a lower amount, they will automatically choose that number. For example, if you've asked for $10,000, but you could eliminate one element of the project that costs $1,500 and still make it work, let them know that, so they don't trim the award to $5,000, an amount that doesn't relate to any particular budget items.

How to Deal with a Lower Award

Be prepared to answer a question often posed by grantmakers: "What will you do if we are unable to grant the entire amount requested?" There are several answers to this question, and only your organization can determine which is true for you.

1. **"We can reduce the scope of the project."** Perhaps you can interview or serve fewer subjects or clients. Perhaps the geographic range could be narrowed, or the length of time. Maybe you don't really need the extra support staff or that fancy computer component. Be clear about

what constitutes a suitable fallback position, or decision makers may not know what would be a helpful amount if they can't award the full request. For example, if they can't give you $50,000, perhaps they could give you $47,000 if they knew you could make that work.

2. **"We will look for other funders."** This shows the grantor that you fully intend to carry out this proposal whether they fund it or not, and that you will continue to search for support until you garner what you need. Contrary to popular thought, this does not necessarily make your request look dispensable. Rather, it makes you look determined, and confident that someone else will find it valuable.

3. **"We must scrap the project."** This signals that the amount you suggest is indeed exactly what it will take to implement the proposal, and it must remain intact, exactly as described, or the project isn't worth doing.

Advice from Funders

The following budget pointers are offered by experienced grantmakers:

- The budget for a proposal can be developed only after the proposed program has been carefully planned and all activities detailed.

- The budget must be developed with the same care and deliberation as other parts of the proposal. Individuals experienced with budgeting can provide help, but decisions on time and cost can be made only by someone who thoroughly understands the intended operation of the project.

- The proposal writer must be aware of all pertinent regulations, both those of the applicant organization and those of the funding source.

- Keep a record of the method used in computing all budget items (spreadsheets or worksheets used to develop the budget) so you can answer questions during review, negotiation, or project operation.

- Thoroughly document all budgeted expenses included in the application, either in the narrative or through the use of appendices.

- Make sure the items in your budget reflect the narrative text. Seeing items in the budget that were not explained in the body of the proposal raises doubts in the minds of reviewers.

- Make sure your revenue and expense columns add up to the same total!

- Make sure the project budget is sufficient to perform the tasks described in the narrative.

- Check to make sure that all budget items reflect the values of the applicant and are not at cross-purposes with the funder's goals.

- Include estimates from vendors if you request funds for capital expenditures. Funders want to know you sought out the best value for their dollars.

- Don't be greedy. For example, don't ask for a $25,000 van when renting one for the occasions you need it during the year would cost only $5,000.

Chapter 13

Review, Submission, Notification, and Renewal

This chapter discusses the final steps in the proposal-development process and describes what typically occurs after the proposal is submitted. It also provides several perspectives on why proposals fail and suggests issues to consider when trying to renew or refund a project.

REVIEW OF THE FINAL PROPOSAL

By now you have completed the proposal, prepared it in the required format, and are ready to move on to internal review and signoffs. Right? No, not yet. Before you take these steps, it is important to get a final reading by the most critically minded person you can recruit. Otherwise, you will likely commit at least one of the "seven deadly sins of proposal writing" (see Figure 13-1). These fatal flaws were the most frequently mentioned problems in proposals cited by over 100 public and private grantmakers during interviews held in late 2002.

Internal Reviews Before Submission

Every institution or organization has a slightly different procedure and timeline that must be followed, but most typically include the following:

- **Program Director or Department Chair.** Determines consistency of proposal with internal program, budget priorities, and personnel assignments, and ensures professional or scientific competence of the application.

- **Division Director, Principal, or Dean.** Approves alignment of proposal with priorities at a broader level and confirms that any needed matching funds are either available or will be included in the next budget request.

- **Budget Office.** Ensures that the cost of all items has been identified correctly, that proposed salary levels and fringe benefit and indirect cost rates are appropriate, and that the budget totals are accurate.

- **Internal Review Boards.** Depending on the nature of the project, several internal committees may need to screen and approve the proposal's submission. These might include an Institutional Review Board (IRB) dealing with human subject protection or the Institutional Animal Care and Use Committee (IACUC) that ensures compliance with the institution's animal subject regulations. Your organization may also limit the number of applications that can be submitted simultaneously to the same funding source and have special procedures to decide whose proposal can be submitted when.

Figure 13-1. The Seven Deadly Sins of Proposal Writing

1. **The application doesn't have a clear focus.** It does not concisely and compellingly convey what you want to do, why it is important, how it relates to the interests of the funding source, and why you are the best qualified to carry it out. This is especially critical in the abstract or executive summary. A proposal can also look unclear if it is riddled with jargon or isn't written clearly and directly.

2. **Presentation is sloppy.** An application with any misspellings, typos, poor grammar, and coffee stains (or other unidentifiable blobs) signals a sloppy mind and disrespect for the recipient. It is **really** important to correctly spell the name of the funding source to which you are applying. One program officer recalled a proposal that spelled the name of her foundation seven different ways, apparently operating on the erroneous assumption that at least one of them would be right and the other six forgiven. **Do not rely solely on the word processor's spell checker. Proofread carefully.**

3. **Proposal is unsound.** This is often a sin of commission—of simply biting off more than you can chew and promising far more than can reasonably be accomplished. Funders of research particularly cited "unrealistic plans" as something that quickly kills their interest in a proposal. But it can be a sin of omission, too—of simply failing to show how the project's proposed goals, procedures, and resources tie together in a coherent, creative, and manageable project. **A colleague can help you judge if the internal logic of your project is adequately conveyed in the proposal. If not, do a rewrite.**

4. **The proposal has an "internal" rather than an "external" focus.** Most funding sources give money to improve the lives of people, build better communities, advance society, create new knowledge or for other high-minded reasons. They seldom make awards because an organization needs a new way to pay its staff, a faculty member cannot receive tenure without a funded project or an applicant wants

to upgrade facilities. Unfortunately, every day, public and private funding sources receive literally hundreds of proposals that are preoccupied with how the requested money will benefit the applicant, rather than a real commitment to the problem the grantmaker is trying to solve. **You must demonstrate that the project that has not been designed in isolation from those it is to serve or from other organizations whose cooperation is essential for success.** "Working with," as opposed to "doing things to" others (especially your clients) is the message you want to convey.

5. **Budget problems.** Experienced grantmakers who see lots of proposals can quickly judge whether the budget is unrealistic (either over or under a feasible budget), is larded with nonessential expenses or is "asking for the moon." Padded budgets are proof of either incompetence or bad faith. Ask for what you need. **Many reviewers look at the budget first as a way to decide whether they want to bother reading the rest of the application.**

6. **Instructions weren't followed.** Most funding sources sincerely expect that you will give them the courtesy of answering all the questions they have asked and following the instructions. You may feel there isn't much logic in their forms, but now is not the time to demonstrate your creativity by coming up with your own proposal format. **Double check that you have included all of the information requested. Obey word and page limits. Omit irrelevant supplementary materials. Send the right number of copies. "Not following the rules" is one of the quickest ways to ensure your proposal isn't funded.**

7. **Deadline was missed.** Good proposals take time to prepare, and every organization has internal review steps that must be completed before the proposal can be submitted. Some programs require additional reviews at the state or regional level or, because of the nature of the project, expect approvals by professional

---

Figure 13-1. The Seven Deadly Sins of Proposal Writing (continued)

committees of one kind or another. If you plotted these out on the timeline recommended in Chapter 5 and built in a factor for inevitable delays or last-minute negotiations, you should be okay. **Few funding sources will consider a proposal if it has missed the application** **deadline.** Be certain you know if it is a "postmark deadline" (the proposal was stamped at the post office by a certain date) or a "receipt deadline" (it is in the hands of the grantmaker by a certain date).

For applications to corporations or private foundations, that decision may be made by your development office.

- **Executive Director, President, Superintendent, Governance Board.** Typically the last level of internal review and approval before the proposal is cleared for submission. It is intended to ensure that the proposal has institutional-level priority, that the applicant agrees to fulfill all commitments, both programmatic and budgetary, made in the proposal. This level normally results in a signature on a transmittal letter.

Other Reviews

Where another organization's involvement is essential to the proposal, you may also need to plan sufficient time for a similar hierarchy of reviews at that agency. Some government programs also require grant reviews at the state or regional level, particularly if tax revenues from the state or a regional allocation from a federal budget are involved. And some corporations and foundations have geographic committees that must first review and comment on proposals before they can be sent to the home office.

SUBMISSION

The following checklist will help you sort out the information you need in order to submit your proposal. Most of the answers to these questions are available from the funder's Web site, program announcement, or guidelines. When in doubt, contact the program officer. Advice from others who have received grants from this funder can be helpful, but you should always verify this information for yourself. Regulations and processes can change quickly.

Checklist 13-1. Questions to Answer Prior to Submitting Your Proposal

❑ **Will the funding source accept my proposal electronically or must it be sent as hard copy through the mail?** Many corporations and an increasing number of private foundations will only accept proposals on-line. State and federal government sources have announced plans to shift to this approach in the near future and several have already done so.

It can take weeks to get the proper permissions and identification numbers so that you can file electronically. Start early. Find out if the grantmaker wants a follow-up, faxed or mailed hard copy or whether that is prohibited. Most funding sources provide that kind of guidance on their Web site.

❑ **How many copies of the proposal should I submit?** Government sources tend to ask for more copies than private foundations and corporations. Be sure you comply with any requirements about how many of the copies need to carry original ink signatures from your agency's administrators. Have them use a color of ink that copies well.

❑ **What type of cover letter should accompany the proposal?**

For government sources, the letter typically says that the application for the particular program is being officially submitted on behalf of the applicant organization. The letter can also briefly summarize

---

the purpose of the project, show how it relates to the interests of the funding source, and emphasize how important the proposal is to the applicant agency's clientele. Never rely solely on a transmittal letter to make an important point that is not repeated in the body of the proposal.

For private funding sources, the content of the letter and the position of the signer(s) are much more important. Typically, foundations and corporations like to see letters signed by the chair of a nonprofit's governing board in addition to the chief executive.

The letter of transmittal can also be used to underscore points essential to your project. For example, you can:

- Emphasize the importance of your project to solving a problem.

- Include a sentence reiterating the project's tie to the interests of the funder.

- Restate the priority of the project to your agency.

- Underscore your familiarity to the funder by thanking them for past support.

- If relevant, mention that this proposal is for only a portion of the project's budget.

❑ **How should I send the proposal?** Many government sources will not accept proposals addressed to a specific individual when a receipt of delivery is requested. Some private foundations require that proposals go to a box office rather than a street address, thus limiting the type of delivery that can be used. Other foundations and corporations require that you send the proposal by registered mail with return receipt, thus reducing calls to check that the proposal has arrived. If this information is not provided in their guidelines, call and ask.

❑ **How long before I can expect acknowledgement of receipt?** Most government sources send out notification that they have received your application and give you a file number to use in all future correspondence. This typically arrives 30–60 days after you've put the proposal in the mail. The same practice tends to be followed by large private foundations and corporations that accept only hard-copy proposals.

Funders that accept electronic submissions typically notify you of receipt via e-mail. But since some receive hundreds to thousands of applications each week, do give them a few weeks before sending a query to check on status. The Foundation Center says that, on average, you should receive acknowledgement within four to six weeks (1). After that, call the program officer to check.

❑ **Should I solicit letters of endorsement from prestigious individuals or have someone on my board call someone on the funding source's board?** The culture of each foundation, corporation, and government organization is different. Some are really irritated if such contacts are made, while others just consider it part of the game.

This is a very important decision, and you should know in advance whether such testimonials will help or hinder your application. Some funders directly state their views on their Web site or in their guidelines. Seek advice from program officers or others who have received support from this source.

One experienced researcher recommends the following: In a prominent place in the application (or transmittal letter), list the names, affiliations, and contact information for "others who can provide a perspective on this application." This allows you to diplomatically "drop names" and make the point that individuals of influence and reputation are willing to stand behind you. But it leaves it up to the program officer whether to solicit that input. Never include the name of someone unless you have checked with them in advance about this proposal.

REVIEW BY THE FUNDER

Internet Resources

The Internet has helped make review processes much more transparent. Many Web sites provide a step-by-step description as well as details on the criteria used to judge applications. Some helpful resources are:

Proposal Writing Short Course, What happens next? The Foundation Center. http://fdncenter.org/learn/shortcourse/prop2.html

Proposal Writing: The Business of Science, The NIH System of Review, Wendy Sanders. http://www.whitaker.org/sanders.html

Peer Review, *The Art of Grantsmanship,* Jacob Kraicer.
  http://www.med.uwo.ca/physpharm/courses/
  survivalwebv3/grantsmanship/content.htm

OER: Peer Review Policy and Issues.
  http://grants1.nih.gov/grants/peer

NSF Proposal Processing and Review.
  http://www.nsf.gov/pubs/2003/nsf032/start.
  htm

Steps in the Review Process

While the processes of corporations, foundations, and government agencies vary, there are some common elements. The steps below are typical of most funding sources.

Step 1. Proposal Screened

Most are given an initial screening. This is often done by administrative staff with a checklist to see if the proposal meets the basic specifications and purpose of the program and/or funding source to which it was submitted. This person also checks the mechanics: Did the application make the deadline? Is the applicant eligible? Does the applicant match any geographic requirements?

Mary Hall found, as a result of interviews with over 100 corporate foundation and government program officers, that, even given these minimal requirements, as many as 60 percent of the applications they receive are immediately rejected because they do not match their guidelines. (2) The initial turndown rate for government funders is less because many prefer to have the rejection documented somewhere later in the review process. This preliminary step usually takes 30–45 days to occur. At its conclusion, the applicant is usually sent a notification that the proposal has been rejected or that it has been received and a processing number assigned. The applicant is then expected to refer to that number in any subsequent communications about the proposal.

Step 2. Additional Reviews

Proposals that are worthy of further consideration get additional reviews. Some common review modes are:

- **An internal review by the programmatic staff** of the funding agency or others in their organization.

- **A written and/or oral review by a group of outside experts,** an advisory body or the donor's representative in the community in which the applicant organization is based.

  This often involves the reviewers reading and scoring applications on their own and then meeting to discuss and give further consideration to those applications that have survived the initial triage process. Most governmental sources now furnish the names and affiliations of their reviewers, although they may not tell you on which specific panel each individual serves. They also typically tell you to which panel the proposal has been assigned, based on your proposal's title and abstract. This is another reason for careful title writing. If you are assigned to what you think is an inappropriate panel, you can call and ask for a change prior to further review.

- **An on-site visit.** These are becoming increasingly rare because of time and travel costs.

- **A telephone or e-mail interview** by staff of the funding source or their representative is more typical, particularly if a significant sum is at stake.

- **A fiscal and/or legal review.** Some federal agencies have a separate staff that does cost analyses to ensure that the proposed expenditures are allowable and reasonable.

- **An administrative review of the entire proposal or its abstract.** This can be done by top officials in the agency, members of the foundation's board, or a firm's contribution committee to see if they concur with staff and/or reviewer recommendations.

- **An informal check-in with their colleagues.** Many funders will do this to see if others have heard of or funded the organization. This happens frequently enough that you should assume it is going to occur. Grantseekers may not realize how often funders compare notes. This is another reason why it is so important to maintain good relations with prior supporters and never say that you've received a pledge towards a project if that has not actually occurred.

Different grantmakers require different amounts of time for review. Many can take the better part of a year, so check each funding source when doing your *initial* research and build that interval into your proposal development timeline.

Step 3. Criteria Applied

Specific, weighted criteria are used to judge the merits of the proposal. Government agencies usually describe these criteria and tell what weight will be given to each factor on their Web site or reference them in the program announcement. Many foundations and corporations are doing likewise.

If you have done your homework, you will know what the criteria for a specific grant program are and will have tailored the proposal to match it. Examples of proposal criteria from several sources are provided in Attachment 13-1.

Step 4. Decision Made

With both private and public funders, some proposals are so good that they immediately rise to the top of everyone's list and some are so bad that they're dropped to the bottom with little or no discussion. So reviewers and program officers spend the majority of their time on the applications in the middle. For those, mushy things like reputation and strength of leadership can be deciding factors. However, at some point a final decision is made as to who will be funded during this round of awards.

Applications typically finish the review process in one of these categories:

- **Approved.** The proposal is worthy of support as proposed.

- **Approved, but for less than requested.** If this happens, you should always scale back what you've promised this funder that you will accomplish.

- **Provisionally approved.** Some element of the project or its budget needs to be modified or clarified before a final decision will be made.

- **Disapproved.** Not fundable at this time.

- **Deferred.** Consideration postponed until the next round of review. This is often done if the grant program's budget fluctuates for some reason.

Some government sources use numerical scores. For example, Ries and Leukefeld (3) provide a guide to the system used by the National Institutes of Health, summarized below.

- **400–500.** These proposals often are not salvageable without major effort.

- **300–399.** These proposals generally have a number of problem areas identified. Usually, applicants resubmit proposals with scores in this range if not explicitly discouraged by the review panel.

- **149–299.** These proposals are candidates for resubmission. If possible, that should occur in the next review cycle, so the revised proposal will be reviewed by many of those who participated in the first review.

- **100–150.** These proposals generally require very few modifications, and those at the lower end of the range are funded.

Funders normally do some kind of final weighting to prioritize all of the proposals that have been recommended for approval or provisional approval.

- In government agencies, this may be the final review score each proposal received, perhaps modified slightly to ensure appropriate geographic distribution of recipients. A cutoff point on the rank order list is then established, based on the congressional appropriation for the program.

- In corporations and foundations, this final ranking may be more subjective. Here, the culture of the funder's organization can come into play. Those that are risk averse may give priority to well-known organizations or those they have funded in the past.

Most funders record why a proposal was approved or disapproved, and this is either automatically shared with the applicant or can be requested. Most government sources are required to provide at least a summary of reviewer comments. Foundations and corporations are not, so be polite if you request such feedback.

Step 5. Notification

Government Funders. All government agencies will eventually notify you whether the proposal has been approved, rejected, or must be discussed further. You may receive funding notification in several ways. With federal agencies, an announcement that you are to receive an award may first be sent to you by members of your congressional delegation. As a courtesy to those who approve their annual budgets, most federal agencies tell members of Congress of an award they plan to make at least 24 hours before the notice is sent to the applicant. This allows the politicians to give you the good news first. Or, you may simply get an official *Notice of Grant Award* (NGA).

Never start spending money just because you hear that your application is successful. Until you receive an official confirmation of expenditure authority from a government agency (a signed NGA) and have been notified how to request a draw on the award, any expenditure may be disallowed. Instructions for how to access the funds are typically described in a *Payee's Guide* that arrives close to the award date. This document contains information and instructions to follow so that you can request funds through the Federal Grant Administration and Payment System.

And remember, the principal investigator or project director is not the official award recipient. While that person may be the one receiving the notification, the application is submitted and the award received on behalf of the *organization*. So the payee on the check must first deposit the funds, and then those monies must be spent according to the policies and procedures of the applicant organization. It is here that your earlier consultations with the internal legal staff and business office of your organization will pay off. If they are familiar with the project, steps like getting signatures on contracts and setting up accounts are done quickly. But if you have not involved them previously, your

project start may be delayed for months while internal issues get resolved.

Private Funders. With private foundations and corporations, you may or may not receive formal notification of the outcome of your application, especially if the answer is "No." Smaller private donors who do not have professional staffs often do not bother to communicate with those they do not intend to support. If you have not received word after several months, call and check.

Foundations and corporations that have approved a grant normally send a letter pledging a certain sum towards the project or organization and indicating that the actual check will be furnished at some later date, or according to some type of payment schedule, or after the applicant has met certain *contingencies* (such as raising the remainder of the money needed for the project or furnishing further information). All corporations and foundations will ask you either to sign a form or send them a letter specifying that you agree to use their money in a certain way and promising it will not be spent on the types of activities that may be prohibited by law (such as partisan lobbying). This agreement may need to be furnished before a check is sent or, in some cases, you are asked to furnish it within 30 days of receiving the check. Be certain to furnish the requested form or letter and keep a copy for your own files. Larger grantmakers now keep automated records of who has and has not responded, and your organization may be prohibited from receiving additional awards until the form or letter is received.

NEGOTIATIONS

You may be asked to negotiate further before receiving a final award announcement and/or check. These negotiations are typically one of three kinds:

1. **Fiscal.** In an effort to spread their money further, many programs will offer to give you less than you originally requested. **Never agree to this without doing a commensurate scaling down of the scope of your project.**

2. **Substantive.** Some program officers will ask that you make significant changes in what you

propose to do or how you plan to do it. Listen carefully, because highly experienced grant-makers can sometimes help you avoid major problems by adjusting your plans at the outset of the project. But sometimes these requested changes are capricious or based on the grant-maker's inexperience. **Do not agree to changes that will so significantly alter your project that it is no longer of interest or worth to you.**

In some government programs, if there is a significant change to a proposal, a program officer may contact the prospective grantee to make a *funding offer* before issuing the grant award. The applicant can either accept or reject the changes and the funding offer. These offers are usually subject to further negotiation.

3. **Legal.** Most often, this involves executing some type of written agreement that will constrain how you are to use the funds and establish re-porting or expenditure requirements. Founda-tions and corporations tend to call these docu-ments *letters of agreement* or *memorandums of understanding.* In some federal agencies, this negotiation is called a *post-award performance conference.* This initial one-time discussion takes place shortly after an award date. Its purpose is to establish a mutual understanding of the specific outcomes that are expected and to establish measures for assessing the project's progress and results. It also clarifies how moni-toring and communication will take place.

In many federal programs, a grantee indicates acceptance of the terms of an award by requesting funds from the grant payment system. These terms will have been spelled out in the *Notice of Grant Award.* If you cannot accept those terms, the grant will be voided. Typically, they are not subject to appeal.

All funding sources have rules about how much variation you are permitted in spending the money differently than specified in the original budget. Be certain that during the negotiation phase you are clear about those rules. If not, expenditures that exceed permissible variations may be disallowed later. This can be financially, and sometimes le-gally, disastrous.

DISAPPROVAL

Government and private funders tend to reject applications for one or more of the following reasons:

- The project simply doesn't match the priorities or guidelines of the funding source.

- The need for or importance of the project wasn't substantiated.

- The proposed methods appeared unsound or unfeasible.

- The competence of the applicant and/or the organization was questionable.

- The budget was either unclear or inappropriate.

- The proposal was poorly written. Remember, a well-written proposal cannot hide basic flaws in concept or planning, but a poorly written one can result in a good project being disap-proved.

If your proposal is rejected, contact the funder to ascertain the reasons. Explain that you want to improve your next application or find out if you should reapply. **Do not use this opportunity to argue with the decision.**

RESUBMISSION

The only people who never get rejected are those who don't submit proposals. In fact, some indi-viduals and organizations with the best ideas get turned down the most often because they are "ahead of the curve" in their thinking. Few per-sons are fortunate enough to receive a significant grant in any highly competitive field on their very first try. So, give yourself a day to wallow in grief and self-pity, then get busy deciding how your ap-plication can be made stronger and whether you should resubmit it to the same source or look for other potential funders.

Always secure copies of review comments, if available, and study them carefully. Reviewers are your friends, even if you fail. They tell you how your proposal didn't work. Only then can you judge whether the idea is still worth pursuing or whether you might as well move on to another project.

RENEWAL

A similar challenge faces the principal investigator or project director whose proposal is successful, particularly if support is secured for only one year at a time. **Always ask in advance if the funding source would entertain a request for multiple-year support. If they do, ask for it.** It takes just as much effort to write a request for a one-year $50,000 proposal as it does for a three-year $150,000 proposal.

More commonly, however, you are faced with submitting a request for renewal even before the first year of the funded project is even half over. Usually, this is done in accordance with well-established procedures of the funding source and, in most cases, will involve both a progress report on the project and the presentation of the next year's operation and budget. The refunding document is seldom as lengthy as the original application, but still requires careful thought. It also takes time, so it is important that you plan for this. Additionally, you will want to plan the project's evaluation so that data useful in this renewal application is produced early.

Typically, funders have separate pots of money for first-time and renewal awards. If budgets start to get tight, however, different funders will make different decisions about whether to give priority to renewals or new grants. So stay in touch with your funder(s) even after receiving your first award.

CONTINUITY

In many cases, funders will only commit to a one-year grant and will expect you to find other sources of support to continue a project. You should think through how to do this at the outset of the project, because normally, your plans for continuing the

project will be an essential piece of information requested in the original proposal. *Sustainability* has become a buzz word with both private and government funding sources. Your ability to demonstrate the potential longevity of the project is a key element in how competitive your proposals will be.

There are several words of wisdom to observe here:

- **Do not promise that a project will be supported in the future by your own organization's budget unless this commitment has actually been made by the appropriate administrators and is substantiated in your application in some definite way.** Public school districts, particularly, have a reputation for promising to use their own funds to continue innovations and, unfortunately, seldom do so. Most grantmakers know this and consider such undocumented promises in an application as evidence of either lack of candor or inexperience.

- **Realize that the principal staff on the currently funded project will need to be heavily involved in the development of applications for continued support even if the proposal document is being written by someone else.** Plan for their time accordingly. Consider the poor project director, 150 percent of whose time has already been promised and who must now repeat the entire process of determining appropriate funding sources, writing abstracts or letters of inquiry, and submitting additional applications.

- **If possible, include some resources in the budget of the first award that can help you secure funding for continuation.** This may involve such things as travel funds to visit other prospective grantmakers or appearances at professional events that can help you document the significance of your work in future applications.

- **Keep tuned to new needs or ideas produced in one project that can be explored in follow-up proposals.** Being able to show how a future project is building on a previous one will often enhance your chances with new funding sources. They like to be associated with success.

All these concerns may be rather overwhelming to the person who has just completed a first proposal and has vowed never to do another one (or at least not immediately). But writing proposals is akin to the well-known potato chip ad: It is difficult to stop at one. One mark of a good project is how it prompts exciting new ideas that are worthy of external support. Once you have realized that the proposal preparation process is similar from application to application, the second and third proposals really will go much more smoothly.

CHAPTER REFERENCES

1. *Proposal Writing Short Course,* The Foundation Center, http://fdncenter.org

2. Hall, Mary, results of interviews with over 100 corporate, foundation and government program officers during June–September, 2002.

3. Joanne Ries and Carl Leukefeld, *The Research Funding Guidebook: Getting It, Managing It & Renewing It,* (Thousand Oaks: Sage Publications, 1998) p. 9–11.

ATTACHMENT 13-1.

EXAMPLES OF REVIEW CRITERIA

Sonoma County Community Foundation

1. **Appropriateness.** How well does the project to be funded by this proposal meet SCCF's grant guidelines?

2. **Significance.** If the project does meet grant guidelines, how significant is the issue or opportunity and how meaningful will the project's outcome be?

   - Is the issue/opportunity one that is significant in our community?

   - Is evidence offered to substantiate the problem described?

   - If the project succeeds, will it make a meaningful contribution?

3. **Capacity.** How capable does this organization appear to be in carrying out the proposed project successfully?

   - Does the organization have a credible record of performance with the issue addressed by this proposal?

   - Does the applicant's staff have experience working with the issue/populations/services involved?

   - Does the applicant have sufficient staff to carry out the project?

   - Does the applicant have sufficient organizational stability to carry out the project?

   - Is the project's budget appropriate for level/types of activities proposed?

4. **Method.** Given the project's proposed outcomes, does the plan of action seem appropriate and will it be effective in achieving its goals?

   - Does the plan of action give you a clear enough picture of how the project will proceed?

   - Does the plan of action clearly relate to the stated problem/opportunity?

   - If this is a new program, is there a credible basis for the plan of action?

5. **Clarity.** Are the problem statement, plan of action, and proposed outcomes stated clearly so that you fully understand what is involved in the project? When you finish reading the proposal, are you confident you understand why the project matters and what will happen if it is funded?

For more information, see http://www.sonomacf.org/grants/grantlinks/grant_review.html

National Science Foundation

1. **What is the intellectual merit of the proposed activity?** How important is the proposed activity to advancing knowledge and understanding within its own field or across different fields? How well established is the proposer (individual or team) to conduct the project? To what extent does the proposed activity suggest and explore creative and original concepts? How well conceived and organized is the proposed activity? Is there sufficient access to resources?

2. **What are the broader impacts of the proposed activity?** How well does the activity advance discovery and understanding while promoting teaching, training, and learning? How well does the proposed activity broaden the participation of underrepresented groups (e.g. gender, ethnicity, disability, geographic, etc.)? To what extent will it enhance the infrastructure for research and education, such as facilities, instrumentation, networks, and partnerships? Will the results be disseminated broadly to enhance scientific and technological understand-

ing? What may be the benefits of the proposed activity to society?

For more information, see http://www.nsf.gov/pubs/1999/nsf99172/nsf99172.htm

National Institutes of Health

Unsolicited Research Grants and Other Applications

- **Significance:** Does this study address an important problem? If the aims of the application are achieved, how will scientific knowledge be advanced? What will be the effect of these studies on the concepts or methods that drive this field?

- **Approach:** Are the conceptual framework, design, methods, and analyses adequately developed, well-integrated, and appropriate to the aims of the project? Does the applicant acknowledge potential problem areas and consider alternative tactics?

- **Innovation:** Does the project employ novel concepts, approaches, or methods? Are the aims original and innovative? Does the project challenge existing paradigms or develop new methodologies or technologies?

- **Investigator:** Is the investigator appropriately trained and well suited to carry out this work? Is the work proposed appropriate to the expe-

rience level of the principal investigator and other researchers (if any)?

- **Environment:** Does the scientific environment in which the work will be done contribute to the probability of success? Do the proposed experiments take advantage of unique features of the scientific environment or employ useful collaborative arrangements? Is there evidence of institutional support?

While the review criteria are intended for use primarily with unsolicited research project applications to the extent reasonable, they will also form the basis of the review of solicited applications and non-research activities. In addition, in accordance with NIH policy, all applications will also be reviewed with respect to the following:

- The adequacy of plans to include both genders, minorities, and their subgroups as appropriate for the scientific goals of the research. Plans for the recruitment and retention of subjects will also be evaluated.

- The reasonableness of the proposed budget and duration in relation to the proposed research.

- The adequacy of the proposed protection for humans, animals, or the environment, to the extent they may be adversely affected by the project proposed in the application.

For more information, see http://www.whitaker.org/sanders.html.

Appendix A

Proposal Development Checklist

KEY POINTS FROM EACH CHAPTER

Chapter 1. Getting Started

Have you

❏ Decided what type of grant you are seeking?

❏ Identified basic information needed to

    Document your project's need?

    Identify similar past efforts?

    Search for likely sources of funds?

❏ Decided whether your proposal will likely be an unsolicited or a solicited application?

❏ Determined that you have enough time for proposal planning and writing?

Chapter 2. Assessing Your Capability

Have you

❏ Considered whether your idea to start a new organization is really valid—and whether external funders will likely agree?

❏ Determined whether an agency or program already exists where your idea can be implemented?

    If so, have you started discussions with them?

❏ Determined if your project idea is consistent with the mission of your agency or matches current priorities?

❏ Determined if your project idea is worthy of the resources needed for the proposal preparation and submission?

❏ Analyzed your personal ability to compete for external funds?

❏ Considered your professional reputation, prior experience, and ability to write effectively?

❏ Identified actions that may increase your likelihood of success (e.g., securing a more experienced project director, joining a consortium of applicants, or asking another organization to be the fiscal agent)?

❏ Made certain your organization is legally eligible to apply?

❏ Analyzed your organization's ability to compete for external funds?

○ Determined that it has a strategic plan and adequate governance?

○ Listed those things about your agency that will especially appeal to funding sources for this particular project?

○ Identified anything, such as your organization's past performance or reputation, that might hinder your submitting a successful proposal?

❑ Determined the kind and amount of help you will need from others in your organization to prepare the proposal and made certain this help will be available?

❑ Decided whether you currently have access to the right staff for this project or can get qualified people in the necessary time?

❑ Identified who else is doing similar work and whether you can articulate what makes your project distinctive, collaborative, useful?

❑ Determined the kind and amount of help you will need for individuals or agencies outside of your organization and made certain this will be available?

❑ Analyzed the environment in which your project might be implemented, including any political support or opposition?

❑ Reviewed the potential fiscal impact of the project on your organization and determined if you should go forward?

❑ Determined if your organization has the infrastructure needed to effectively compete for and administer external funds if received?

If not, have you considered whether these could be provided by others and started negotiations?

Chapter 3. Developing the Idea

Have you

❑ Developed a clear-cut statement of the problem or need that your idea is trying to address?

❑ Determined what the experience of others has been with similar project ideas?

❑ Gained an understanding of the previous literature and research addressing this same problem or idea?

❑ Made sure the funding will meet a need in the community not just a need of your organization?

❑ Assessed the priority of this idea given other problems and needs that your organization should address?

❑ Determined whether the idea is related to your organization's goals and mission?

❑ Discussed the idea with colleagues and administrators in your organization to see if they are willing to provide support for further planning and development of a proposal?

❑ Ensured that your organization has the capability and resources to accomplish this?

❑ Determined what makes your idea compelling, necessary, timely, significant?

❑ Identified the population that will benefit most from implementation of your idea and documented the extent of their need?

❑ Determined that this approach will affect a significant enough number to merit the required resources?

❑ Discussed the idea with potential participants or secured the opinions of the population to be served?

❑ Gathered relevant statistical data—both locally and nationally—to document the need and its importance?

❑ Considered alternative approaches and means of implementing your project and analyzed the cost-benefit and potential impact of each?

❑ Determined that yours is the most effective approach among all the options?

❑ Identified the constraints or difficulties that should be anticipated in implementing the idea?

❑ Met with external stakeholders and collaborators to see if they are interested in participating in the project or are supportive of its goals?

❑ Determined how this approach could be replicated and sustained?

Chapter 4. Selecting the Funding Source

Have you

❑ Considered the full gamut of types of funding sources that might be interested in your idea—private foundations, state agencies, federal agencies, private businesses, and professional associations?

❑ Researched appropriate information sources to develop a preliminary list of possible sources of support?

❑ Gathered the necessary information to identify those sources most worthy of immediate attention?

❑ Identified the person with whom to communicate for each source?

❑ Made an initial inquiry to verify which of these sources might be most interested in your idea?

❑ Asked these sources to provide any comments or suggestions on ways to improve your project idea?

❑ Contacted the most likely prospects to gather all information necessary to guide proposal preparation?

    ○ Determined deadlines, writing instructions, forms, regulations, guidelines, priorities, any legal or fiscal requirements?

❑ Identified the criteria and process used for proposal review and selection?

❑ Talked to others familiar with the funding sources and reviewed previously approved proposals to gather informal information on things such as language preference, proposal style, etc.?

❑ Assessed the preferences, interests, and priorities of the funding sources and the capabilities of your organization and selected the most appropriate source(s) for the proposal?

❑ Tailored the proposal to the characteristics of the type of funder?

❑ Articulated why your project fits the guidelines of this particular funder?

❑ Cultivated a relationship prior to submission?

❑ Completed any preliminary steps necessary to proceed such as a letter of inquiry?

Chapter 5. Writing the Proposal

A. Planning

Have you

❑ Identified the specific information the funding source expects you to provide?

❑ Developed an outline of your proposal showing how the outcomes, need statement, methods,

evaluation/dissemination/qualifications, and budget all logically connect with each other?

❑ Collected all of the other information necessary for writing the proposal?

❑ Created the necessary proposal development team or identified others who need to provide certain types of information during development?

    ○ Secured their participation?

❑ Arranged for the necessary support systems for the proposal's development?

❑ Established a careful timeline for the writing, internal review, submission, and funding source review of the proposal, so that there is enough time to complete all the necessary steps?

❑ Identified all individuals and groups that must review and approve the proposal prior to submission?

    ○ Studied each of their requirements and processes?

❑ Identified what compliance statements must accompany the proposal?

    ○ Made certain these will be available when needed?

❑ Arranged for one or more colleagues to read the proposal after it is written to check for typographical errors, clarity, effectiveness of communication, and compliance with informational requirements of the funding source.

B. General Criteria

Does the proposal

❑ quickly inform the reader what you want to do?

❑ Immediately grab the reader, conveying that this idea is really important, needed, effective, and feasible?

❑ Establish clearly that you are the best choice (or at least, highly qualified) to do this project?

❑ Establish early in the proposal that your project matches the funding source's interests?

❑ Show how it meets all review criteria?

❑ Provide all the information requested by the funding source, in the required format?

❑ Appear professional, including correct spelling, grammar, and style?

❑ Read easily?

❑ Convey the key points clearly?

❑ Guide the reader to the most significant parts of the proposal?

❑ Flow logically from section to section?

❑ Include enough detail, but not exceed page limits?

❑ Identify constraints or problems associated with the idea or its implementation and indicate how these will be handled?

❑ Include appropriate citations to prior work and related literature?

Chapter 6. Title Page, Abstract, and Accompanying Forms

Have you

❑ Secured all the necessary assurances of compliance and other signatures and requirements for the cover sheet or title page?

❑ Crafted an abstract that summarizes the entire proposal succinctly and compellingly?

❑ Secured and included all the required or essential accompanying forms?

Chapter 7. The Purpose Statement

Does the purpose statement

❑ Include a clear description of the purpose, objectives, hypotheses or research questions, aims and/or outcomes?

❑ Make the purpose compelling?

❑ Show that the project is significant?

❑ Tell the funding source how problems it cares about will improve as a result of the award ("so what" question)?

❑ Use language that emphasizes consistency with the funding source's guidelines?

❑ Include outcomes that are clearly achievable and feasible?

❑ Avoid over-promising results?

❑ Display the goals/objectives/outcomes appropriately and with logic?

○ Guide the reader's attention to the most important first?

○ Show how they relate to each other?

○ Include a program logic model if required by the funding source?

❑ Match the type of purpose statement to the nature of the project (e.g., include process or product objectives only if those are a significant part of the project's results?)

❑ For research projects, demonstrate that the project's outcomes are conceptually sound and rest on sufficient evidence?

❑ Include sufficient information to justify the budget?

Chapter 8. The Statement of Need

Does the statement of need

❑ Clearly convey the need for the project early in the narrative?

❑ Demonstrate a precise understanding of the problem or need that the project is attempting to address?

❑ Obviously relate to the purposes of the project?

❑ Indicate the relationship of the project to a larger set of problems and explain why its particular focus has been chosen?

❑ Establish the importance and significance of the problem/need—especially to a national audience?

❑ Signify the potential generalizability and contribution of the project to the field?

❑ Indicate why the issue is timely or more urgent than others?

❑ Provide effective coverage of related research and demonstrate how the project will build on these earlier studies?

❑ Show how your proposed approach is distinct from similar efforts?

Chapter 9. The Procedures

Does the proposal

❑ Include procedures for every objective?

❑ (For research) Include procedures for every hypothesis or research question?

❑ Justify that the approach and methodology are suitable to the stated objectives or purpose?

❑ Provide sufficient detail on the procedures so that their adequacy can be evaluated?

❑ Demonstrate that the procedures are feasible and likely to succeed?

❑ Explain why the procedures are suitable for the time and resources requested?

❑ Provide a clear description and justification of the theoretical basis of the methodology?

❑ Describe the procedures clearly so that the reviewer easily understands what will take place during the project period?

❑ Make appropriate use of tables, diagrams, and other visual displays and summaries?

❑ Include information that addresses all the funder's questions about the approach?

❑ Present the procedures in a format so that they follow logically from section to section?

❑ Demonstrate why the procedures are technically sound?

❑ Clearly describe the project's population and how it will be selected?

❑ Include a description of any prior accomplishments of the applicant that bear specifically on the project?

❑ Describe any data to be gathered, including instruments to be used, and the timetable and procedures for collection, analysis, reporting, and utilization?

❑ Direct the reader to a summary of the intended results, benefits, or anticipated products of the project?

❑ Demonstrate that the procedures are imaginative?

❑ Describe how the project will make certain that its results are generalizable and usable?

❑ Address how any potentially contaminating factors will be identified and controlled?

❑ Include a discussion of how unanticipated events and problems will be addressed?

❑ Make clear the intended role of the funder in monitoring implementation of the procedures?

○ Indicate the type and amount of information to be provided to the funder to assist with its monitoring?

Chapter 10. Evaluation

Does the proposal

❑ Clearly tell how you will judge whether the project is a success?

❑ Make explicit the purpose of the evaluation.

❑ Identify the audiences to receive the evaluation results?

❑ Demonstrate that the scope of the evaluation is appropriate to the project?

❑ Describe standards that will be used in judging the results of the evaluation?

○ Set performance targets, if appropriate?

❑ Demonstrate that the evaluation plan is appropriate to the project and will produce information needed to answer key questions?

❑ Provide a model for the evaluation and justify its technical and theoretical soundness?

❑ Describe what information will be needed to complete the evaluation, the sources for this information and the instruments that will be used for its collection?

○ Show how these are appropriate and technically sound?

❑ Clearly state what information will be provided to the funding source, when, and for what purposes?

❑ Indicate what reports will be produced, when, for whom and to guide what types of decisions?

❑ Specify who will play what roles in doing the evaluation?

❑ Provide other justification as needed for evaluation-related costs in the budget?

Chapter 11. Qualifications and Personnel

Have you

- ❑ Described the role, responsibilities, or assignment of each member of the project staff?

- ❑ Identified the roles and responsibilities of consultants?

- ❑ Shown how the project staff and major consultants complement and balance each other and provide the breadth of experience and skills necessary for the project?

- ❑ Provided names and qualifications of all key project staff and given sufficient detail on their experience and training to justify their capabilities?

- ❑ Described how any staff and/or consultants not yet identified will be recruited and the criteria for their selection?

- ❑ Indicated how state and federal laws governing affirmative action and non-discrimination in personnel selection will be implemented?

- ❑ Described the organizational and management structure of the project to show that you have the infrastructure necessary to succeed?

- ❑ Demonstrated that you have a strong, competent, engaged board?

- ❑ Defined any intended role of advisory boards?

- ❑ Included evidence that consultants and external organizations essential to the project's success have agreed to participate?

- ❑ Demonstrated appropriate community support?

- ❑ Clearly indicated which staff will be responsible for what set of procedures and other project activities?

- ❑ Clearly identified the facilities and major equipment needed for the project?

Chapter 12. The Budget

Does the budget section

- ❑ Show that the applicant is aware of all regulations of either the local organization or the funding source governing the project's budget development and administration?

- ❑ Include sufficient resources to carry out the project's procedures and achieve its objectives?

- ❑ Provide some way to refer the reader back to that portion of the proposal's narrative which justifies major budget categories?

- ❑ Use the format desired by the funder, including all pertinent support documents?

- ❑ Provide sufficient detail so that the reviewer can understand how various items were computed?

- ❑ Project reasonable sources of anticipated income?

- ❑ Separate direct costs from indirect costs and describe what is covered in the latter, if appropriate?

- ❑ Include sufficient flexibility to cover unanticipated events?

- ❑ Organize expenses so that the general use of dollars can be compared to phases of the project?

- ❑ Specify the type and amount of any matching funds or cost-sharing?

- ❑ Include any attachments or special appendices to justify unusual requests (e.g., estimates from vendors)?

- ❑ Show who else is supporting the proposed work and to what extent?

- ❑ Indicate how the project will be continued in the future?

Chapter 13. Review, Submission, Notification, and Renewal

Have you

- ❑ Read the final proposal carefully to check for misspellings, poor grammar or any other problems that might hinder its overall presentation?

- ❑ Verified that it clearly provides all the information requested by the funding source and in the required format?

- ❑ Checked that the proposal explicitly addresses the review criteria of the funding source?

- ❑ Ensured that the proposal has an "external focus" and makes a compelling case for why it is essential to issues of concern to the funding source?

- ❑ Reviewed your proposal against the reasons why proposals fail and made certain you've avoided the same mistakes?

- ❑ Ensured that the budget is adequate?

❑ Ensured that the indirect cost and fringe benefit rates used are correct?

❑ Ensured that all the numbers total correctly?

❑ Justified the amounts in the narrative?

❑ Determined if the submission deadline is a mailing deadline or a receipt deadline?

❑ Arranged for internal reviews by cooperating agencies, if necessary?

❑ Made preliminary contacts with everyone who must review and approve the proposal prior to its submission?

  ○ Allowed the time necessary to complete these steps?

  ○ Informed all of these sources about the deadline that mustn't be missed?

❑ Obtained the necessary original signatures on the correct number of title pages?

❑ Made the necessary number of copies of the proposal?

❑ Secured an appropriate letter of transmittal?

❑ Included letters of support if appropriate?

❑ Identified whether to submit the proposal electronically or by mail?

  ○ If electronically, verified if the funding source also wants a "hard copy?"

  ○ If by mail, determined how it should be sent—receipt requested or registered?

❑ Determined how and when you will be notified of the proposal's receipt?

❑ Determined how and when you will be notified of the final decision?

❑ Made arrangements to obtain copies of the reviewers' comments?

❑ Discussed with more experienced persons how to approach negotiation?

❑ Arranged to have your organization's administrator or business officer present during negotiations?

❑ Identified ways in which the budget might be cut and the project modified if necessary?

❑ Determined, if possible, what procedures the funding source will follow for negotiations?

  ○ Allocated sufficient time in case this process occurs?

❑ Requested government funding sources to give you, in writing, in advance, the major items that they expect to negotiate?

❑ Determined when you will have to start efforts to get your proposal refunded?

❑ Identified what information will be required in the continuation or renewal request?

  ○ Initiated steps to see that this information is collected?

❑ Planned a timeline for and allocated personnel to develop the renewal request?

❑ Begun preliminary discussion and contacts with other possible funders and developed a long-range plan for continued financing of the project activities and its possible spin-off ideas.

Appendix B.

Resources for Teachers

SYLLABUS FOR A NINE-SESSION COURSE

SESSION 1

Content

- Types of funding sources.

- Characteristics of each type and distinctions among them.

- How to determine most appropriate funding sources for project.

Classroom Exercises

- Form small groups and ask each to role-play a particular type of funder (government, corporate, family foundation, trade union, etc.). See how the motivations, the questions they ask, and the answers that would appeal to each might differ).

- Form small groups and ask each to brainstorm what type of funder might be appropriate for sample projects (disease prevention research versus social service versus environmental conservation versus art exhibit).

Assignments

- Read Chapter 4, except how to research potential funders.

- Envision a match between a potential project and a type of funder, using some of the examples in Chapter 4, Finding Common Ground, as inspiration.

SESSION 2

Content

- Ask for feedback, questions stemming from Session 1 assignments.

- Organizational background: importance of clearly defined mission, goals, objectives, major activities, constituency served, accomplishments, compliance with funder regulations.

- Grantseeking process: order of steps (as in Attachment I-1 on page xi), players involved in each step, timeframe.

- Where and how to research potential funders.

Classroom Exercises

- Ask what they would want to know about an applicant organization and what would make one look more appealing than its competitors (see Suggested Assignments, Chapter 4, item 3 on page 171).

- Ask who should be included in each stage of the planning process (internal and external).

- Offer time in class for each student to name which staff members and which cooperating agencies or organizations should be included.

Assignments

- Read Chapter 1.

- Read Chapter 4, how to research potential funders.

- Research and identify two suitable funders for a proposal idea.

SESSION 3

Content

- Ask for feedback and questions stemming from Session 2 assignments.

- Assessing need: how to find statistics to corroborate need, how to find out who else has done or is doing similar work, what the literature and research have found.

- Qualifications: how this work is distinct from similar work being done or how it complements or furthers others' work, why this organization is uniquely suited to carry out this work. Is there infrastructure in place? Is there strong leadership among board and staff? Are necessary partnerships already built?

- Proving that the proposal meets an external rather than internal need.

Classroom Exercises

- Ask what types of organizations, agencies, or governmental entities might have statistics to corroborate need.

- Ask from whom an applicant could glean input if there are no statistics available about your topic.

- Ask how a group could determine who else is doing similar work.

- Ask what types of things could distinguish them from others.

- Ask what they would want in an organization, if they were to fund them with their own money.

Assignments

- Read Chapters 2, 3, and 11.

- Draft a section on organizational background.

- Draft a one-paragraph statement of need.

SESSION 4

Content

- Review of writing assignments.

- Statement of need.

- Purpose and procedures.

- Outputs, outcomes, objectives.

- Logic model.

Classroom Exercises

- Review writing assignments in small groups and report out.

- Using two organizations from the class, have students work through differences between outputs and outcomes.

- Using one of the groups in the class or a made-up project, have students discuss possible outputs/outcomes.

- Give students silent time to come up with their own outputs and outcomes, then share with the class and work through hard ones.

Assignments

- Read Chapters 7 and 8.

- Revise original draft of statement of need. This version should be more externally focused and more polished.

- Devise a logic model format proposal.

SESSION 5

Content

- Review of statements of need and logic model.

- Abstracts and executive summaries.

- Letters of inquiry.

- Tailoring letters to different sources.

Classroom Exercises

- Review statements of need in small groups and report out.

- Review logic model exercise and report out.

- Practice writing opening paragraphs of letters of inquiry or abstracts to bring out common issues; share in small groups or have selected students read theirs aloud for group critique.

Assignments

- Read Chapter 6.

- Review "letter of inquiry" section at end of Chapter 4.

- Draft a two-paragraph executive summary.

- Draft a letter of inquiry to a government or foundation funder.

- Draft a letter of inquiry to a corporate funder.

SESSION 6

Content

- Review of assigned drafts.

- Evaluation: deciding what to measure and how.

- Putting together pieces into a whole proposal.

Class Exercises

- Review assigned drafts in small groups and report out lessons learned.

- Brainstorm ideas for cultivating relationships with funders prior to submission, once letter of inquiry is approved.

- Have small groups discuss what stakeholders could be involved in evaluation, what methods are available, and/or how they could determine the most important thing to evaluate.

Assignments

- Read Chapters 5, 9, and 10.

- Draft a whole proposal—including organization background, need, approach, procedures, qualifications, and evaluation—and bring enough copies to next class to share in small group review.

SESSION 7

Content

- Review of draft grants.

- Discussion of patterns, strengths, and challenges in draft proposals.

- Lessons from experienced grantseekers.

Class Exercises

- Have a panel of seasoned grantseekers participate in the group review of draft grants (one grantwriter per group).

- Have the panel discuss what patterns, strengths, and challenges they saw in the draft proposals.

- Have panel share lessons they've learned from experience.

Assignments

- Fine-tune proposals using feedback from class (Session 9 panelists will read them ahead of time).

- Read Chapter 12.

SESSION 8

Content

- Budgets: elements, how to determine costs, stories budgets tell, different formats.

- Future funding.

- Other support documents.

Classroom Exercises

- Have small groups review examples of real budgets to see what they can ascertain about a group simply from the numbers.

Assignments

- Read Chapter 13 and Appendix A, Proposal Development Checklist.

- Draft one-year project budget with income and expense items.

SESSION 9

Content

- Panel review draft proposals.

- What to do in the event of rejection.

- What to do once you get funded: reporting, stewardship, etc.

- Questions.

Classroom Exercises

- Have panel of funders review four or five draft proposals in front of the students as if they were in a determination meeting. If possible, choose one from government, one from a corporation, one from a private foundation and one from a family foundation, service club, professional association, or employee giving group, so students can see distinctions.

- Discuss what to do in the event of rejection.

- Discuss what to do once you get funded: reporting, stewardship, etc.

- Answer any remaining questions.

SYLLABUS FOR ONE-DAY WORKSHOP

Morning—Part I

- Go over types of sources and the distinctions among them, asking students to help name broad categories (e.g., government) and specific types (e.g., Rotary).

- Break into groups and role-play different types of funders to see how motivations, questions, and answers might vary.

- Bring guidelines from government, corporate, and foundation funders and review them to see which groups in the class might fit them best. Stress the importance of finding the best match of project and funder goals.

Morning—Part II

List elements of standard applications and discuss lengths and formats, then cover three most important areas listed below.

Need

Go over importance of need, then ask students:

- How they could determine and corroborate need.

- Where they could look for statistics.

- From whom they could glean information if no research had been done.

- How they could determine who else is doing similar work.

- How they could distinguish their organization or work from others.

Purpose

Tell them how to describe their proposed solution, then using groups in the class, help distinguish between outputs and outcomes.

Evaluation

Help them understand:

- Why grantseekers should conduct an evaluation.

- What needs to be evaluated.

- Who should be involved.

- How an evaluation can be conducted.

Afternoon—Part I

- Show how to write an abstract or letter of inquiry.

- Let them practice, then have small groups critique what they wrote.

Afternoon—Part II

- Go over elements of budgets. Have pairs of students come up with revenue and expenses categories and show how they are usually formatted.

- Have groups study sample budgets to see what they can tell from the numbers.

- Describe the entire proposal process, the timeframe, and the people involved in each stage.

- List common challenges and how to address them:

  - How much money to request.

  - How to respond if offered a lesser amount.

  - How to answer the question about future funding.

  - How to get others in the organization to cooperate in the planning process.

- Answer final questions from participants.

SUGGESTED ASSIGNMENTS FOR EACH CHAPTER

The following are optional assignments instructors can use to enhance classroom instruction and textbook review.

Chapter 1: Getting Started

1. In small groups, have students discuss trends that are affecting proposal writing, as mentioned in the book's introduction. Ask them to select the most important and report to class, with a rationale for their choice.

2. Ask students to list the three reasons why it matters whether a proposal is *solicited* or *unsolicited*.

3. Assign students to identify and bring to class a Request for Proposals (RFP) and a Program Announcement that they have found through the Internet. Examine these and discuss how they differ.

4. Ask students to define the difference between a *grant* and a *contract*.

5. Have students build a profile of the characteristics of a project for which they will be writing a proposal. Discuss how the different characteristics will affect the search for funders and the content of a proposal. Discuss whether each project is likely to need a *solicited* or *unsolicited* application and whether it will likely result in a *grant* or a *contract*.

Chapter 2: Assessing Your Capability

1. Choose an RFP through the Internet (see Chapter 4 for details). Assign students (or teams of students) a short paper assessing whether their employer should apply for this RFP using the criteria of eligibility, interest, feasibility, flexibility, capability, and competitiveness. If they are not currently employed, have them do the assessment from the perspective of the institution, organization, or agency that is offering this course.

2. Ask students to briefly describe a project of interest to them. Have small groups select one and assess the capability of the proposing individual to seek funds for that project. Each group should develop a short list of strengths and weaknesses. Debrief each group's conclusions.

3. Give students the opportunity to assess their capability by focusing on something personal, such as buying a car, getting married, or getting a new job. Have them use the criteria in Chapter 2 to do the assessment and then report their insights to the class.

Chapter 3: Developing the Idea

1. Have students locate statistics from government sources that prove the need they intend to address.

2. Have students research who else is working on the issue locally.

3. Name three ways of addressing the need, then see what information students can find on those approaches that might indicate which method would be most appropriate.

4. List which internal stakeholders and which external stakeholders should be included in their own or a sample proposal idea.

Chapter 4: Selecting the Funding Source

1. Have students come up with four different types of funders who might support their proposal and share how they would justify the match.

2. Compare the guidelines of four different funders to see how responses to them might differ.

3. Assign students to small groups, each assuming the role of a different type of funder (government, private foundation, corporation, employee giving group, professional association, etc.). Have each group compile a list of questions they would ask applicants and decide what answers would appeal most to that type of funder. Reconvene groups and share their

responses to see distinctions among types of sources.

4. Prepare a letter of inquiry for the same proposal idea to (1) a government funder, (2) a staffed private foundation, and (3) a corporate giving officer.

Chapter 5: Writing the Proposal

1. Ask students to identify an Internet site that has useful information on proposal writing and to give a short report in class describing the site and its contents. Prepare a short summary of all of the identified sites and distribute to the class.

2. Have teams of students identify proposal requirements on a Web site for a private foundation and a site for a government agency. Have them prepare a 1–2 page paper discussing how a proposal would need to differ for the foundation versus the government program. Discuss their reports in class.

Chapter 6: Title Page, Abstract, and Accompanying Forms

1. Find an RFP that requires a cover sheet or use a sample from Chapter 6, and assign students to gather all the necessary information.

2. Assign students to draft a two-paragraph abstract or executive summary. Have them review one another's writing in small groups, emphasizing the need for clarity among those unfamiliar with your work.

3. Hand out a sample audited financial statement or an IRS Form 990 from an organization and have the students analyze it to see how much a reviewer can tell about an applicant from one.

4. Have students bring board of directors member lists to class to see how different each one looks.

Chapter 7: The Purpose Statement

1. Have students write a goal, objective, output, and outcome statement for a project in which they are interested. Critique these in small groups. Ask the students to debrief the exercise. As writing good purpose statements is so essential to successful proposals, you may wish to have students repeat this assignment at least twice.

2. Form students into small groups and tell them to produce a goal, objectives, outputs, and outcomes for a potential project. Have these critiqued in class by a panel of representatives of local funding sources or other individuals with experience in proposal writing. This works best if those on the panel have the opportunity to study the student products prior to the discussion.

3. Give students a sheet with several different purpose statements on it. In teams, have them decide which is a goal, objective, outcome, or output. Debrief each team's results.

Chapter 8: The Statement of Need

1. Offer the students two sample issues that need to be addressed in your community and have them write two draft statements of need. Have them review these in small groups to see how they differed from or paralleled one another's. Ask them to watch for internal versus external needs.

2. Have students research a particular issue to see where they can locate statistics that corroborate the need. If they can't locate any, determine whom they would include in a focus group or interview to assess the need using anecdotal evidence.

Chapter 9: The Procedures

1. Name three different approaches to addressing the same need. Have students research all three to see which one seems most appropriate, based on the experience of colleagues in the field, research, and absence of potential barriers.

2. Present a sample statement of need. Have students draft a plan of action to address this need which matches the scope of the need with the scope of the procedures and desired outcomes.

3. Draft a two-paragraph plan for dissemination of results, including anticipated audiences.

4. Present a proposed project and have students brainstorm potential deliverables.

Chapter 10: Evaluation

1. Ask students to identify three Internet sites that provide particularly useful guidance on evaluation and to report on their favorite to the whole class. Compile these into a reference to hand out to everyone.

2. Assign teams of students to create a program logic model for a project. Critique these in class or arrange for a panel of grantmakers to give a critique of the models.

3. Have students submit a paragraph describing a particular evaluation problem they are experiencing in writing their proposal. Bring in a panel of experienced evaluators to discuss these problems and suggest optional solutions.

4. Have students do an assessment of optional methods of evaluation for a particular project in order to better understand the trade-offs that must be faced in doing an evaluation design. Ask them to identify which method is most appropriate. Most useful. Easiest. Cheapest. Discuss their choices in class.

5. Ask students to develop an evaluation design to be included in a proposal for an outcome (one you give them or one they prepared in an earlier class). Critique these designs in small groups and discuss insights with the full class.

Chapter 11: Qualifications and Personnel

1. Ask students to name an organization and articulate what characteristics would make its board, staff, volunteers, participants, or part-

ners more appealing to funders than those of a competitor.

2. Ask students to list what infrastructure elements make their organization look more fundable.

3. Have students determine how they would assert their capability if the applicant (either an individual researcher or an organization) is inexperienced or newly formed.

Chapter 12: The Budget

1. Have small groups list the expense categories that would appear on most organization's budgets. Then have them list potential revenue sources.

2. Pass out budgets submitted to a funder by four or five organizations and have the students compare them in small groups to see how much they can tell about each organization just by looking at the numbers.

3. Assign students to research a funder that accepts indirect costs and determine which costs in their organization would be included in that category.

4. Have students create a three-year budget for a startup project that hopes to remain in place after the grant, showing which costs might be incurred in each phase of implementation.

5. Have students create a mock budget with multiple sources of revenue, including in-kind contributions of expertise and goods, some from the sponsoring organization and some from external sources.

Chapter 13: Review, Submission, Notification, and Renewal

1. Have students identify an Internet site for a funding source and do a short analysis of its implicit or explicit review criteria, pointing out what topics should be emphasized in a proposal in order to increase the likelihood of success.

2. Have teams of students identify a project and do the research needed to create a plan specifying how various funding sources might be used to provide support over several years or through different phases of the project's development.

3. Have students use the Internet to identify a good source of information on why proposals do not get funded. Do a quick "show-and-tell" on the best of these.

Index